W9-CCO-191

MAY   2007

HAVING A MARY SPIRIT

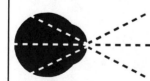

This Large Print Book carries the
Seal of Approval of N.A.V.H.

HAVING A MARY SPIRIT

ALLOWING GOD TO CHANGE US
FROM THE INSIDE OUT

JOANNA WEAVER

THORNDIKE PRESS

An imprint of Thomson Gale, a part of The Thomson Corporation

Des Plaines Public Library
1501 Ellinwood Street
Des Plaines, IL. 60016

THOMSON

GALE

Detroit • New York • San Francisco • New Haven, Conn. • Waterville, Maine • London

THOMSON

GALE

Copyright © 2006 by Joanna Weaver.

All Scripture quotations, unless otherwise indicated, are taken from the Holy Bible, New International Version®. NIV®. Copyright © 1973, 1978, 1984 by International Bible Society. Used by permission of Zondervan Publishing House. All rights reserved. Scripture quotations marked (ASV) are taken from the American Standard Version. Scripture quotations marked (KJV) are taken from the King James Version. Scripture quotations marked (NASB) are taken from the New American Standard Bible®. © Copyright The Lockman Foundation 1960, 1962, 1963, 1968, 1971, 1972, 1973, 1975, 1977, 1995. Used by permission (www.Lockman.org). Scripture quotations marked (NKJV) are taken from the New King James Version®. Copyright © 1982 by Thomas Nelson Inc. Used by permission. All rights reserved. Scripture quotations marked (NLT) are taken from the Holy Bible, New Living Translation, copyright © 1996. Used by permission of Tyndale House Publishers Inc., Wheaton, Illinois 60189. All rights reserved. Scripture quotations marked (Phillips) are taken from The New Testament in Modern English, Revised Edition © 1972 by J. B. Phillips. Copyright renewed © 1986, 1988 by Vera M. Phillips.

Thomson Gale is part of The Thomson Corporation.

Thomson and Star Logo and Thorndike are trademarks and Gale is a registered trademark used herein under license.

ALL RIGHTS RESERVED

Thorndike Press® Large Print Inspirational.

The text of this Large Print edition is unabridged.

Other aspects of the book may vary from the original edition.

Set in 16 pt. Plantin.

LIBRARY OF CONGRESS CATALOGING-IN-PUBLICATION DATA

Weaver, Joanna.
    Having a Mary spirit : allowing God to change us from the inside out / by Joanna Weaver.
        p. cm.
    Includes bibliographical references.
    ISBN-13: 978-0-7862-9168-7 (lg. print : alk. paper)
    ISBN-10: 0-7862-9168-0 (lg. print : alk. paper)
    ISBN-13: 978-1-59415-176-7 (lg. print : alk. paper)
    ISBN-10: 1-59415-176-8 (lg. print : alk. paper)
    1. Christian women — Religious life — Study and teaching. 2. Spirituality — Study and teaching. 3. Large type books. I. Title.
    BV4527.W385 2007
    248.8′43—dc22

                                                            2006101056

Published in 2007 by arrangement with Waterbrook Press,
a division of Random House Inc.

Printed in the United States of America on permanent paper
10 9 8 7 6 5 4 3 2 1

To my Mary-spirited husband, John
You have taught me so much
through your life,
your humility, your servant heart.
Thank you for being Jesus to me.
The heart of this book was formed
through watching you live.
I am so blessed to call you mine.

CONTENTS

ACKNOWLEDGMENTS

They say writing is a lonely occupation, but in my particular case, nothing could be further from the truth.

While completing this book has required long hours in front of the computer, those long hours have been filled with notes of encouragement, phone-call prayers, friends dropping by to help out, willing wonderful baby-sitters (thanks, Grandma and Grandpa Gus, Trish, and Kerry), and beautiful places to write (thank you McLoy's, Creech's, and Glacier Bible Camp!).

But none of it would have been possible had my family not come alongside me. Thank you, John, for encouraging me to follow God's call on my life. Thank you, John Michael and Jessica, for believing in me and telling me not only it could be done, but it *would* be done. Thank you, sweet Joshua, for never crying when Mommy had to go to work — not once! And for all the sweet hugs and cuddles when I got home.

Thanks as well to my dear friends who allowed me to share our story, to other friends who shared their stories as well, and to all the women who faithfully prayed and lifted me up as I wrote — I couldn't have done it without you. I literally felt your intercession, and I thank you from the bottom of my heart.

To my agent, Janet Kobobel Grant, who walked with me through six years of writing silence — your consistent encouragement to write only when the Holy Spirit gave me something to say reinforced what I already knew. You are a gift from heaven, and I thank God for you!

And to my Anne, my dear funny marvelous editor, Anne Christian Buchanan — thank you once again for helping me shape the words to best express the message that so fills my heart. Working with you felt like coming home again. Thank you for being my friend.

To WaterBrook Press and all the wonderful people that make you such a wonderful company to work with — my deepest gratitude as well!

And to all the saints who have gone before, who, through their examples in Scripture or through their writings, show us the path to

Christlikeness — Oswald and Hannah, C. S. and Catherine, not to mention Paul, Mary and Martha of Bethany, Mary Magdalene, and Mary, mother of Jesus — thank you for living lives of such passionate God pursuit that we can't help but follow.

But most of all, to You, Lord Jesus, I give my deepest thanks. For it is in You and through You that we find our life and have our being. You take what we are and make us what we were meant to be. Partakers of Your divine nature. Reflections of Your glory.

Soli Deo Gloria.

To You alone.

1
A MARY SPIRIT

Create in me a clean heart, O God;
and renew a right spirit within me.
PSALM 51:10 (KJV)

I've always dreamed of being much more
than I am. More organized, more disciplined, more loving . . . much more "much
more," if you know what I mean! Each January I set out on a new self-improvement
program.

This year I'll get in shape.

This year I'll keep my house clean.

This year I'll send out birthday cards. On
time.

This year — really — I'll be the loving, forgiving, obedient woman of God I long to be
instead of the willful, stubborn, disobedient
Christian I sometimes see staring back at me
in the mirror.

All noble goals. And truth be told, I am
much more at peace when my house is

clean. And I believe that if you really love people, you ought to care enough to send the very best — or at least one of those ninety-nine-cent cards from Wal-Mart! And I know that genuine happiness only comes from living close to God and obeying Him.

I really do want to be different. I want to be changed.

As the saying goes, "There's a skinny woman inside me just struggling to get out." Unfortunately — as the saying continues — "I can usually sedate her with four or five cupcakes."[1]

Working toward these noble goals has left me with little more than a cupboard full of half-empty vitamin bottles, several pairs of slightly worn running shoes, and enough cleaning products to Lysol a small third-world country. Not to mention a shelf filled with dust-covered devotionals.

Is that true for you as well?

Maybe you've discovered, as I have, that most of your New Year's resolutions have little effect on day-to-day life except to add a burden of guilt and a feeling of failure. Continually striving, yet never arriving. Hoping, praying to be different, only waking up to find you're not as far along as you'd hoped to be. Sometimes feeling like you're right back where you started — again!

I know. I've felt that way too.

In fact it was one of those discouraging moments that prompted me to write this book.

LEARNING FROM MARY AND MARTHA

It all began about seven years ago, with two sisters I'd met in the Bible — Mary and Martha of Bethany.

As a pastor's wife and — at the time — the mother of two almost-teenagers, my life was busy and often crazy. There was so much to do and so little time. Yet while I tended toward drivenness, my heart longed for intimacy with God. Maybe that's why I was drawn to take a new look at the story that had intrigued me for years. Luke 10:38–42 reads:

> As Jesus and his disciples were on their way, he came to a village where a woman named Martha opened her home to him. She had a sister called Mary, who sat at the Lord's feet listening to what he said. But Martha was distracted by all the preparations that had to be made. She came to him and asked, "Lord, don't you care that my sister has left me to do the work by myself? Tell her to help me!"
>
> "Martha, Martha," the Lord answered,

"you are worried and upset about many things, but only one thing is needed. Mary has chosen what is better, and it will not be taken away from her."

After hearing several hundred sermons on these two women, I assumed the meaning was fairly straightforward. Mary was the heroine. Martha was the villain. And too much of the time I was Martha! I felt the Lord convicting me of my tendency to rush around, busy with "many things" while ignoring the "one thing" that was needed — to sit at Jesus's feet.

But as I studied the rest of the sisters' story in John 11 and 12, I discovered something so beautiful, so amazing, that I felt compelled to share it in a book. For I saw two women change before my eyes, both of them experiencing a holy makeover when they encountered the living Lord.

And so, six years ago, *Having a Mary Heart in a Martha World: Finding Intimacy with God in the Busyness of Life* was born.

Perhaps the most comforting thing I learned as I worked on that book was that none of us has it all together. Even on our best days and with our best intentions, we all eventually blow it. We start out operating in our gifts and talents — excited to be serving the Messiah — only to have our efforts morph into a full-blown pity party when we don't get enough help, or we aren't appreciated, or someone else gets the attention we *know* we deserve.

But what stood out most to me was the fact that when Jesus scolded Martha about her busyness, He wasn't condemning her efficiency and hard work or her can-do personality. He wasn't telling her she had to be just like Mary to please Him. Jesus simply didn't want Martha to be so caught up in kitchen service *for* Him that she missed out on the joy of living-room intimacy *with* Him.

Jesus challenged Mary as well in John 11. When her brother, Lazarus, was sick and dying, Jesus waited two days before making His way to Bethany. By then, Lazarus was dead. And Mary, apparently paralyzed by grief, declined to go out to meet Jesus and stayed in the house instead. Later, she cried out her questions to Him. But while Jesus didn't answer her, He felt her pain. The Bible tells us He wept.

Neither Mary nor Martha got what they expected from Jesus. Instead, they received much more. For God never withholds good except when He has something better to give. Whether it's refusing more help in the kitchen or the miraculous healing of your brother, you can be sure Jesus knows what He's doing when He says no to our earthly requests in order to say yes to His heavenly plan.

But these two sisters had to accept Christ's better way — for it was a choice. Only as they humbled their hearts and learned from Him were they changed. Martha learned to be still and listen. Mary learned to pour out her heart as well as her expensive perfume in service. As they received Jesus's teaching, they learned the balance between a soul at rest and a body in motion,[2] between working hard for Christ and sitting at His feet.

And I was learning right along with them. My Marthalike tendencies were being tempered by the tender grace of God. Because I no longer felt as if I had to earn the Father's favor, I was finally able to enjoy His lavish love. Rather than striving, I was learning what John 15's abiding in the vine really means. As a result, like Mary and Martha, I, too, was being changed.

I'm so glad we have a Savior who loves us just as we are, but loves us too much to leave us that way. After all, Christ's main purpose is to return to us the glory of God we were meant to reflect in this world. As author Donna Partow puts it: "Our task here on earth is to show the world an accurate reflection of what God is like. To show them, through our lives, who God is."[3]

In other words, the whole purpose of our holy makeover is to make us more and more like Jesus.

But that divine transformation only happens as we choose to have a Mary spirit and accept the Lord's rebuke.

Even when it hurts.

BRICK WALLS AND LEARNING CURVES

After completing *Having a Mary Heart in a Martha World,* I decided to take a six-month sabbatical. After being "spilled" out in my writing, I knew I needed time to be refilled.

I had no idea six months would turn into six years.

Not that they were barren years. No, far from that! During that time God taught me so much. He walked me through some valleys and up some mountaintops. I had the privilege of watching my son, John Michael, and my daughter, Jessica, grow up into wonderful young people. Then, three years ago, God surprised us with a baby we named Joshua — a truly unexpected blessing. Plus, our growing church purchased land, and we were finally ready to build our new facility — the one that had been years in the dreaming. But it was that dream-coming-true that showed me just how far I still had to go. It also birthed this sequel. A book I didn't know existed.

I was so certain I was on the right track with the church building project. As the daughter of a part-time contractor, I was familiar with the construction process. As plans progressed, I discovered in myself a vision and a passion I hadn't felt in a long time.

With the official launch of our fund-raising just weeks away, I was running full tilt. There was so much to do — floor plans to finalize, brochures to design, numbers to crunch. I'd go to bed thinking about all the details and wake up with a focused energy and purpose that propelled me through my to-do list and beyond. It felt wonderful to be doing something for the Lord.

My pastor husband, John, tried to warn me. "Honey, I think you need to slow down. You're going to burn out." Of course I should have listened. My husband, unlike me, is not inclined to give his opinion 24/7. I should have realized that God was trying to get my attention through my spiritual covering. But I brushed away John's concern.

Sure, this was a crazy time, I told myself. Getting a ball rolling takes a lot of effort. I'd slow down later.

I slowed down, all right.

Brick walls have that effect on people.

The brick wall, in this case, was a lack of funding. We were unable to raise enough pledges to complete the project, and we felt strongly that we were not to borrow funds. Plans would have to be scaled back. So many dreams and ministries we'd envisioned launching would have to be downsized as well.

I tried my best to hang on to the initial vision. My Martha fix-it mode kicked in, and I scrambled to come up with ways to still fulfill the dream. But every option I came up with was discarded and, to be honest, my insistence began to wear on people.

Finally, I had to admit that God must have other things in mind. The vibrant passion I'd had for the project began to dwindle as discouragement and disappointment flooded in to take its place.

"Why, God? I don't understand," I wailed. "I so wanted to do this right. What did I do wrong?"

In that moment this book was born.

THE MARTHA IN ME

Joanna, I sensed the Lord whisper to my tired soul. *You have a Martha spirit. You're a good girl wanting to do the right thing. But sometimes you do it the wrong way.*

A Martha spirit? Oh, man. I knew what that meant. Martha was trying to reassert herself in my life. Not the grown-up, lesson-learned, Jesus-changed Martha we meet near the end of the Gospels, but the old Martha. The high-octane, high-anxiety, chronically overachieving woman Jesus had to rebuke at her own dinner party. The Martha who loved the Lord but just couldn't be bothered to actually listen to Him. Who kept rushing in to do things her way and complaining loudly whenever anyone dared do things differently.

She was the Martha I thought I'd left behind — but she seemed to be running the show once again.

When you run ahead of Me, the Lord impressed on my heart, *you end up doing what I've asked you to do in your own strength rather than Mine. Instead of being cloaked in the sweetness of My Spirit, your efforts are cloaked in your flesh. And sometimes, my dear daughter, your flesh ain't that easy to receive.*

It was hard to hear, but I knew it was true. My woman-on-a-mission mode was rarely attractive. While I always strived to keep a sweet demeanor on the outside, my inner spirit — my heart attitude — often had an

22

edge to it. Especially when I was busy. Especially when I was tired. Especially when things didn't go my way. You can only imagine the cosmic repercussions when the planets of those three *especially*'s happened to align!

What made the truth even harder to bear was that I had learned — or thought I'd learned — this lesson before. More than once, in fact.

It was the same truth God had sought to teach me back at the beginning of our ministry. And again shortly after I finished *Having a Mary Heart in a Martha World,* when a misunderstanding led to a painful falling-out with friends.

Now here I was once again. Facing the same old flaws in myself. Struggling with a Martha spirit that continually tried to overshadow my Mary heart.

"Lord, change me," I prayed in all sincerity.

But, I must confess, with my repentance came an underlying fear. After so many years of being taught the same lesson over and over, would I ever be truly changed? Was lasting transformation even possible?

I knew in my heart it was. After all, I had experienced God's hand in my life over the years. But how would it happen now? And how could I better cooperate with the process?

You need a Mary spirit, the Lord whispered. And once again, in the quiet of that moment, I understood what He meant.

A NEW KIND OF ATTITUDE

In order to really change — and keep on changing — I needed the kind of heart attitude Mary had when she left her duties and spent time with Jesus, basking in His presence. The same kind of attitude Martha displayed when she chose to be teachable rather than offended by Jesus's rebuke.

A Mary spirit is not a personality type. It isn't about being an extrovert versus an introvert or an active person versus a more contemplative type. Having a Mary spirit is about our attitude toward what God wants to do in our lives. The spirit behind our response to Him makes all the difference.

Mary of Bethany seemed to have a Mary spirit from the beginning. And although it took the tough love of Christ, her sister Martha eventually had it too. But there are two other Marys I want to mention (both of whom we'll discuss in greater detail later) — women who shared with Mary of Bethany not only a name, but also the grace-filled peace of a heart in tune with God.

First, Mary, the mother of Jesus, displayed a willing Mary spirit when she told the angel Gabriel, "Let it be to me according to your word." Although everything within her must have balked at the implications of mothering the very Son of God, and although she must have known in her heart that doing so would be costly, still she said yes to God's plan.

Second, Mary Magdalene exhibited the gratefulness of a Mary spirit after Jesus set her free from seven demons. Rather than settling down to a "normal" life, she abandoned it all in order to follow the One who had brought her out of darkness and into His marvelous light. That grateful and persistent love for the Lord, that desire to always be near Him and follow wherever He leads — that's also part of a Mary spirit.

And that, I realized, is what I wanted.

You see, Joanna, the Lord seemed to be saying, *I delight in a heart that welcomes My work rather than resents it. A willing, teachable spirit is all I'm looking for. A life so surrendered to Me, I can do My work unhindered.*

As God began to work these truths in my life, I realized this was the book He'd had me wait six years to write. For just as *Having a Mary Heart in a Martha World* shows us how to make room in our outer lives for intimacy with God, *Having a Mary Spirit* is meant to

This book is different from *Having a Mary Heart in a Martha World* in several ways. Rather than following a biblical story line, for instance, it delves into spiritual truths — truths that, I must confess, are sometimes beyond me.

You see, I am not a scholar, and this is not a theological treatise. The thoughts in this book come from studying the Word as well as from my own personal experience of having God work in my life so that He might change me. There may be places where you disagree with me. But I hope what you read here will spark a desire in your heart to wrestle with your issues before God just as Jacob did — until He blesses you. Until you are made over in His image.

The first half of this book attempts to build a foundation for this inner work of

show us how to give God access to the deep, hidden corners of our hearts. Those dark, sin-ridden parts of our lower nature that continually cause us to stumble when we so desperately want to walk in the light. Those secret, not-so-silent kingdoms Christ came

the Lord by outlining how the process of change happens and why God is so intent that it does. The second half focuses on the more practical application of training our minds, guarding our hearts, and purifying our ways. At the end of the book, you'll find appendices of practical resources as well as a fourteen-week guide for individual or group study.

As you read, I pray that the Holy Spirit will lead you into all truth. For the Spirit is our teacher, and He makes real in our lives even that which we don't fully understand.

I pray also that the eyes of your heart
may be enlightened in order
that you may know the hope to which he
has called you.

EPHESIANS 1:18

to conquer as well as redeem.
So that we can be made holy as He is holy.
Changed from the inside out.

GIVING GOD ACCESS

I don't know your situation. I don't know

what God is walking you through right now. But I suspect He's been stirring in you a divine discontentment — a hunger for something more, a desire to *be* something more. Otherwise you wouldn't have picked up this book.

May I tell you that such spiritual discontentment is a gift from God? For He only stirs us when He wants to change us. He only makes us feel uneasy with where we are so we're willing to do whatever it takes to get where He is.

So if you're feeling those discontented stirrings, if you're tired of taking one step forward only to fall two steps back, if you, like me, would like to stop learning the same lessons over and over again, then I'd like to invite you to join me on an adventure of change.

And I can't think of a better place to start than with this prayer:

Lord Jesus, I give You my life.
I invite You to have Your way in me.
Take me and break me. Shake me and make me.
Fill me and spill me. Change me and rearrange me.
But whatever You do, Lord . . . don't leave me the same.

Spirit of wisdom and revelation, I wel-
come Your work.
Open my eyes so I can see . . . my ears so
I can hear . . .
I choose truth over comfort, challenge
over complacency.
Lord, make me forever Yours.
And most of all, make me like You.
Amen.

2
CHANGE ME, LORD

*Being confident of this, that he
who began a good work in you
will carry it on to completion
until the day of Christ Jesus.*

PHILIPPIANS 1:6

I started praying the prayer early in our ministry, and I meant it from the bottom of my heart: "Lord, make me perfect by the time I'm thirty."

My inadequacies and imperfections were causing a lot of problems. Certainly God would honor my prayer and deliver me from myself.

I tried to enlist a couple of friends to pray on my behalf, but they just howled with laughter. "Yeah, right!" they said. "Perfect by thirty? Like that's going to happen."

Okay, perhaps I was a little naive. But the idea wasn't mine. Jesus Himself had said it in His Word: "Be perfect, therefore, as your heavenly Father is perfect" (Matthew 5:48). If God required perfection, I reasoned, certainly He would give me the tools to accomplish it.

And, in many ways, He has. God has not only provided the tools for my transformation, but His Holy Spirit has also been at work in me, actively moving me toward the perfect wholeness God intends for my life. For this is what the word perfect means in the Bible.

Teleios. Mature. Complete.[1]

However, the process of moving toward perfection hasn't happened nearly as quickly as I hoped. In fact, at times I've felt that heaven itself was working against my best efforts. And perhaps it was — because God's plans for making us like His Son have very little to do with mere self-improvement.

You see, I assumed that Christian perfection was an outer work *I* had to do. A cleaning up and purifying of my words, my life, and my actions. If I could just be good enough and do the right things, then I would please God. But in my heartfelt desire to serve and honor the Lord, I fell prey to the same lie that deceived the Pharisees so long ago.

The lie that holiness is all up to us.

You, Me, and the Pharisees

The Pharisees were godly men, at least on the outside. Their sole purpose in life was to obey all of God's commands, so they made up hundreds of rules and regulations to help them follow the original Law God had given. The summary of those rules is known as the Mishnah. Translated into English, it is a book of almost eight hundred pages. Later, Jewish scholars added commentaries on how to fulfill the Mishnah. Known collectively as the Talmud, these commentaries fill at least twelve volumes.

The Pharisees were famous for their scrupulous observance of the Law. Yet even the Jews recognized the hypocrisy that sometimes accompanied the Pharisees' pious attempts at religious perfection. The Talmud itself distinguishes seven different kinds of Pharisees.

1. There was the *Shoulder Pharisee,* who meticulously followed the Law but wore his good deeds on his shoulder to be seen of men.
2. There was the *Wait-a-Little Pharisee,* always able to offer a valid excuse for putting off doing a good deed. He spoke, but he did not do.
3. There was the *Bruised* or *Bleeding*

Pharisee, so intent on avoiding evil that whenever a woman approached, he would close his eyes and therefore run into things. He then displayed the bruises to prove his piety.

4. There was the *Humpbacked* or *Tumbling Pharisee,* so determined to look humble that he bent completely over, shuffled his feet . . . and often tripped over obstacles.

5. There was the *Ever-Reckoning* or *Compounding Pharisee,* forever counting up his good deeds in the belief that each one put God further in his debt.

6. There was the *Timid* or *Fearing Pharisee,* always in dread of divine punishment, constantly cleansing the outside of the cup and the platter in an attempt to escape God's wrath.

7. Finally, there was the *God-Fearing Pharisee,* defined by the Jews themselves as one who truly loved God. Only one out of seven was admired as a man who found delight rather than drudgery in obeying God's Law no matter how difficult it might be.[2]

To be honest, I've been all of these Pharisees to one degree or another, with most of my time spent acting out versions of the first six. For no matter how pure my intent, the only result of making outward purity my goal has been an unhealthy self-obsession and a self-worth that swings wildly between feelings of inordinate pride or overwhelming failure — depending on how well I think I've done that day.

Oswald Chambers warns against this dangerous preoccupation with our own "personal whiteness," as he calls it, referring to the unhealthy kind of introspection that focuses on our inadequacies rather than on God's power to redeem and change our lives. "As long as our eyes are upon our own personal whiteness," he writes in *My Utmost for His Highest,* "we shall never get near the reality of Redemption." Later he adds, "The continual grubbing on the inside to see whether we are what we ought to be generates a self-centered, morbid type of Christianity, not the robust, simple life of the child of God."[3]

Jesus wasn't quite so nice when He denounced the Pharisees and their attempts at self-induced holiness. He ripped off the religious facades they tried to hide behind (as most of us do at times), calling these religious leaders, "whitewashed tombs . . . full of dead men's bones" (Matthew 23:27).

Whitewashed tombs were common in

Jesus's day, especially during the Passover and other religious festivals. Graves were painted bright white so no one would accidentally touch them at night, becoming ceremonially unclean and thus unfit to worship. Such tombs might look beautiful on the outside, Jesus reminded the crowd, but their insides were filled with dead, rotting things and "everything unclean."

Jesus was indirectly warning ordinary people who admired the Pharisees and their superficial show of holiness to avoid them at all costs. *Ignore the outside,* Jesus advised, *no matter how brightly it shines. It's what is inside that counts.*

Over and over in the New Testament, Christ confronted those who had succumbed to the whitewashed-tomb syndrome — the dangerous belief that we can somehow make ourselves presentable to God through our own human effort. Not only were such efforts pointless and even dangerous, Jesus said, but they were no longer necessary. God had a better plan.

The Sin Bearer had come.

SCANDALOUS GRACE

Jesus offered another way to holiness, and you'd think the Pharisees would have been relieved by this incredible news. They no

Like the Pharisees, you may be depending on your own goodness to make it to heaven. What a heavy load to bear! Jesus came and paid the price so we no longer have to strive and strain to be right with God (Titus 3:5).

Won't you take a moment and receive the forgiveness Christ freely offers? In many ways, it's as simple as A-B-C, and a prayer:

A — Admit your need (Romans 3:23).

B — Believe in Christ (Acts 16:31).

C — Commit your life to following Him (John 1:12).

"Lord Jesus, I need You. Thank You for taking the punishment for my sin when You died on the cross. I give You my life — be my Savior and Lord. Take the throne of my heart and make me the kind of person You want me to be. Amen."

Yet to all who received him,
to those who believed in his name,
he gave the right to become
children of God.

JOHN 1:12

longer had to pose and posture, grovel and beg, barter or try to blind themselves to avoid sin.

But sometimes good news can be just too good to receive. After all, the free grace that Jesus Christ offers to anyone who believes in Him can be quite scandalous. Imagine what would happen if we stopped resisting God's love and started resting in it? To those of us who are used to thinking that we're in charge of our spiritual development, that prospect can be hard to accept, even downright threatening.

Author Donald Miller describes this beautifully in his wry account of his own struggle with the message of grace. He tells about a time when "I used to get really ticked about preachers who talked too much about grace, because they tempted me to not be disciplined." Miller writes, "I believed if word got out about grace, the whole church was going to turn into a brothel." (He adds, pointedly, "I was a real jerk, I think.")[4]

Miller had fallen into the Pharisee trap that tends to trip us all; as he puts it, "trying to discipline myself to 'behave' as if I loved light and not 'behave' as if I loved darkness." But the only thing this macho, legalistic type of self-improvement — which Miller calls living "like a Navy SEAL for Jesus"[5] —

brought him was failure and despair.

It's the same failure and despair the Pharisee/Navy SEAL in all of us feels when we depend on ourselves for salvation. More to the point, it's the cycle of failure and despair Jesus destroyed when He died on the cross. As the apostle Paul writes in Romans 8:2, "Through Christ Jesus the law of the Spirit of life set [us] free from the law of sin and death."

The Law outlined in the Old Testament serves an important purpose: It illuminates the sin in our lives. But that's all the Law can do. It can show us what's wrong with us, but it is absolutely powerless to make us right. By itself, it is incapable of bridging the chasm that sin made between *Abba* God and His children — the gaping crevasse in our souls that leaves us forever lonely, forever removed from the only love that can make us whole.

Bottom line, self-induced holiness is a miserable exercise in futility. For no matter how strictly we observe it, the Law will never make us righteous. It will never come close to making us changed, different, Christlike people.

Paul learned this lesson the hard way. All his years of militant religion and his obsession with keeping the Law did little but make him hate people who were free. It wasn't until Paul was blinded by the Light of the World and knocked off his spiritual high horse that he was released by grace to be all that he could be.

Thank the Lord that His grace is available to us as well! When I shared Oswald Chambers's term *personal whiteness* at our women's Bible study a few years ago, one of the ladies began to laugh. She'd just been to the store to pick up paint for her living room and discovered there were approximately 586 shades of white to choose from. Five hundred and eighty-six shades! You could spend a lifetime trying to get just the right shade. And some of us do just that!

But — praise God — we don't have to! "Though your sins are like scarlet," God promises in Isaiah 1:18, "they shall be as white as snow."

Christ offers us a fresh start. A clean slate. A "personal whiteness" so white that the human mind cannot comprehend, but only receive it. It doesn't come through our striving, our internal grubbing and external scrubbing. Only the power of the Holy Spirit can make us truly new. Only the mighty power of God working within us — the same power that raised Christ from the grave — can change us from the inside out.

You see, God doesn't want us whitewashing our tombs.

He wants to raise us from the dead.

FICTION AND FAIRY TALES

I don't know how I missed this amazing and important reality. I was raised in a grace-filled home and a grace-filled church. But, as a young adult, I somehow fell for the lie that when I accepted Jesus as my Savior, the rest was up to me. As though, after an initial warm hug of welcome, God had tossed me into the sea of life, stepped back, and crossed His arms as if to say "It's up to you now, sweetheart — sink or swim."

So swim I did. I swam like crazy — pouring myself into all kinds of good works. I led music. I taught Sunday school. I worked hard to be "all things to all men" — and women, boys, girls, infants, toddlers, senior citizens, teens, college and career, young marrieds. Well, you get the picture. I was a pastor's wife, for goodness' sake!

But no matter how fast I paddled, no matter how hard I tried to keep my head above water, my efforts were never enough. I could feel myself going down. One night I finally reached the breaking point. Sobbing, I clung to my husband. But nothing he said could comfort me, and I was at a loss to explain what was wrong except . . .

"Tell me the good news," I begged him between sobs. "I honestly can't remember. Tell me the good news."

I've told that story many times before. I told it in my last book. But I felt I had to repeat it here because it's such a vivid picture of just how far away from God's grace a Martha spirit can take a person. The only thing my inner Pharisee had given me was deep despair and hopeless frustration. But coming to the end of myself also turned me toward freedom — because it pushed me to confront my own faulty theology.

It was the same turning point Brother Lawrence came to more than three hundred years ago. Desperate to serve God with his whole heart, he joined a monastery. But as hard as the poor monk tried to be holy and without sin, he constantly failed. Finally, as he describes in his timeless book *The Practice of the Presence of God,* he began to converse openly and honestly with the Lord. Looking to Christ rather than to his own character for strength, Brother Lawrence flung himself entirely upon God's mercy and grace.

When faced with an opportunity to practice a virtue, he prayed, "Lord, I cannot do this unless Thou enablest me."

And when he failed, he was quick to acknowledge, "I shall never do otherwise if You leave me to myself; it is You who must hinder my falling and mend what is amiss."

After doing that, his biographer writes, Brother Lawrence "gave himself no further uneasiness about it."[6]

Do those words minister to you as they do to me? To think we can have such an intimate relationship with the Almighty that we no longer have to whitewash our faults or deny our need of Him — well, that blesses me. After all, a true relationship must be based on honesty. The only way we will ever experience lasting change is to be willing to stand naked and needy before our heavenly Father. Honest and bold in our requests. Yearning for His transforming touch, yet secure in His steadfast love.

We can do that because we have a Savior who understands that we are caught in a human body of contradictions. Wanting God one minute and chasing the world the next. Desiring holiness, yet settling for compromise. Hungering for the divine, yet willing to trade it for a bowl of stale porridge and a nap in the shade.

But here's the best news of all: Jesus not only understands our weaknesses, He has the power and the know-how to help us change.

However, let me warn you. The process of transformation is not nearly as passive as that statement makes it sound. Instead of speaking a word and instantly changing our lives, God asks us to partner with Him in our own transformation.

I like how author Andrea Wells Miller describes this process. Too often, she says, when confronted with the challenge to change,

> I spiritually lie down on the operating table, grab the ether mask, and get ready for surgery and the healing that will follow, saying "Okay, Lord, here I am . . . 'yielded and still, mold me and make me after thy will.'"
>
> It's as if the Lord says, "First, fold your arms across your chest."
>
> "Great!" I answer.
>
> But then he says, "Now, sit up and lie back down 100 times."

"That's *not* what I had in mind!" Miller concludes.[7] But it is what God had in mind when He made us. The Lord knows that we need the process as much as we need the product. For it isn't just our holiness God is after. He also wants to make us wholly His.

But beware — we have an enemy who wants to thwart God's work every which way he can.

Because Satan hates God so much, he hates God's children. So his favorite pastime is whispering lies to us. Lies that tell us we're enough on our own . . . or that God could never love us.

And — the worst lie of all — the insinuation that our transformation itself is a fairy tale.

For Satan loves to twist our salvation stories and insist that, while for a moment our pumpkins may have become carriages and our rags glistening gowns, midnight has tolled, and it's time we face reality. He insists we're nothing more than barefoot Cinderellas, beggar girls trying to find our way back home, with no happily-ever-after to close our stories and no handsome Prince to call our own. That no matter how we wish and hope and dream, we will never experience lasting change. Not here on this earth, at any rate.

But nothing could be further from the truth. Yet that doesn't change the fact that many of us are living far more like paupers than princesses. Like slave girls rather than daughters of the King.

I read an unsettling statistic recently. Researcher George H. Gallup Jr. reported in his 2004 poll that while 42 percent of Americans claim to be born-again Christians, only 10 percent of those polled can point to a transforming encounter with Christ.[8]

In other words, nine out of ten Christians report that, while they may be going to heaven, nothing much has changed for them here on earth. They may have secured an eternal fire-insurance policy, but they haven't experienced the life change Christ came to give. And while occasionally they may get spiritual warm fuzzies, they can't point to any noticeable reconstruction going on in their lives.

If that statistic is true, it absolutely breaks my heart, and I can only imagine what it does to the heart of God. To think that Christ gave us so much only to have us experience so little brings tears to my eyes.

I can only pray that this statistic is incorrect. That people were confused by the wording of the question. Or that Satan has somehow blinded them to the changes the Spirit has made in their lives.

I know that's what happened with me.

Because of my perfectionism and the fact that I failed more regularly than I succeeded when it came to living the Christlike life, I assumed one of two things had to be true. Either I was miserable scum — unworthy of God's love and unable to change.

God has used many practices and experiences to shape my life. I've found that these six regular disciplines have helped me grow and become more like Christ. I recommend them all to you. (For more on these tools, please refer to the appendices in the back of this book.)

Developing a Quiet Time. Carving out a regular time and place to hear from God has truly transformed my life. As I sit quietly before Him, read my Bible and other devotional materials, write in my journal, and pray, He leads me in the way I should go. (See Appendix C.)

Memorizing Scripture. When I'm struggling in a certain area, I've found that memorizing verses on that topic is especially helpful. Hiding God's Word in my heart not only changes my thinking; it stores up spiritual provision for future need. (See Appendix E.)

Listening to Others. I'm thankful for the Christian wisdom I glean from books, sermons, Bible studies, and godly friends — faithful mentors who proclaim, "This is the way, walk ye in it" (Isaiah 30:21, KJV).

Journaling the Journey. It isn't

enough for me to see my face in the mirror of God's Word; I must respond with obedience. I've found that regular journaling — keeping track of both my own thoughts and what I perceive the Lord is saying to me — reminds me of God's faithfulness and keeps me accountable. (See Appendix D.)

Gathering with the Body. I pursue every opportunity to meet with God's people — from prayer groups to church services to retreats and conferences. When two or more are gathered together, God is there and we are changed.

Altar-ing My Ego. Responding to God by going to the altar has changed my life. Whether I'm at home or church, bowing my knee as well as my heart nails down my commitment to obey what He is speaking to my heart.

The Spirit of the LORD will come upon you in power ... and you will be changed into a different person.

1 SAMUEL 10:6

Or true victory over sin in this world was impossible, so I'd just have to hang on until the end and hope the good in my life outweighed the bad.

If George Gallup had come to my house back then and surveyed me, I'm certain I would have counted myself among the 90 percent of born-again Christians who say they have not experienced a significant life change since meeting Christ. The twisting of the good news by the enemy had convinced me to paint my entire life with a broad, black stroke. Convinced me that anything good and holy God might be doing in my life didn't count because I wasn't currently measuring up to some self-imposed standard of holiness.

In other words, because I wasn't *all* good, I assumed I was no good at all.

No wonder Mama warned me not to talk to strangers.

Unfortunately, there's always a grain of truth in every one of Satan's lies. It's true that many of us are not living as we ought to live — the way Christ called us to live. Statistics reveal that much of the Body of Christ in our culture prefers self-gratification over true transformation. Comfort over character. Ignorance over belief.

Pollster George Barna reports that 54 percent of adults think a good person can earn a place in heaven. One-third of born-again Christians believe that people can gain salvation through a route other than Jesus.[9] And Gallup says we've become so biblically illiterate that nearly half of all Christians don't know who delivered the Sermon on the Mount.[10]

No wonder we are experiencing a powerless Christianity. Too often we have dethroned God and enthroned ourselves. We've thrown out the Cross as well as the mandates of Scripture. In doing so, we've put up significant obstacles to our true, long-lasting, joy-producing change. Both as a church and as individuals, we've chosen stagnation over transformation, and our homes and lives suffer because of our choices.

Yet I believe there is also an awakening taking place. There is a hunger for God's Word and God's presence all around the world. Church Bible studies and home groups are springing up as people search for truth. Worship is exploding in all denominations as God stirs the hearts of His people.

For in His mercy, our heavenly Father does not leave us to ourselves. He woos us. With open arms, He lovingly draws us to Himself — for He wants a people to call His own.

But we must come. And we must be willing to be changed.

Which brings us back once more to a Mary spirit.

"Change Me, Lord"

God was good to place an important book in my hands early in my adulthood.

Every Wednesday morning in Libby, Montana, Grandma Rayson would gather a group of women in the back of the church sanctuary for Bible study. A joyful, gray-haired pack of dynamite, she'd get us giggling, and then crying as we made our way through the lesson for that day. It was in this study I first read Evelyn Christenson's wonderful book *Lord, Change Me!*

As a nineteen-year-old newlywed and a youth pastor's wife, I desperately needed this study because I was struggling. With my deep need to succeed being thwarted on every level, my performance-driven Martha was in high gear. And all that my inner Pharisee could see was where everyone *else* needed to change.

If my husband were only like this . . .

If the youth would only respond like that . . .

If only . . . if only . . .

But as I read Evelyn's book, I saw myself.

She, too, had a lot of passion and vision. Like me and Martha, she tended to think that her way was the right way, and this assumption often got her in trouble. Through a series of humbling circumstances, God brought Evelyn to her knees in more ways than one. Her book journals the changes in her heart and life as she chose to adopt a Mary spirit, receiving rather than resisting the rebuke of the Lord.

"I have discovered through the years," Evelyn writes, "surprising things happen when I pray, 'Lord, change *me* — don't change my husband, don't change my children, don't change my pastor, change *me!*'"[11]

Oh, Father, I thought when I read that paragraph, *that's what I need.* And so Evelyn Christenson's lifelong prayer became mine as well:

"Lord, change me!
Whatever you do, don't leave me the same.
Make me like you."

THE GREAT BECOMING

While God has faithfully answered my prayer for transformation, it almost never happened the way I wanted.

Definitely not the way I planned.

I wish I could tell you how wonderful I am now. How put together and perfect-by-thirty

I've become. How I nearly never get angry and hardly ever sin. But if I did that, I'm afraid my family (not to mention my church!) could sue me for false representation and "inflammation of character."

Now fourteen years past my target date, I wish I could tell you that my struggle against sin has been easy and is relatively complete. I can't tell you that either.

But to say I haven't been changed would be a lie as well.

What is true is that I am *being* changed.

Whether I can see it or not, my holy makeover is well underway.

And though I sometimes wish for quicker results, I am really grateful that God doesn't just barge in and perform radical surgery on my character. Instead, the Lord knows me so completely, so intimately, that He takes me at a pace I can go. He nurtures me, challenges me, builds my strength and understanding. Then when I am most ready, most able to respond with repentance, my loving Savior reveals an area of sin in my life and shows me exactly what needs to change. He knows I would be completely undone if He revealed all my sin at once.

Like someone peeling an onion, the Lord reveals one layer of sin in my life at a time. He gently exposes my failings, my prejudice, and my pride. Then He invites me to repent. To turn away from my destructive bent. To take advantage of His grace and the new paths of life He shows me.

And then, step by step, to move toward becoming what I was meant to be.

PRESSING ON

Over the years, the apostle Paul has become one of my dearest friends. He not only identifies with my struggles; he puts into words the frustration and the exhilaration I've experienced in my own walk with God. Through the inspiration of the Holy Spirit, Paul points out what I'm not, but he's also quick to tell me what I can become — and how it can happen.

"Not that I have already obtained all this, or have already been made perfect," Paul writes in Philippians 3:12–14, "but I press on to take hold of that for which Christ Jesus took hold of me. Brothers, I do not consider myself yet to have taken hold of it. But one thing I do: Forgetting what is behind and straining toward what is ahead, I press on toward the goal to win the prize for which God has called me heavenward in Christ Jesus."

I press on. Those words echo in my heart, bringing me comfort and courage.

No, I haven't achieved all my goals. I'm

not yet perfect. I'm still a recovering Pharisee in many ways, still more eager to whitewash the outside of my life than to do the hard work of cooperating with God's inner renovation. But rather than giving in to the enemy's condemnation of my shortcomings, I am determined to "press on to take hold of that for which Christ Jesus took hold of me."

My deepest fear is waking up twenty years from now still the same woman I am today. With the same annoying habits and petty attitudes; with the same besetting sins and false beliefs. I can't imagine anything more terrible than getting to the end of my life only to discover that God had so much more in mind for me — more freedom, more joy, more peace, more true effectiveness. And I had missed it all, simply because I refused to change.

So I press on, and I hope you will too. Believe me, dear sister, we can trust God. If we allow the spotlight of heaven to shine on the dark recesses of our souls, God will scrub off the old layers of whitewash. He'll remove those pockets of Martha drivenness and Pharisee pride. By the power of His Holy Spirit, He will transform us from glory to glory (2 Corinthians 3:18, NKJV).

Until one day, to our surprise, we'll wake up and realize that we look just like . . . Jesus!

I'm not saying it will be easy. Or fully accomplished here on Earth. Even with God doing the real work, we'll have to cooperate. We will have to change, and change hurts.

But I can promise you this. It hurts good.

3
TWISTED SISTERS

Therefore, if anyone is in Christ,
he is a new creation;
the old has gone, the new has come!
                              2 CORINTHIANS 5:17

It's a shock, I tell you.

I had no idea she lived inside of me. For a very nice, exceptionally sweet (well, sometimes) Christian girl like me to have the likes of her not only as a neighbor but as an actual roommate, well, the discovery was nearly more than I could bear. I tried to deny it, to pretend she didn't live with me. I explained away her dirty laundry and the messy dishes she left in the sink. But it was no use. Even I wasn't convinced. Finally, I decided to face her down myself.

"You have to leave," I told her. But she simply ignored my efforts to evict her. So I lectured her, hoping she would change her despicable habits. When the lecturing didn't work, I resorted to crying and begging. Then I got mad. But she seemed completely unmoved. In fact, she seemed to enjoy my displays of distraught emotion (i.e., tantrums).

Finally, I had to face the truth. Though I'd heard it said and I'd read it in the Bible, the complete reality of my predicament hit me for the first time.

Paul was right: "In me . . . dwelleth no good thing" (Romans 7:18, KJV).

WHAT WE'RE REALLY LIKE

My sister, Linda, knew it all along. We were in the middle of one of our notorious teenage squabbles when she pulled out her secret weapon, the one thing that could bring me to my knees.

"They all think you're so wonderful," she sneered, her blue eyes narrowing, her little pug nose twisting with the effort. "If they only knew what you're really like."

Bam, pow, wham! It was a knockout punch delivered right on the chin. She said the words slowly, making sure each one found a resting place. And, oh boy, did they. I can still hear their echoes today.

My sister had me. I knew she was right. The way I lived at home didn't always match up with my at-church-and-out-in-public persona.

Cross me at church and I did my best to be nice about it. Cross me at home — and watch out! (There would be a cross all right — but I wouldn't be the one on it.) Ignore or insult me at school, and I would try to return good for evil. But if you left me out or neglected my needs at home, I turned into an Emmy award–winning drama queen. Whining. Complaining. Conniving. Fighting for my rights. Insisting everyone follow my agenda.

Nobody knows the trouble I've been — I mean, seen!

Not that I meant to be a hypocrite. Nor did I set out purposely to deceive. It was just so hard lining up what I knew I ought to be with what I actually was. My heart agreed with God's law, but other parts of me seemed to have a rebellious streak. When I got home, with the people I knew would love and accept me as I am, I tended to collapse from the effort of trying to be a godly person: *Nobody's perfect. The pressure's too much. Why even try?*

All I could do was pray that the outside world never found out what I was really like. Because I wasn't certain I could be any different.

I'll never forget the relief I felt when we

studied Romans 7 in youth group one night.

I don't understand myself at all, for I really want to do what is right, but I don't do it. Instead, I do the very thing I hate. I know perfectly well that what I am doing is wrong, and my bad conscience shows that I agree that the law is good. But I can't help myself, because it is sin inside me that makes me do these evil things.

I know I am rotten through and through so far as my old sinful nature is concerned. No matter which way I turn, I can't make myself do right. I want to, but I can't. When I want to do good, I don't. And when I try not to do wrong, I do it anyway. But if I am doing what I don't want to do, I am not really the one doing it; the sin within me is doing it.

It seems to be a fact of life that when I want to do what is right, I inevitably do what is wrong. I love God's law with all my heart. But there is another law at work within me that is at war with my mind. This law wins the fight and makes me a slave to the sin that is still within me. Oh, what a miserable person I am! Who will free me from this life that is dominated by sin? (Romans 7:15–24, NLT)

Finally! Someone had put into words the wretched wrestling I had felt in my heart for so long. It was as if two people lived inside of me — one bad, one good. And both of them pulled for my attention, my cooperation, in an unholy tug of war, the outcome of which felt strangely like a matter of life or death.

Because, of course, it was.

You see, I've come to realize that Satan is not nearly as disappointed at losing me from his kingdom as he is determined to keep me from being effective in God's kingdom. If Satan can't make me fall away from God's grace, he will do everything he can to keep me from fully embracing God's grace. Satan wants me — and he wants you! — to be so constantly preoccupied with what we're not that we never get around to realizing all that God is. Our enemy wants to keep us so consumed with our inadequacies that we never get around to appropriating the love and transforming power God has made available to us through His Son.

And, in reality, when you look at all the evidence, Satan is right. Because of the Fall, we are — all of us — twisted sisters. Unworthy of salvation. Unlikely candidates for anything but destruction. The only appropriate response we — like Paul — can give to our circumstances is an anguished cry: "Oh, what a miserable person I am!" (Romans 7:24, NLT).

But then Paul continues. "Thank God!" he writes in verse 25 (NLT). "The answer is in Jesus Christ our Lord."

Woohoo! Preach it, brother! I love a happy ending.

The trouble is, Paul doesn't end the verse there. Instead, he reiterates that, though in our hearts and minds we want to obey God's laws, our "sinful nature" makes us slaves to sin.

Wait a minute! Let's go back to the victory-in-Jesus part. I thought we were new creations when we got saved. I thought the old had gone and the new had come (2 Corinthians 5:17). I thought we'd signed on for a holy makeover.

Well, yes, we are. Yes, it has. And, yes, you did.

But Flesh Woman doesn't know it yet.

UNLEASHING TWANDA

Whether we realize it or not, we all have a little Dr. Jekyll and Ms. Hyde going on inside. No matter how sweet and compliant we may seem, we all feel the influence of Flesh Woman — that unholy roommate I told you about earlier. For she lives inside all of us. She's that contrary, rebellious, incredibly self-centered version of you who shows up when things don't go the way you planned and life seems habitually unfair.

I must warn you, however, that on the surface Flesh Woman doesn't always appear so bad. Instead of wearing leather and tattoos, my Flesh Woman prefers lace and carefully coiffured hair. She goes to great lengths to be respectable because she feeds on people's praise and applause.

You see, Flesh Woman doesn't need dark alleys and smoky bars to work her worst. I'm discovering she may flourish most in religious surroundings, carefully disguised in church-lady clothes.

You know the kind of outfits I mean. The critical attitude we call discernment. The righteous indignation we use to justify our not-so-righteous anger. The flattery we pour on in order to secure coveted positions. The false humility in which we cloak ourselves while secretly hoping to be admired.

Unfortunately, we rarely pause to wonder if what we're doing is wrong, for it feels so right. And that's just as Flesh Woman wants it to be. For if you were to pull off her mask, you'd know what she's really up to. Her main goal is not your benefit, but her power base. Though Flesh Woman would never admit it, she's determined to do whatever it takes to remain in control of your life.

Martha felt her bold presence that busy day in Bethany as she worked and her sister played.

Mary felt her dark embrace the day her brother died and Jesus was a no-show.

And I . . . well, I've felt Flesh Woman's influence more times than I care to recall. Just put me in a position where I feel treated unfairly, forgotten, or left out — and you'll hear my case. Again and again and again. Because nothing brings out the worst in me more than injustice.

But at least I haven't pulverized a VW convertible with my midsize sedan like Kathy Bates's character did in the movie *Fried Green Tomatoes.*

After a couple of snotty bimbo Barbie dolls steal her parking space, saying, "Face it, lady. We're younger and faster," Bates decides to take matters into her own hands. Tired of being ignored by a sports-crazed husband and bypassed by life, she decides to awaken what she calls the "Twanda Amazon Woman" inside her. She stands up for herself and takes control.

Well, she takes control all right. After repeatedly smashing their Volkswagen's rear end, Bates drives away after telling the upset Barbies, "Face it, girls, I'm older and I have more insurance."[2]

The first rule of warfare is knowing your enemy. E. E. Shelhamer's famous "Traits of the Carnal Mind" can help you identify the Flesh Woman inside you so you can begin to put an end to her evil designs. Here are some of the telltale signs:

1. *A prideful spirit.* Do you have an exalted feeling because of success or position, good training or appearance, or natural gifts and abilities? Do you show an important, independent spirit? Do you tend to be married to your own opinion?

2. *A love of praise.* Do you have a secret fondness to be noticed? Do you draw attention to yourself in conversation? Does your ego swell when you have the opportunity to speak or pray before others?

3. *A touchy temper*. Do you cover up irritability or impatience by calling it nervousness or holy indignation? Do you have a touchy spirit, a tendency to resent and retaliate when reproved or contradicted? Do you throw sharp words at others?

4. *A willful attitude.* Do you show a stubborn, unteachable spirit? Do you like to argue? Are you harsh, sarcastic, driving, or demanding? Do you come across as unyielding or headstrong? Do you tend to criticize and pick flaws when you are ignored or decisions don't go your way? Do you love to be coaxed and humored?

5. *A fearful heart.* Does fear of what others think cause you to shrink from duty or compromise your principles? Are you afraid your commitment to righteousness will cause some prominent person to think less of you?

6. *A jealous mind.* Do you hide a spirit of envy in your heart? Do you harbor an unpleasant sensation in view of the prosperity and success of another? When someone is more talented or appreciated than you, are you tempted to speak of his faults rather than his virtues?

7. *A dishonest disposition.* Do you evade or cover the truth? Do you hide or minimize your real faults and

attempt to leave a better impression of yourself than is strictly true? Do you show false humility or exaggerate, straining the truth? Do you show one face to one person and the opposite to another?

8. *A lack of faith.* Are you easily discouraged in times of pressure and opposition? Do you lack quiet confidence and settled trust in God? Do you worry and complain in the midst of pain, poverty, or trials that God allows? Are you overly anxious about whether situations will turn out all right?

9. *A wandering eye.* Do you entertain lustful stirrings, showing undue affection and familiarity to those of the opposite sex? Do you act out sexu-

The movie struck a deep chord in women everywhere, garnering many awards and becoming a box-office hit. The problem is, it was just a movie. Kathy Bates's character never had to address the painful consequences of unleashing Twanda on the world. For how do you turn off that selfish I'll-get-

ally and dwell on romantic fantasies?

10. *A spiritual deadness*. Are you complacent about the lost? Is your relationship with God characterized by dryness and indifference? Does your life lack spiritual power? Do you regularly meet God?

11. *A love of self*. Do you cater to your appetites and hanker repeatedly for short-lived pleasure? Do your joys and sorrows fluctuate around your personal interests? Do you yearn for money and earthly possessions?[1]

Search me, O God, and know my heart . . . see if there is any wicked way in me, and lead me in the way everlasting.

PSALM 139:23–24, NKJV

mine-no-matter-what attitude once you've released it? How do you handle the guilt, the wrecked relationships, and the ongoing frustration when tantrums don't solve anything? And what do you do with the reality that the Twanda inside of you has very little interest in following God or anyone else?

You see, what Kathy Bates's character calls "Twanda," the Bible calls "flesh" — and Scripture makes it clear that the Flesh Woman in each of us is energetically opposed to the kind of transformation God wants for us.

Most of us are used to thinking of *flesh* as either the physical part of us or as unhealthy indulgences like illicit sex or overeating. But the word translated *flesh* in the Bible — *sarx* — is much broader. According to my online Greek lexicon, it "denotes mere human nature, the earthly nature of men and women apart from divine influence, and therefore prone to sin and opposed to God."[3] The New International Version of Romans 7 translates it "sinful nature," while the New King James Version vividly refers to it as "body of death." *Vine's Expository Dictionary* connects *sarx* or *flesh* with several things, including "the weaker element in human nature" and "the seat of sin in man." But I like another of *Vine's* definitions best: "The lower and *temporary* element in the Christian"[4] (emphasis mine).

What a relief! I may struggle with my fleshly Twanda here on earth, but she's temporary. I may lose a few battles with my lower nature, but I won't forever!

And here's the kicker: Not only will I be

free of this "body of death" one day when I get to heaven, but I can have the satisfaction of overcoming Flesh Woman today.

Right here.

Right now.

Because Paul was right. The answer to our stubborn Flesh Woman problem really is in Jesus Christ our Lord.

REAL-LIFE WRESTLING

My Grandma Nora loved All-Star Wrestling. I don't mean the respectable Greco-Roman wrestling you see in the Olympics — the kind with tidy mats, safety helmets, and clear-cut rules. No, Grandma loved the cheesy Saturday-afternoon variety. The kind with colorful masks, wild hairdos, the occasional makeup and feather boas. No real rules. And no holds barred. Or so we believed.

Our favorite wrestler was a huge African American named Rufus. Now Rufus didn't need a cape or a mask. He didn't boast and shout like the other wrestlers did about how great he was; he didn't proclaim he was his opponent's worst nightmare. He just smiled a lot — because he had something they didn't have. Rufus had his belly.

Every Saturday afternoon when it looked for certain that our ol' buddy Rufus had finally met his match, when some evil-eyed, wild-haired maniac had Rufus in a headlock-turned-full-nelson, Rufus would just smile at the camera. Then he'd start shaking his belly. He'd start out slowly at first, but the jiggling momentum would build until his great mound of a stomach trembled so violently it not only knocked his competitor off him but threw the poor guy to the ground.

Each time this happened, we'd scream and clap with delight. And every Saturday afternoon, as though he could hear us, Rufus would turn and smile an extra big smile at the camera. Then he'd leap into the air and — as if in slow motion — fall with an earth-shattering thud on top of the dazed and soon-to-be comatose masked man lying helpless on the mat.

It was years before I finally accepted the fact that all those moves were rehearsed and the outcomes predetermined. And though I wouldn't recommend All-Star Wrestling to anyone, I did learn something valuable from watching it those many years ago. Especially from the tag-team wrestling that my sister, Linda, and I loved to act out with the good sport we call "Dad."

Each evening after dinner our father would get down on his knees, and one of us would meet him in our make-believe center ring. The fighting would begin. But no matter how hard we tried, Dad would always get the best of us. Pinned and nearly counted out, the sister about to lose would stretch one arm as far as she could toward the sister outside the ring until finally our fingers met and deliverance was nigh. With a mighty leap into the ring, the other sister would join the fray, body-slamming our competitor and rendering him helpless. While one sister pinned him to the ground, the other would slap the floor with her hand — one, two, three!

Dad was out for the count. He was done for. We were victors once again.

Of course, our after-dinner tag-team bouts were just as fake as those we watched on television. But the life-or-death struggle we wage against Flesh Woman each day — well, there's nothing fake or rehearsed about it. We all have times when we feel overwhelmed and overpowered by our lower nature, gripped in the choke hold of bad habits, the headlock of secret vices. On our own, we have little chance of winning.

So aren't you glad we have the best tag-team partner of all?

Just when we think we can't make it, just when we feel helplessly pinned down by some sin or compromise, the Lord calls from outside the ring, "Can I give you a hand?"

We don't have to squirm and scramble to find Him; we simply have to admit our need. With our asking, Jesus comes — and then all hell breaks loose. Literally. The hopeless, helpless, paralyzed feeling lifts as we see the King of the universe rushing to our aid to rescue us from our fiercest competitor, our most dangerous adversary.

Ourselves.

But we have to invite Him. We have to call Him into the ring. That's definitely a place to start. But getting the help we need is a bit more complicated than just calling out for it. For if we ever hope to have real victory over Flesh Woman, we must give Jesus the right to rule our lives.

WHO'S ON THE THRONE?

Ray Stedman's book *Authentic Christianity* [5] has helped me understand the struggle between my flesh and my own best intentions — and why, though I really am a new creature in Christ, an ongoing war still seems to rage "in my members," as Paul put it in the King James Version of Romans 7:23.

You see, God created each one of us as a three-part person: body, soul, and spirit. The *body* is the physical, outermost part of us, the tent of skin and bone we live in that makes contact with the world around us. The *soul* is our inner person — thoughts, emotions, and will. It is the part of us that reasons, feels, and make choices, allowing us to know and love God in a practical way.

But it is the innermost part of us, our *spirits,* that are awakened only by salvation. Previously dead because of sin and the Fall of man, the spirit is the hidden place where the Holy Spirit takes up residence when we invite Christ into our lives. When the Spirit comes, He throws open the shutters that have darkened our spiritual understanding and turns on the lights, filling us with God's presence, with His sparkling joy and peace. At that very moment, in our spirits, we become completely new creatures in Christ. We comprehend truth as never before. And our holy makeover — that is, our perfecting by grace — begins.[6]

These three basic areas of our lives, though closely connected, operate more or less independently. Especially in terms of who's in charge. Until we come to Christ, Flesh Woman sits upon the throne of both body and soul. (*Flesh,* remember, doesn't just mean our physical bodies, but our natural selves unchanged by God; our lower natures, tainted by sin.)

Even after salvation, Flesh Woman tends to

call the shots. Because, although we've given Christ complete dominion over our spirits, He must also be welcomed into the other areas of our lives. The dark corners of our hearts still need to be evangelized. Kingdoms in our souls have yet to hear the good news. And that multilevel transformation doesn't happen all at once.

Though our spirits are brought to life when we meet Christ, the other, more outward parts of us remain largely unchanged at first. We may feel the effects of the good news — we are happier, and we enjoy a peace and a lightness we've never experienced before. Yet Flesh Woman still rules in these areas — and she's not at all happy about our conversion.

After all, she has enjoyed unchallenged power in our lives since the day we were born. She will not give up such deep-rooted dominion without a fight. And fight she does — in any area of our lives where she's challenged.

When we accept the gift of salvation, the Spirit of God penetrates our spirits with the life of Jesus. But, as Ray Stedman wrote, "The soul is still under the control of the flesh and remains so until the Spirit successively invades each area or relationship and establishes the Lordship of Jesus within."[7] This is important to understand: *There is a throne in every area of the human soul!*

The question of Jesus's lordship must be fought anew in each area of our physical, mental, and emotional lives. This means we can be living by the Spirit in one area (say, daily devotions) and still be totally controlled by the flesh in another area (for instance, our choice of entertainment or patterns of escape). The process of unseating Flesh Woman in all these areas and making Jesus Lord of our bodies, souls, and spirits can literally take a lifetime.

In his powerful book *The Pursuit of God,* A. W. Tozer describes this process another way:

There is within the human heart a tough, fibrous root of fallen life whose nature is to possess, always to possess. . . . The ancient curse will not go out painlessly; the tough old miser within us . . . must be torn out of our heart like a plant from the soil; he must be extracted in agony and blood like a tooth from the jaw. He must be expelled from our soul by violence, as Christ expelled the money changers from the temple. And we shall need to steel ourselves against his piteous begging, and to recognize it as springing out of self-pity, one of the most reprehensible sins of the human heart.[8]

This work that Tozer and Stedman (and many other Christians) describe — the process of dethroning Flesh Woman and giving the Spirit of God the right to rule our entire lives — is traditionally called sanctification ("being made holy"). But *sanctification* seems a fairly tame word for what is really an ongoing battle to overthrow the flesh and enthrone Christ in every corner of our lives.

It's the original All-Star Wrestling match, strenuous and even painful. For while Jesus has already done the work when He died and rose again, we still have to be in the ring with Him.

Because when it comes right down to it, we have to choose which side we want to win.

THE INTERNAL TUG OF WAR

It didn't happen very often. But once in a while, back in elementary school, two girls would want to play with me at the same time. Teasing, yet serious, they would both begin to tug on my arms, pulling me one way and then the other.

"Come play tetherball!"

"No, we need you for kickball!"

For a sports-impaired ten-year-old who was usually chosen last, this was a dream come true! They wanted me. Two things to do. Two ways to go. But it wasn't the strength of their pull that determined my choice. It was the side I chose to give in to.

Paul tells us that deposing Flesh Woman and living victoriously over sin requires the same kind of daily choices. "Live by the Spirit, and you will not gratify the desires of the sinful nature," the apostle reminds us in Galatians 5:16. "The one who sows to please his sinful nature, from that nature will reap destruction," he adds. "The one who sows to please the Spirit, from the Spirit will reap eternal life" (Galatians 6:8).

With the Lord's help, we can have victory in the ongoing conflict between our Christ-controlled spirits and the parts of our lives still ruled by our flesh. But the victory is determined by whose side we take.

When John Michael and Jessica were small, I used an analogy I'd heard to try to explain this dilemma that even little children feel. "It's like you have a good dog and a bad dog inside you," I explained one night as I tucked them into bed after a particularly difficult day. "The good dog belongs to Jesus, and the bad dog belongs to the devil. They fight and fight. And they'll keep on fighting until you decide which one you want to win. If you feed the good dog, the good dog will win. But if you feed the bad dog, the bad dog will win."

When we were in the car a few days later, I

noticed John Michael glance over at his sleeping sister as though he was trying to figure something out. "What's the matter, Michael?" I asked, catching his eye in the rearview mirror.

"I think I got the bad dog inside me, Mom," he said in all seriousness. "He wants to hit Jessica *so* bad!"

Don't you wish we outgrew such inner turmoil? But we don't. At least not naturally. Oh, we may no longer have a desire to hit our sister (except when she really deserves it!), but we may struggle with feelings of envy and resentment when someone else gets something we've wanted — like the promotion we deserve or the new car we need. We may smile on the outside and offer our congratulations, but inside the bad dog howls as Flesh Woman stalks the halls of our hearts, ranting and raving at the injustice of it all.

And, if we're left to ourselves, this is our destiny. But this Twanda torment is exactly what Jesus came to save us from. For while the Law helps us recognize sin as sin, it has no power to deliver us from sin's destructiveness. It can point out Twanda's rampages and make us feel bad that she lives in us, but it can't make her stop being Twanda. And it can't get her out of our lives.

Only Jesus can do that. Only Jesus can rescue me "from this body of death." But I have to be willing to be rescued. And I'm learning that I must hate my sin if I ever hope to be rid of it.

I have to get so sick and tired of spiritual tug of wars and playground games that I finally pray, "Lord, I want to be on Your side.

"I choose You."

CONVICTION OR CONDEMNATION?

Isn't the tender mercy of the Lord wonderful? One of the sweetest realizations I've come to is that He knows my frame. He understands my limitations and, as my Creator, is keenly aware that I am only dust (Psalm 103:14). He's also well aware of how influential Flesh Woman can be. Which means He isn't nearly as surprised at my sinful failures as I am. That's why God put into place the pattern of redemption.

It's right there in Romans 8, directly after the passage that so vividly describes our weary internal wrestling:

Therefore, there is now no condemnation for those who are in Christ Jesus, because through Christ Jesus the law of the Spirit of life set me free from the law of sin and death. For what the law was powerless to do in that it was weakened by the sinful nature, God did by sending his own Son. (Romans 8:1–3)

God knew that, even on my best days, I could never stand up to my un-holy roommate or escape her corrupting influence. So, in His mercy, God clothed Himself in humanity and descended to dwell on this earth. Taking my sin and paying for it by His death, Christ became what I was . . . so I could become what He is.

And Christ's sacrifice was enough. Nothing I could ever do would add or take away from it. Nothing — except my refusal to receive what He has so graciously given.

Which is why our choosing is so important: it's our part in the redemption process. We must choose to agree with God's judgment against our sin and accept His remedy for the Flesh Woman problem in us all.

It's simple, really — though we usually manage to make it complicated. I know I did. For years God couldn't shine the spotlight of conviction on my heart without Satan pushing that conviction into extreme condemnation. I couldn't admit my shortcomings to myself without being overwhelmed by shame and guilt.

But lately the Lord has been giving me a larger view, a kind of third-person perspective that allows me to back up and see what He sees and then call it what He calls it.

Falling short. Missing the mark. Sin.

Instead of fighting against the revelation or grieving myself into paralysis over its implications, I'm learning to simply confess my faults, my weaknesscs, and even my willful sin, accept God's forgiveness, and move on with my life.

Somehow in the past I had confused repentance with penance. "Bad me, bad me," I'd cry in my heart as I beat myself bloody for my failures. "How could I have done this? How can God still love me?" You see, I had picked up the false belief that I had to feel really bad for a certain amount of time before I could be forgiven; that I had to add something to the Cross and the shed blood of Christ.

But the problem with this twisted way of thinking was that by the time I had "felt" bad enough for my sins to receive forgiveness, I had usually sinned again. Which, of course, launched me into another round of guilt and shame. "Bad me, bad me." Around and around I'd go in the downward spiral of condemnation. I never experienced any release from the heavy load of guilt. I felt the weight of sin piled upon sin piled upon sin.

No wonder I couldn't remember the good

Have you ever wondered what the difference is between conviction and condemnation? We need to know — for one leads to life, the other to death.

CONVICTION from God
- Pinpoints problems
- Targets specific actions
- Leads to repentance (godly sorrow)
- Offers solutions
- Makes us hopeful
- Enables us to change
- Brings us closer to God

CONDEMNATION from Satan
- Obscures problems
- Makes general accusations

news. Spiritual amnesia had wiped out the power of the Cross and left me with only myself as a savior. And, try as I might, I could never deliver myself from this particular body of sin and death.

For there is only one Messiah.

Only one perfect Lamb.

One Lion of Judah who can break every chain.

- Leads to regret (worldly sorrow)
- Appoints blame
- Makes us hopeless
- Keeps us from change
- Drives us away from God

WARNING: What starts as conviction by the Holy Spirit can quickly turn to condemnation from the enemy if we don't respond immediately with repentance. Be quick to obey and don't grieve the Holy Spirit, for He desires to help you.

Blessed are they whose transgressions are forgiven, whose sins are covered.

ROMANS 4:7

DE-DRAGONING

In *The Voyage of the Dawn Treader,* C. S. Lewis tracks the adventures of a boy named Eustace Grubb. Obnoxious in the extreme, Eustace is always demanding his own way and is certain everyone is against him. When his ship *Dawn Treader* stops at an unknown island for repairs, the boy wanders off on his own. Stumbling across a great pile of treasure in an abandoned dragon's lair, Eustace stuffs his pockets with jewels and gold and then falls asleep on the dragon's hoard. As he sleeps, dark dragonish thoughts fill his heart, and Eustace wakes to find that he himself has become a dragon.

Dismayed by this and other events, Eustace wants to be different. He tries to be different. But at the end of every day, he remains the same — a boy trapped inside a dragon's body.

Then one night Eustace meets the great lion Aslan, who leads him to a clear pool. Certain the water will ease his discomfort, Eustace decides to bathe. But Aslan tells him he must undress first. Three times Eustace scratches at his scales and sheds his dragonish skin. But each time he does, he finds yet another layer underneath.

"You have to let me undress you," the Lion tells him. Here's how Eustace describes it:

The very first tear he made was so deep that I thought it had gone right into my heart. And when he began pulling the skin off, it hurt worse than anything I've ever felt. The only thing that made me able to bear it was just the pleasure of feeling the stuff peel off. . . . Well, he peeled the beastly stuff right off — just as I thought I'd done it myself the other three times, only they hadn't hurt — and there it was lying in the grass: only ever so much thicker, and darker, and more knobbly looking than the others had been.[9]

Naked and trembling, Eustace bathes in the pool and is once again a boy. Aslan gives him a new set of clothes and transports him back to the beach where the ship waits.

Back to his new life. His transformed life.

How we all need de-dragoning, every single one of us. Left to ourselves we can only scratch and claw at our dragonish skin. We make small amounts of progress, but little semblance of change. Until we lay our lives before the great Lion of Judah, asking Him to do the transforming work, our efforts at self-improvement will only yield one layer of dragonish skin after another.

Perhaps that's why Paul implores us to, in view of God's mercy, offer ourselves "as living sacrifices, holy and pleasing to God" (Romans 12:1).

Climb up on the operating table, Paul advises. Put your entire self in the trustworthy hands of Christ. Let the divine Surgeon remove the fleshly encasement of sin that has bound you too long. Lie still under the razor-sharp scalpel of Christ's unfailing love and allow Him to release what you were created to be.

I love how C. S. Lewis concludes this story. "It would be nice, and fairly nearly true, to say that 'from that time forth Eustace was a different boy.' To be strictly accurate, he began to be a different boy. He had relapses. . . . But most of these I shall not notice. The cure had begun."[10]

And so has it begun for us as well.

Though I'm not yet what I ought to be, thank God, I'm not what I was.

And neither are you. For "he who began a good work in you will carry it on to completion until the day of Christ Jesus," Philippians 1:6 assures us. Though we may not see the finished product until heaven, you can be sure that what God has started, He will finish. And as long as we daily relinquish control of our lives to Jesus Christ, our transformation will continue.

Flesh Woman, though still our roommate, will no longer run the house. Instead of wreaking chaos and anarchy, she will be forced to bow her knee and submit to the Spirit of God and His rule.

Oh, she'll fuss and fret. She'll pout and moan. But she will no longer have the power to completely control and manipulate us. For we are different; we are new creatures in

Christ Jesus.

And yes, we may have relapses. But these we shall not notice, except to confess them, repent of them, and accept the forgiveness Christ so freely gives.

For the cure — our holy makeover — has begun.

From glory to glory Christ is changing us. And we will never be the same.

4
SPIRIT CHECK

*Let us examine our ways and test them,
and let us return to the LORD.*
LAMENTATIONS 3:40

There was a tension in the air that day.
They all could feel it. Mixed with the dust
that swirled up around them at every step
was a purpose the disciples didn't fully understand.

Jesus had tried to explain. Something
about Jerusalem and betrayal. Something
about going there to die. But it didn't make
sense. *Probably another figurative story,* they
reasoned. *Another parable.*

The Master was quiet as He walked. His
face set still as stone as He gazed down the
road toward the Holy City and the upcoming Passover.

As for James and John, they could only
shake their heads over what had just happened.

For a backwater, God-forsaken Samaritan village to turn away a request from the King of kings for a simple place to lay His head — it was intolerable. Racial animosity often closed doors to Jews on their way to worship in Jerusalem, but this was Jesus! This was the Man who'd healed their sick and made their blind see. Surely they should have made an exception.

Now Jesus and the disciples would have to sleep outside on the hard ground. It was more than they could take. More than they *should* have to take!

After a whispered conference, the two brothers concocted a plan. They caught up to Jesus and discreetly asked, "Lord, do you want us to call fire down from heaven to destroy them?" (Luke 9:54).

It was a brilliant idea, they thought. Like the children of Israel when Elijah called down fire and destroyed the prophets of Baal, all of Samaria would know that Jesus was the Messiah — the one, true God. And all of Israel would know as well. After all, there's no object lesson as effective as a smoldering, black heap of ruin. Remember Sodom and Gomorrah?

At least that had been their reasoning. But the brilliance of their plan began to fade as they saw Jesus staring at them in unbelief.

"You do not know what manner of spirit you are of," Jesus said in a low, pained whisper. Gripping James and John gently by the shoulders, He spoke the words that would forever echo in their minds: "The Son of Man did not come to destroy men's lives but to save them" (Luke 9:55–56, NKJV).[1]

WHAT SPIRIT ARE YOU OF?

That story never fails to pierce my heart. It is sobering to realize that, like the disciples, I can walk with Jesus, be taught by Jesus, yet still act and react out of human rationalization rather than the principles by which He told us to live. Even after serving the Lord for so long, I still tend to take matters in my own hands when it appears that no one else is going to take care of the situation. When things move too slowly for my comfort. When doors remain shut that I'm certain God wants opened.

"Do you want me to take care of this, Lord?" I ask, flexing the strong arm of my flesh. "I'm really good at it, you know." And instantly Twanda's in her prime. Flesh Woman is strutting her stuff. Taking care of business. Setting everybody straight.

And when that happens, I need to ask myself, "Of what manner of spirit am I?"

Because, to be honest, I can see myself

standing eagerly beside James and John that day offering Jesus my services, more than willing to teach the world a lesson. The whole fire-breathing-dragon role comes far too easily to me.

And that is my problem — our human problem — in a nutshell. Left to ourselves, we will always default to the *carnal,* which is really just another word for *flesh.* Just as my computer defaults, or automatically goes, to one program even when I want access to another, so our reactions tend to revert to our fleshly thinking.

I don't have to decide to lash out when my spouse says something that hurts me. The angry retorts just happen.

I don't have to consciously choose to be impatient with the kids. Just let them be slow getting ready, and my mind (not to mention my mouth!) starts fuming without any prompting.

I don't have to force myself to tell those little (or big) self-protective lies. They just slip out.

Carnal thinking and carnal responses come *naturally* to us humans. Preprogrammed into our operating system since the Fall, our lower nature is our default mode. But what seems right to our natural minds rarely aligns with what God would have us do. In fact, Paul said the carnal mind "is hostile to God" (Romans 8:7). It not only refuses to submit to God's will; it is powerless to do so.

Because when we're living carnally, the spirit we're of is not God's, but what 1 Corinthians 2:12 calls the "spirit of the world." It's Flesh Woman all over again, stubbornly holding out in one area of our lives or another. And we might not even know she's there — because one of the hallmarks of carnal thinking is self-deception.

Renew a Right Spirit

"Create in me a clean heart, O God," David wrote in Psalm 51:10–11, "and renew a right spirit within me. Cast me not away from thy presence; and take not thy Holy Spirit from me" (KJV). I've prayed that prayer thousands of times over the years, but perhaps no one has prayed it with as much heartfelt sincerity as the man who wrote it.

King David, you see, was a man found out. All his dirty little secrets — his lust for Bathsheba, his plot to have her husband killed, his willingness to lie about it to himself as well as his subjects — had been exposed by God through the prophet Nathan. As I read the psalm, I can almost feel the weight of failure pressing down upon

David's soul.

Yet when he finally faced the reality of who he was and what he'd done, David went to the only appropriate place any of us can go when our inner darkness is finally revealed: he poured out his heart to God.

He did the same in Psalm 139:23–24, "Search me, O God, and know my heart. . . . See if there is any offensive way in me."

Don't let me fool myself any longer, he was saying.

Show me what spirit I am of . . .

I pray that prayer constantly as well because self-deception comes quite easily to me. To all of us. Because we live such surface lives, we find we can gloss over sin just as we cover our kids' crayon marks with a coat of paint. It is possible to become so adept at leading the "unexamined life,"[2] as Socrates called it, that even the author of the psalms could steal another man's wife, have him murdered, father an illegitimate child, and justify it all in his mind.

But God never deals in deception — or denial. In His mercy, He confronts what we ignore and reveals what we are much too willing to hide. Though we may put our fingers in our ears and hum loudly like a rebellious child, God will still find a way to put the truth in front of us.

Why do we need God to renew a right spirit within us? Because the wrong spirit infiltrates our hearts and minds far more easily than we realize. That's why the Bible warns of many kinds of wrong attitudes. Here are five I consider very dangerous, especially for women:

1. *A Competitive Spirit*: A woman with a competitive spirit needs to achieve, to be the best. She gloats over winning and pushes others to succeed so she looks good. Although she chases position and craves achievement, she can never get enough. And because no one can win all the time, she is often deeply frustrated (see Ecclesiastes 2:22).

2. *A Controlling Spirit*: A controller micromanages people and situations out of a desperate "need to know" all that's going on. She freely gives advice and expects compliance. Her belief that she must make things happen can lead to weary despair when no one cooperates (see 1 Peter 4:15, NKJV).

3. *A Critical Spirit:* A woman with this attitude expects the worst rather than the best from people and situations. She cancels out positives with her constant negativity. No matter the achievement, she believes that *someone* should have done better. Her secret self-criticism may cause depression or anger (see Isaiah 58:9).

4. *A Contentious Spirit*: This woman loves to argue and debate, and she flies off the handle easily. She corrects others' versions of a story and creates drama by picking fights. She fiercely defends her children even when they're wrong — but she's hard on them too. Wound tight, she may suffer physical ailments (see 2 Timothy 2:23).

5. *A Discontented Spirit:* Never at rest in her own skin, this woman is always on the go. She accumulates possessions and relationships in an attempt to fill her emptiness. Flitting from one thing to another in search

of meaning, she starts projects but rarely finishes them. Disappointment with what isn't swallows the joy of what is (see Philippians 4:12).

The LORD'S searchlight penetrates the human spirit, exposing every hidden motive.

PROVERBS 20:27, NLT

He may send a friend to confront us, as God sent Nathan to expose David's sin. He may speak through the pages of a book or the words of a counselor, or He may nudge us into awareness in the depths of our souls. But one thing we can count on — God will eventually show us our sin.

And aren't you glad He does? After all until we see how dark our hearts can be, we will never cry out for a heart like His. We'll continue living our lives with the wrong spirit, the wrong attitude, rather than calling out for a heart made new in the likeness of Christ. And we'll keep lying to ourselves about who we are and why we do what we do.

Perhaps that is why many of us struggle in our relationships and why our best efforts are misunderstood and unappreciated. We live life out of the natural, the carnal. We do what we think is best, never realizing that the selfishness and sin built into our basic natures can infect even our best intentions.

We're good girls wanting to do good things. But because our hearts have not been completely reprogrammed to operate according to God's truth, our best gifts tend to be tainted by a Martha spirit and distorted by a sharp edge, a haughty attitude, and a hidden agenda or two.

They'd better appreciate what I've done!

It's high time they asked me to teach a Bible study.

If I do this, then they'll have to do that . . .

We don't say such things out loud, of course, and perhaps we only rarely think about them. But, subconsciously, such ulterior motives often shroud our offerings. No wonder they are poorly received. For God wants to change our carnal behavior, not reward it.

I'm convinced that's why God refused to allow my Flesh Woman drivenness to accomplish what I desired for our church's building project. You see, God is more concerned about shaping the eternal in His people than about building an external kingdom that will someday pass away.

Though we may be eager to do things for God, it's important to realize that ministry, like any kind of power or position, can be fancy food for the flesh. Our carnal nature can grow up around our call (and even our careers) like a wild vine, choking out the sweetness of Jesus, leaving behind the foul stench of selfish ambition and vain conceit.

And all the while, Jesus is whispering, *You do not know what manner of spirit you are of.*

If we don't pause and listen to Christ's correction, God often allows us to run into a continuous string of mishaps and misunderstandings at church, at home, and on the job. We speak the truth in love only to have people misinterpret our words as judgmental. Or mislabel our gift of administration as controlling. Or misconstrue our desire to help as meddling. Our families may even accuse us (unfairly, of course) of loving everyone else except them.

As we continue our wrong-spirited, carnal-minded efforts, we'll inevitably find that people neglect — or refuse outright! — to follow the scripts we've so carefully prepared for them. They won't do what we want. They won't say what we need to hear. And we're left with hurt feelings and rejection.

In fact, life may come to feel as though it's made up of one self-fulfilling prophecy after another: *I knew they would leave me out. I knew they'd give that position to someone else. No one appreciates how hard I work.* As though, unbeknownst to us, we wear a big neon sign pasted on our foreheads that says "Hurt me! Reject me!" — and people seem to line up around the block to comply.

Do you see how twisted this whole process can become? For not only are our best intentions misinterpreted, but Satan manages to secure our insecurities by using them against us. During those times when we are genuinely hurting, he will see to it that our legitimate needs for affirmation and encouragement go unmet. That no one calls. That no one seems to care. And with each hurt we experience, Satan just stands back and chuckles, watching as we add yet another brick to the wall we're building around our hearts.

Continuing to wonder why people don't treat us right.

Never realizing that the problem may lie within us.

HOW DOES YOUR BREATH SMELL?

It had been a hard day. Once again my four-year-old son and I were in a tug of war of the wills. We pulled back and forth, neither of us willing to give in, to admit that perhaps — just perhaps — we might be out of line. I'd ask him to do something, and he wouldn't. He wanted to play, and I couldn't. Total frustration and nap deprivation on both our parts brought us to a nose-to-nose confrontation midafternoon.

"Your attitude stinks, John Michael!" I said sharply, one hand on my hip, the other shaking a finger in his upturned little face.

There. I'd summed up the problem in just three words. He was being a pill, and he needed correcting.

But rather than seeing the light dawn, I saw something else in his eyes. It was as though I'd taken his heart and crumpled it like a juice box. While his defiance may have melted slightly, I could see hurt flooding in to take its place.

"Oh yeah?" he said in a small, trembling voice. A voice I needed to hear. "Well, your breath doesn't smell very good either."

From the mouth of babes . . . God continues to use this shrewd analysis to change my life. Because even when we're right, we can be wrong.

How does your attitude smell? What spirit are you of?

Wouldn't it be great if we had a spiritual breathalyzer test available at all times?

Rather than measuring drunkenness and our ability to drive, it would indicate the sweetness of our spirits. But even if such an instrument existed, it could only tell us what's wrong. It couldn't renew a right spirit in us.

One of the most beautiful promises and prophecies concerning Christ's new covenant work is found in Ezekiel 36:26–27:

> I will give you a new heart and put a new spirit in you; I will remove from you your heart of stone and give you a heart of flesh. And I will put my Spirit in you and move you to follow my decrees and be careful to keep my laws.

Listen to those verses! What Jesus did on the cross not only saved us from our sins, but it can also save us from ourselves — from our lousy attitudes, our default-y thinking, our stubborn self-deception. And the Lord does this not by pointing out where we should change or by calling us to wrestle Flesh Woman to the mat.

He does transforming work by filling us with Himself.

For I need more than a right spirit to live a life that pleases God. I need God's Holy Spirit alive and active in me.

When Jesus breathed on the disciples in John 20:22 and said, "Receive the Holy Spirit," He was, in essence, both answering David's prayer and fulfilling Ezekiel's prophecy. The word for spirit in the Greek is *pneuma*. In the Old Testament Hebrew it's *ruach*. Both can be translated "breath."[3]

Jesus came to breathe His breath — His sweetness, His completeness, His very being — into you and me so that He is the operating system to which we default. So that in Him "we live and move and have our being" (Acts 17:28).

Trying to live apart from the Holy Spirit is like a goldfish trying to survive outside water. We may look alive. We may flop around a lot and move our mouths, making strange gasping noises now and then, but we will never know what it means to really live. To glide free, breathe, and live effortlessly in the liquid life of grace.

Too often, I fear, we Christians settle for this fish-out-of-water kind of existence. "Well, I'm just a sinner saved by grace," we gasp, as though that somehow excuses and explains away our spastic, flip-floppy behavior — almost holy one moment, completely unholy the next.

As though Christ's coming and dying did

nothing more than secure for us a place in heaven.

As though spiritual mediocrity is the best we can hope for here on earth.

As though God created us to be captives even though everything in the Bible says we've already been set free.

Pastor and author Mark Buchanan, describes this halfway life too many Christians settle for as "conversion without regeneration, an initial encounter with Jesus that doesn't lead to a life abiding with Jesus." He calls it "borderland."

People on borderland have grown comfortable with boredom. They have settled for a God "on call," a God available for crises and fiascos, who does a bit of juggling with weather patterns and parking stalls but who otherwise remains unobtrusive as a chambermaid, tidying things up while you're at brunch, leaving a crisp sash of tissue around the lid of the toilet bowl to let you know all is in order. The problem, obviously, is that this god — so kind, so shy, so tame — has nothing whatsoever to do with the God of the Bible. This god resembles not even remotely the God whose Spirit broods and dances, the God who topples entire empires, sometimes overnight, the God who reveals himself in the Christ who looks big men in the eye and says, "Follow me," and then walks away, not waiting for a reply.[4]

This is a God bold enough to call us away from borderland and kind enough to provide a way out. For we have not been left helpless. "The Christ you have to deal with is not a weak person outside you," the Phillips translation of 2 Corinthians 13:3 declares, "but a tremendous power *inside* you" (emphasis mine).

THE SPIRIT THAT CHANGED IT ALL

This powerful Presence, this dynamic Christ-in-Us, is the third Person of the Trinity. The indwelling aspect of God we call the Holy Spirit. And oh, if we only realized the difference the Spirit can make in our lives — just as He has done throughout the centuries.

For He's the same quickening power that turned Peter from shifting sand into a solid rock upon which Christ could build His church.

He's the transforming power that turned Saul, a murdering persecutor of the body of Christ, into Paul, a church-planting father of the faith.

He's the revolutionary power that took a handful of believers in a Jerusalem upper room and used them, in the words of their detractors, to turn "the world upside down" (Acts 17:6, NKJV).

It wasn't until after the Spirit came, in fact, that Jesus's disciples made any kind of impact on their world. Though they had lived and walked with Jesus for three years, being in His presence hadn't changed them all that much. I know that may sound blasphemous, but keep reading.

These twelve handpicked men had left their families and livelihoods to follow Christ. Yet after being privy to all the inner workings of God on earth, after enjoying front-row seats to hundreds of miracles never seen before by the human eye, they still doubted Jesus when they faced impossibilities like really big storms, really bad demons, and really hungry people. Even as Jesus walked toward Jerusalem and the Cross, His disciples were still arguing about who would be greatest in the kingdom that they were certain He came to build. They were just as clueless at the end of Christ's time on Earth as they were at the beginning of His ministry.

Because here's the bottom line: We can *know* what we ought to do. We can even have

God physically there beside us, a flesh-and-blood example of what life should be — yet still be powerless to live as we ought to live.

In order to truly change — to stop our self-sabotage, oust Flesh Woman, and open our lives to transformation — we need a Helper. A Strengthener. An internal Source of power.

Praise God, that's exactly what Jesus sent the Holy Spirit to be for us. Fifty days after Christ appeared to His disciples, after He breathed on them saying, "Receive the Holy Spirit," the Spirit came at Pentecost (Acts 2).

And nothing has ever been the same.

MARKED BY LOVE

No wonder Satan has tried for so long to squelch the Spirit's work, going so far as to make the precious gift of the Holy Spirit a lightning rod for controversy in the Body of Christ. We've gotten so mired in the peripherals of the Spirit's work — tongues and miracles and whether or not these manifestations are valid today — that we often miss an incredible resource.

"There's a whole group of people out there in the Christian world that are more frightened of the Holy Spirit than they are of the enemy," Beth Moore says in her video series

Breaking Free. "And therefore we continue living in defeat. . . . [We must be] totally dependent upon the Holy Spirit and the Word of God to equip us."[5]

For you see, the Holy Spirit came to do more than enable us to live victoriously. He came to help us do the one thing Jesus said would cause the world to stand up and take notice that we were God's children: "By this all men will know that you are my disciples, if you *love* one another" (John 13:35, emphasis mine).

And that is exactly what happened! The baptism of love the New Testament church experienced after the Spirit's coming was unlike anything the world had ever seen. People set aside time daily just to be together, to eat and laugh and sing and worship God. When someone was in need, others sold their possessions — without being asked! — so the needy person could be helped. Slave or free, Jew or Gentile, or even a complete stranger — everyone had a place in God's family. When pagan observers were asked to describe the early church, their oft-quoted comment was "Behold, how they love each other!"

However this was no ordinary human love. Human love wears thin with time and lack of gratitude. Human love is willing to help, but only to a point. (It fears unhealthy dependence, not to mention long-term commitment.) Human love may strive to be pure and giving, but selfishness inevitably creeps into the mix somewhere.

But this love . . . *this* love! There had been nothing quite like it in the history of the world. And it is this same selfless love we are called to live out every day.

But how do we do that? *Really* do that?

I believe the ability to love people as we should only comes from the security of knowing we ourselves are loved. For you cannot share what you do not have. Which is another reason we need the Holy Spirit — for He bears witness with our hearts that we are God's children, and dearly loved as well (Romans 8:15–16, 1 John 3:1).

MORE THAN Y'ALL

The evening had been beautiful. After speaking at an event in the South, I walked a young woman to her car. "So what has God been saying to you lately?" I asked. Her eyes sparkled under the parking-lot lights as she paused. "Well, I've been realizing how much God loves me," she said in her soft southern drawl. "But the most exciting thing is that I just feel like He loves me more than y'all!"

She quickly clarified that she knew God

loved every one of us and that she didn't think she was better than anyone else. "But you know," she confided with a sweet little grin, "I still feel like I'm His favorite!"

Her words quickened something in my heart. After completely stunning me with their innocent boldness, they awoke a longing inside me for the same kind of assurance. The same confidence that not only lit her face, but her life as well.

"How did you get that?" I asked, wanting the same confidence. "What happened that made you feel so secure in God's love?"

She said she wasn't sure. "But I think it began when I had my kids."

I've thought about her words many times since that night, and I believe I'm beginning to understand what she might have meant. After all, the love born in a mother's heart at the birth of her child truly is unique. Unconditional. Sacrificial. Intense and personal. As though there has never been another child in the universe like the child you now hold in your arms. A mother's love really is a reflection of the love God has for us. But to have it translate so deeply into a confidence that makes one feel that she is God's one and only — wow! I want to experience that kind of love.

And in some ways, I have.

How do we cooperate with the wooing and leading of the Holy Spirit? The following is by no means a comprehensive list, but here are some ways I've experienced the Spirit's leading. (I wish I was quicker to recognize His guidance and followed it more regularly!)

1. **Tune your heart to His voice.** God's Spirit speaks in a still, small voice rarely audible to the human ear (at least not to mine!). But as we quiet our hearts, He often uses impressions or our own thoughts to direct us. The more we practice listening for Him, the more we're likely to recognize His leading.

2. **Mind the checks.** This Quaker phrase means that when we feel a strong doubt whether a particular course is right, we should simply wait and do nothing. Direction from God will strengthen with the passing of time. If the course of action is not from Him, in a few days or weeks it will fade or disappear entirely.[6]

3. **Test the message.** We must check

any inner direction we receive against Scripture. If it aligns, then the advice of godly friends, providential circumstances, and what Catherine Marshall calls "sanctified common sense" can also be helpful.[7]

4. **Watch for repetition.** God often sends me confirmations that I've heard His voice through sermons, other people, or miraculous provision. Themes will be repeated because, as my friend Marla says, "God is like your mom. If you don't listen the first time, He repeats Himself!"

5. **Take the next step.** Though God often gives direction, I've found He almost never lays out a road map for the future. He intends this life to be a walk of faith. So, as we obey one step at a time, the next step will come into view. As we practice obedience, the voice of the Spirit becomes clearer, His instructions more definite.[8]

6. **Beware the Spirit's withdrawal.** Our disobedience grieves and hin-

ders the Holy Spirit's work. If He is insistent that you obey in some area, do it — or you'll feel a lack of the Spirit's presence. As Oswald Chambers says, "God will never reveal more truth . . . until you obey what you know already."[9]

7. **Ask for and expect wisdom.** Do not rule out God's help with the small details of life. If we don't allow God to direct our everyday lives, we may not be able to follow Him when crises come.[10] When you ask, believe the Spirit will lead you into all truth. Look for the answer in faith. God is eager to help us!

Teach me to do your will, for you are my God; may your good Spirit lead me on level ground.

PSALM 143:10

For the first sixteen years of my life, Grandma Nora lived with us. She helped raise us kids while my mother worked, and I have so many wonderful memories of my times with her. Cheeseburgers and Pepsi at Woolworth's soda fountain. Chicken and dumplings for dinner and pancakes (so many pancakes!) for breakfast. Taking turns spending the night with Grandma, tucked in her big iron bed, and falling asleep as she prayed for missionaries around the world. Grandma Nora blessed us with a rich legacy of love.

When she passed away, my brother and sister and I sat around sharing all that Grandma Nora had meant to us. "I feel kind of bad," my baby brother Steve said. "I hope you guys weren't mad that I was her favorite."

I looked at him in amazement. "What do you mean?" I asked. "I was her favorite."

Linda looked at both of us and shook her head. "No way! *I* was her favorite!"

We all stared at each other in disbelief and then dissolved in laughter and wonderment. To experience such a depth of love and attention that all three of us would secretly consider ourselves loved "more than y'all" — wow! I want to love like that.

I think this experience might explain what happened to John, the disciple of Jesus. I've always found it odd how John refers to himself in the gospel he authored. Rather than using his name, he refers to himself, again and again, as "the disciple whom Jesus loved" (for example, John 13:23). Scholars have all sorts of explanations as to why John may have done that, but I have a feeling it's because John had an encounter with Christ much like the one my sweet southern belle described. A solid realization of just how personal and passionate God's love for each and every one of us really is.

When you first read it, John's self-description may seem a bit haughty and self-absorbed. But as you continue reading, you realize there's only one main character in John's gospel — Jesus Christ. John disappears. Jesus is lifted up. When inserting himself in the scene seems necessary, instead of using earthly tags and descriptions such as *I* or *me* or even the third-person *John,* the disciple refers to the One who loves him. After all, Jesus's love for him is the key to John's identity.

Instead of defining himself, John lets Christ define him. And the incredible reality of Christ's acceptance goes so deep that it roots out all of John's insecurity and even concern over how other people might interpret his bold ID.

"I just feel like Jesus loves me more than y'all," John declares. But rather than diminishing the love Christ had for the other disciples, John's declaration increases the astounding possibility that Jesus might love the rest of us just as much. So much that we, too, will never be able to look at ourselves — let alone define who we are — the same way again.

TEMPERED BY THE SPIRIT

By the end of his life, John, formerly known as a "Son of Thunder," became known as the apostle of love. The man who had once found people expendable — not to mention extinguishable — now spent the last years of his life calling the body of Christ to one great mission. The same mission Jesus had given the disciples years before — loving one another in such a radical way that it not only drew people to Christ, but it changed the world.

As you read John's later epistles, it's apparent that his fiery, sharp-edged manner had been tempered by the Spirit of Christ dwelling in him. In its place was a winsome Christianity that drew people instead of repelling them. Though John clearly rebuked heresy and false doctrine in his writings throughout his life, his final message embraced one theme. The historian Jerome recorded John's words:

"Little children, love one another . . . this

is the Lord's command, and enough is done when this is done."[11]

Because the same Spirit who lived in John dwells in us as well, we too can be changed. As we surrender our nature to Christ, He replaces it with His own.

Honing our gifts and talents so they can be used effectively by God.

Purifying our motives and intents so we're not undone when He chooses to use someone else.

Mending and healing our past so it no longer affects our future.

Tempering our personalities and spirits so they are not only fit for the Master's use, but also can be received by others with gratitude.

All of this describes the manner of Spirit who desires to live and move in you if you will allow Him access.

For God's Holy Spirit can create in you a clean heart and a right spirit. Restoring to you such joy in your salvation, such compassion in your heart, that you won't feel the need to call down fire from heaven.

For heaven's fiery love will fill your soul.

5

FAULT LINES

Surely you desire truth in the inner parts;
you teach me wisdom in the inmost place.

PSALM 51:6

The ancient city of Sardis sat proudly upon a rock citadel high above a river valley in Asia Minor. A seemingly impenetrable fortress for centuries, it was considered one of the greatest cities in the world. Its most famous king, Croesus, ruled Sardis boldly, amassing great wealth and power. So much that even today "rich as Croesus" is used to describe someone of unimaginable wealth.

But while Croesus brought the city to its zenith, he also plunged it into disaster.

After receiving an oracle's prophecy that if he "crossed the River Halys, a great empire would fall," Croesus confidently led his troops against Cyrus of Persia, only to be severely beaten back. As Croesus retreated to the safety of his citadel, Cyrus followed him and laid siege to Sardis for fourteen days. But the city enjoyed a plentiful supply of food and water, and Cyrus soon realized Croesus would never surrender. So the Persian king offered a reward to anyone who could find entry into the city.

Meanwhile, Croesus assigned only a few guards to the city walls before retiring to his palace. He wasn't worried. Everyone knew his fortress could not be taken.

But one day, one of the Sardinian sentries dropped his helmet. A Persian soldier named Hyeroeades watched as the guard disappeared from his post high above, slipped out from the base of the cliff, reclaimed his gear, and went back into a hidden fold in the mountain. With that careless mistake the sentry revealed a fault in the great citadel, a crack in the seemingly unbreachable wall of rock.

That evening Hyeroeades and a party of Cyrus's troops crept up through the same crevice and captured the unwatched city without a struggle.

The oracle's prophecy was correct. Croesus's crossing of the river brought the end of a great empire. And so Sardis fell.[1]

FATAL FLAWS

Like the citadel of Sardis, we all have fault lines that run through our souls. Weak spots in our psyches that may go undetected — or simply ignored — for years. Living high above the hidden fissures, we may function fairly well in our outer lives. In fact, we may appear as strong and invincible as King Croesus felt. Rich and well fed. Never acknowledging our vulnerability or the need to guard against potential attack.

These are the very places Satan searches for when he prowls around "like a roaring lion looking for someone to devour" (1 Peter 5:8). Because when the Enemy can't storm the gate of our salvation, he looks for a break in the wall, even the tiniest crack. A weak spot he can exploit.

It's a strategy as old as time.

In Genesis 4 when God rejected Cain's offering and accepted Abel's, a jealous breach opened up in Adam and Eve's firstborn. God tried to reason with him.

"Why are you angry? Why is your face downcast? If you do what is right, will you not be accepted?" the Lord asked the young man. God was trying to remind Cain that the problem was between him and his Maker, not between him and his brother. Pointing out the weak spot in Cain's fortress, God warned him, "But if you do not do what is right, sin is crouching at your door; it desires to have you, but you must master it" (Genesis 4:6–7).

Unfortunately, Cain ignored God and carried out his plan. While his brother's blood satisfied his anger for a moment, it placed Cain under a curse and separated him from the One whose approval he craved. "My punishment is more than I can bear," Cain grieved. "I will be hidden from your presence . . . a restless wanderer on the earth" (Genesis 4:13–14).

And so it is today. Sin crouches at our doors, looking for fault lines, searching for a point of entry into our hearts and souls. Which is why it's so important to allow God to expose and confront the cracks in our characters.

Jesus often did this kind of work in the New Testament. When He pointed out flaws in people He met, He wasn't trying to humiliate them. He wanted to alert them to danger and point the way toward their healing.

To the Pharisees intent on appearing religious, Jesus pointed out the fault line of hypocrisy.

To the rich young ruler requesting the way to heaven, Jesus exposed the dangerous tendency of loving money more than God.

And that day in Bethany when Martha came whining to Jesus demanding assistance, it wasn't insensitivity that caused Jesus to rebuke her (Luke 10:38–42). He knew the last thing Martha needed at that moment was more help in the kitchen. What she really needed was to recognize the fault line in her soul.

"Martha, Martha," He told her gently. "You are worried and upset about many things" (verse 41). With those words, Jesus pointed to a weak spot in her psyche — her anxiety, her need to succeed, and to the fear of failure which fed a demanding spirit.

Whether it is resentful anger like Cain's, a Pharisee's need to appear successful, a young ruler's passion for possessions, or a Marthalike pursuit of perfection — we all have fault lines, core issues that fuel our desires and shape our actions. And when we give in to our natural impulses and go against God's ways, we may get what we want but lose what we need most.

An awareness of God's presence.

His blessing on our lives.

What Is Your Weak Spot?

I don't know what your core issue might be, what flaw runs through your soul like Sardis's dark crevice. (The sidebars in the previous chapter might give you some clues.)

I didn't truly become aware of my own fault line until about six years ago. Although I knew I had weak areas and could recognize recurring sins and trigger points, I had no idea what the core problem was until everything in my life began going wrong.

That statement may sound strange to you — or it may sound all too familiar. For there is nothing like adversity to reveal what we're made of. In fact, I'm convinced that trouble and stress are two of the most common ways God shows us the weakness of our flesh and the futility of our self-efforts. In His mercy, He often allows stress to build up until the weak areas in our lives begin to give way under pressure.

That is exactly what happened to me.

The details of my situation aren't important. They never are. My experience was simply the tool God used to open my eyes to the San Andreas fault in my life — my hunger for approval. Though I'd felt small rumblings along this particular line before, it took an 8.5 earthquake on my emotional Richter scale — and watching my own personal Southern California slide into the sea — before I finally acknowledged that I had a problem. A problem I no longer wanted to hide and, more important, a core issue I needed God to deal with.

It all started so innocently — with a difference of opinion between me and a group of friends at church. Talking off the top of my head, I got on one of my opinionated soapboxes, and a flippant remark landed like a spark on my most treasured relationships. These were women I dearly loved (and still love), women who had supported me through the most demanding year of my life, women who had worked (and still work) by my side in several of our church's ministries. And women who, like me, were exhausted and slightly on edge.

Though I knew our common ground was severely parched from lack of time together, I had no idea how damaging my thoughtless comment would prove to be. Like a tourist flicking a cigarette out a car window on the way through Yellowstone, I threw out my careless, self-important words. And suddenly our forest was on fire (see James 3:5–6).

On the surface, it didn't seem like the end of the world. Call the fire trucks, hook up the hose, and put out the blaze. And don't flick cigarettes anymore.

But when my friends and I tried to put out the fire my words had started, it only grew worse. The misunderstanding spread. Resentments flared. Smoldering hurts from the past burst into flame again.

Under ordinary circumstances, the whole thing shouldn't have undone me like it did. Under ordinary circumstances, it would have quickly blown over, and the rift in our friendship would have been fully healed. But I think everyone involved would agree that these were no ordinary circumstances. At the risk of sounding melodramatic, I believe Satan had taken out a contract on our friendships and perhaps our very lives. But God had another plan.

Don't you love those words? *But God . . .* All through the Word (sixty-one times, to be precise), we read that little phrase right before God intervenes in a situation, taking what Satan meant for evil and turning it for good. And God still intervenes today.

But please note. While God may intervene, He doesn't necessarily interrupt. In fact, He may prolong the painful circumstances and injustice in order to work out His perfect purpose in our lives. He may allow us to experience the consequences of our sins in order to wean us from their deceptive embrace. For He is a wise Father, and He knows what we need. Even when we question His ways.

"How long, O LORD?" David asked repeatedly in Psalms. How long must all this go on? How long will I feel as though you have forgotten me? Those words echoed in my heart often during those days when my closest friendships seemed to be going up in smoke. For no matter how we tried, my friends and I couldn't seem to get past our problems. We'd apologize, come to an understanding, repent, forgive, pray together, and think all was well. But then — suddenly — the hurt would erupt somewhere else. And any attempts to rebuild relationships just seemed to make things worse.

A TEN-MONTH MAMMOGRAM

I still shudder when I think of that painful time. So many important people in my life, it seemed, were upset with me — bristling at my words, questioning my motives, even avoiding my company. But I know now, after the fact, that they felt just as wounded, isolated, and abandoned as I did. For Satan doesn't waste his fiery darts on just one person when he has the chance to ruin multiple lives. But be assured that God doesn't waste opportunities either. For He is the one who takes "*all* things" and works them together "for the good of *those*" — note the plural! — "who love him" (Romans 8:28, emphasis mine).

125

Now I can look back and see that God was hemming me in. I remember how I used to find that concept comforting. I love Psalm 139:5 that says, "You have hedged me behind and before, and laid Your hand upon me" (NKJV). It still comforts me to think of God cradling me in His hands, keeping me safe in the midst of the darkest storm. But at that particular time I didn't feel cradled. I felt pressed — as if God were narrowing my life rather than nurturing it. Stripping me of all that (I thought) gave me help and comfort and meaning.

It hurt so bad that I thought I was going to die.

But, as time went on, I began to see a purpose in my pain.

Nearly a year into the experience, I told another dear friend that I'd finally figured out an analogy to describe what I was going through.

"I know what God's doing!" I told Patty as I slapped my hands together and held them tight. "He's got me in a ten-month mammogram!"

"Ouch!" she answered, obviously remembering her own experience with having a very tender part of her squeezed between solid plates — all in the interest of future health.

But the analogy made sense to me. God was using this painful time, this awful pressure, to reveal what lay below the surface of my life. And what it revealed wasn't very pretty. Flesh. Lots and lots of flesh — and one very ugly weak spot.

It was as if the Great Physician had placed the results of the mammogram on a screen so I could finally see what He'd known all along. There, down the center of my being, ran a dark streak, an abnormality that was keeping me from experiencing true health. A vulnerability that, left unchanged, had the potential to destroy me.

The Holy Spirit's diagnosis of my problem? A sinful, self-centered preoccupation with how I was perceived and what other people thought of me. An excessive, deep-rooted need for approval. A desperate hunger for compliments and affirmation, achievement and praise. A tendency to look to people rather than to God for life and meaning.

Now, years later, I can see the Lord's handiwork all over that dark night of my soul. Had God not used the removal of approval, had He not confounded my idolatry of people's opinions, I would have missed the joy of finding all I need in Him alone. Had God not insisted that I focus, as

In *The Search for Significance,* Robert McGee identifies four false beliefs Satan often uses to undermine our sense of worth. While you may see yourself in several, one is usually foundational and relates to your core issue. Prayerfully replacing the lie with God's truth can do a lot to shore up this weak area in your life.

THE PERFORMANCE TRAP

False Belief: "I must meet certain standards in order to feel good about myself."

Symptoms: "Fear of failure; perfectionism; drivenness toward success; manipulating others to achieve success; withdrawal from risks."

Truth: "I bear Christ's righteousness and am, therefore, fully pleasing to the Father (Romans 5:1)."

APPROVAL ADDICTION

False Belief: "I must be approved (accepted) by others to feel good about myself."

Symptoms: "Fear of rejection; attempting to please others at any cost; overly sensitive to criticism; withdrawing to avoid disapproval."

Truth: "Although I was . . . alienated from [God], I am now forgiven . . . [and thus] totally accepted by God (Colossians 1:21–22)."

THE BLAME GAME

False Belief: "Those who fail are unworthy of love and deserve to be punished."

Symptoms: "Fear of punishment; punishing [and] blaming others for personal failure; withdrawal from God and others; drivenness to avoid failure."

Truth: "Christ satisfied God's wrath [against sin] by His death . . . therefore, I am deeply loved by God (1 John 4:9–11)."

SHAME

False Belief: "I am what I am. I cannot change. I am hopeless."

Symptoms: "Feelings of shame, hopelessness, inferiority; passivity; loss of creativity; isolation; withdrawal from others."

Truth: "I am a new creation in Christ (John 3:3–6)."[2]

Sanctify them by the truth;
your word is truth.

JOHN 17:17

Martha Tennison says, "not on what's happening, but on what's really going on,"[3] I would have missed learning what my real problem was.

Or, rather, *who* my real problem was. Because my fatal flaw — like everyone else's — was being gleefully and successfully exploited. By Satan, of course — but in partnership with someone we've already met.

Yep. You guessed it.

Flesh Woman.

No Friend of Mine

I introduced you to Flesh Woman in chapter 3, but did I mention that she is a 683-pound sumo-wrestler chick? And that her favorite stomping grounds in your life and mine are the places along our fault lines?

I had no idea she had grown to such monumental proportions or was wreaking such havoc in my own soul. After all, I had been a good girl all my life. I didn't have regrets that haunted my nights or an abusive past to disturb my days. I wasn't an alcoholic or a drug addict or a porno queen. Not much to feed a lower nature.

Or at least that's what I thought. It was quite a rude awakening to discover just how lost I am apart from Jesus. My core issues might not be as apparent as some people's, but they are just as dangerous. Perhaps more dangerous because they are so easily ignored.

Because you see, it doesn't take outward sin to feed our inner Flesh Woman. In fact, I'm discovering that Flesh Woman often delights most in the inward feast — the hate-filled thought, the pride-filled comparison, the petty nitpicking and backbiting we do in our minds without speaking a single word. These are the dishes she devours. And, unfortunately, many Christians can offer her quite a feast.

If we aren't careful, God's claim and purpose for our lives can easily become food for Flesh Woman's ravenous hunger. We feel the need to *do* something, to *be* something, significant. For God, of course. But also, secretly for ourselves, unconscious as our motives may be. If we're not careful, we can end up like Samson after his haircut, who "did not know that the LORD had departed" (Judges 16:20, NKJV). Still going through the motions of ministry, still living as God's chosen, but doing it in our own strength.

Without His power.

Without His Spirit.

Without His life at work in us.

No wonder we have cracks in our foundations!

You see, it's possible to spend the bulk of our lives fighting the wrong battles. Warring against people and circumstances when the Bible makes it clear that "our struggle is not against flesh and blood, but . . . against the spiritual forces of evil in the heavenly realms" (Ephesians 6:12).

But let me add that sometimes it isn't the enemy of our souls we're wrestling against.

Sometimes it's the very hand of God we resist.

Because God loves us so much, He wrestles against our denial, our naive assumptions, and our willful misunderstandings. He challenges us to see the truth about our situation. Because we have to face our weak areas in order to strengthen them.

Even though the fault line He's revealing may have been created through no fault of our own.

How Fault Lines Happen

Fault lines are an inevitable consequence of living as a fallen human being with other fallen human beings on a fallen earth. Sometimes fault lines can be traced back to a painful event or circumstance in our lives, especially in childhood. Unmet needs or painful trauma can mark us for life, and later events can stir up powerful feelings of fear, anger, guilt, or shame. Those feelings and our lower-nature responses — perfectionism, rage, repression, people pleasing, to name a few — all help create vulnerable spots in our souls.

I can trace the beginnings of my particular weakness back to when I was five. Though it wasn't the only factor, I believe a tearful exchange between my mother and me after I'd misbehaved caused me to embrace the false belief that I had to be good in order to be loved.

It seems so silly now. After all, it wasn't my mother's fault — she was and is the most loving woman I know. It wasn't my fault either — I was just a child. But somehow my lower nature latched on to the lie and carried it as truth into my adulthood.

In *The Search for Significance,* Robert McGee offers a helpful explanation of how this can happen. "We all have compelling, God-given needs for love, acceptance, and purpose," he writes, "and most of us will go to virtually any lengths to meet those needs." The trouble, as McGee points out, is that too often we neglect going to God to have our needs met. Instead, "many of us have become masters at 'playing the game' to be successful and win the approval of others."[4]

Which is exactly what happened to me. I'd picked up the false belief that:

MY PERFORMANCE + OTHERS' OPINIONS = MY SELF-WORTH[5]

Swallowing this lie caused me to live as though I held a mirror in my hand. I held it up to other people, and their response told me who I was. If they smiled, I was a good person. If they frowned, I was bad. If they welcomed me with their expression, I had value. But if they remained detached or looked away, their disinterest wasn't due to fatigue or a bad day. No. I had obviously messed up and deserved their rejection. I had disappointed them somehow, and made myself unworthy of their love.

And, as a result, unworthy of *God's* love as well.

Let me tell you, there is no more miserable, schizophrenic way to live. For that particular mind-set pushes me not only to be what *God* wants me to be, but also what everyone else wants me to be. Including everything I *think* they want me to be! A chronic chameleon, I spend my life constantly changing colors and outfits in order to fit whatever situation I find myself in. It's exhausting. Futile. Hopeless.

Refusing to play the approval game — yet holding on to the lie — can be just as destructive. "Some of us . . . ," McGee writes, "have failed and experienced the pain of disapproval so often that we have given up and have withdrawn into a shell of hurt, numbness, or depression."[6] Shame and regret from the past tell us we will never be different, that we are incapable of changing. Fear of making a mistake may keep us from trying anything at all.

Whether we respond with perfectionism or withdrawal or a combination of the two, the results are just the same, according to McGee. We develop a "have to" mentality toward life rather than a "want to."[7] We settle for legalism rather than grace. We miss Christ's joy and peace in our pursuit of human approval and applause.

Worst of all, we may persist in viewing God as an aloof and distant judge, holding up a scorecard to rate our every attempt to please Him, rather than seeing Him as He truly is — a loving Father on bended knee with hands outstretched and a smile as big as eternity. Praising our every step. Picking us up when we stumble. Helping us walk while He teaches us how to run. Ready with the acceptance and approval we have been killing ourselves to obtain on our own.

Your core issue may not be approval, of course — although I believe it's an issue for many women. It might be something entirely different. Something related to or reinforced by darker, much more terrible memories than mine. Abuse as a child. Rape. Divorce. Mental or physical illness. Sexual promiscuity. Circumstances or events that still leave you feeling vulnerable, victimized all over again every time something triggers your memory. Abandonment. Rejection. Shame and guilt. You may have felt them all.

But no matter the core event that created

your fault line, please hear this wonderful, incredible, life-changing good news: No matter what we've done or what's been done to us, no matter how deep our wounds or how damaged our spirits, we have a mighty God who is able to redeem our darkest moments and deepest fears. A loving Father who promises to keep watch at our points of vulnerability, to strengthen us where we're weak, to correct the lies that have led us astray, and to heal the rifts in our souls.

But only if we give Him access. Unless we adopt a Mary spirit, unless we give God permission to straighten out the twisted mess of our lives, we don't have much hope of avoiding an invasion from the enemy.

It all comes down to this. The pain and injustice of life, our wrongdoing or the wrongdoing of others, may twist and distort us, creating fault lines and weak areas. But it's our response to these issues that makes the real difference. It's what we do — and what we let God do.

As long as we cling to our pain as an excuse for our problems and a reason for being and staying the way we are, we will never experience God's healing.

As long as we deny our weakness, we'll never experience His strength.

We need both His healing and strength,

Structures in earthquake-prone areas require a different building code, and so do we. Because we're prone to fault lines, it isn't enough to throw a life together. Here are some strategies for making sure yours is built strong from the foundation up.

1. ***Invite the Inspector.*** Give God permission to take you on a tour of your life. Let Him look in locked closets, probe dark crawlspaces, and point out danger zones. He can only bring wholeness to your life if you give Him full access.

2. ***Shore Up the Foundation.*** It's what lies beneath the surface that really counts. Maintaining a strong relationship with God is crucial. So is pursuing healing for emotional wounds from the past. If your house isn't built on solid rock, you'll shift like sand.

3. ***Reinforce Your Structure.*** Invest in the primary relationships of your life. Good marriages don't just happen; they're built. Strong friendships take

time, and growing godly children requires wisdom. Work at a strong life. God will help.

4. ***Build in Some Flexibility.*** A building with the capacity to move a little has a better chance of surviving a quake than one that is stiff and rigid. A sense of humor; a relaxed, trusting attitude; being willing to bend on issues that aren't that essential — these can help you survive life's seismic activity.

5. ***Watch for Tremors.*** Tremors usually precede earthquakes. Signs of such fault-line instability may include destructive thoughts, new temptations, or disintegrating relationships. Don't ignore them — these are God's way of warning you. Admit them to a friend and be accountable. Cut out activities that put you at risk.

6. ***When the Earth Shakes, Choose to Stand.*** It really isn't a matter of *if* you'll have an earthquake, but *when*. Please know that life built on Christ can survive nearly anything. The Rock will absorb the shock, and

though you may sway, don't be afraid. God will help you stand.

God is our refuge and strength, an ever-present help in trouble. Therefore we will not fear, though the earth give way.

PSALM 46:1–2

because even those of us growing and maturing in the Lord are vulnerable along our fault lines. As long as we live on this fallen Earth, the tectonic plates of our souls will shift now and then. And when they do, destruction may be just one choice away.

HIDDEN FAULTS

In the early morning of April 18, 1906, San Francisco was awakened by the violent shocks of an earthquake, probably as strong as 8.25 on the Richter scale. Lasting little more than a minute, the earthquake wrecked 490 blocks and toppled a total of twenty-five thousand buildings. Broken gas mains caused fires that ravaged the city for three days. More than 250,000 people were left homeless, and the gold-rush capital that had stood there for a half-century was essentially destroyed[8] — all because a weak spot deep inside the earth — a fault line — gave way. And no one foresaw the destruction until it was too late.

Geological fault lines are hidden until they produce an earthquake. That is often true with spiritual fault lines as well. Sometimes we are unaware of the weak areas of our souls until something triggers them. But while San Franciscans were helpless to stop the seismic activity that destroyed their city, we can shore up our souls.

My friend Tricia never expected to feel the happy stability of her marriage shaken — until an old boyfriend, her first love, contacted her through e-mail. Their correspondence started out innocently. Just catching up on each other's lives. But soon he was writing: "You are the only woman I've ever loved. I never should have let you go."

At nearly thirty-four years of age and after so much time, my friend shouldn't have been so affected by his flattering words. But the same emotionally barren relationship with her father that had left Tricia susceptible to unhealthy relationships as a teenager also made her vulnerable as an adult. His unexpected words rocked Tricia to her core.

"The emotions were so intense. It was like I was fifteen again," Tricia explains. "This guy had been the first man who'd ever shown me love. He had been everything to me. I found myself imagining the unthinkable, and I knew I was in trouble."

With rumblings in her heart pointing to a potentially devastating earthquake, Tricia immediately called for help. She made herself accountable to friends and, with their support, pushed herself to confess the situation to her husband. Together they wrote Tricia's former boyfriend and explained why all contact had to end.

"It took awhile for the emotions to subside," Tricia says. "Even now, a month later, I have flashes of 'what if' thoughts that take me by surprise. But I know I can't entertain them."

Going to God's Word has helped a lot. As Tricia began reading what the Bible says about real love, she says, "I realized what I'd experienced with my former boyfriend was a distorted form of love. It was a counterfeit of the real thing."

She also learned to pray as soon as thoughts came into her head, submitting them to Christ and then deliberately turning her mind elsewhere. For the first two weeks, the spiritual struggle was so intense Tricia's husband would pray over her at night and then call during the day to assure her of his love and pray once again.

Bringing the situation into the open was the crucial first step. "One of the reasons I knew I was in trouble was the fact I didn't want to tell anyone," she points out. "But when I did tell, the power of the lie was broken. God showed me these hidden things for a purpose: He wanted to bring healing in the areas of my life where I was vulnerable."

Though Tricia's world shook, rattled, and rolled during that difficult time, her house stood firm. All because she gave God access to a dangerous core issue — her desperate need for love and attention from a man. As a result, a situation with the potential to destroy actually ended up healing some of Tricia's emotional wounds and strengthening her marriage as well. "Our marriage has become a safe place rather than a place of secrets," she says.[9]

Your life can become a safe place as well. For that's what God creates when we get honest with ourselves and others about our weaknesses rather than trying to deny or hide them.

After all, fault lines left unattended are invitations to disaster.

You'd think Sardis would have learned its lesson the first time. But history really does have a way of repeating itself, especially for those who refuse to learn.

Two hundred years after Croesus's downfall, the city of Sardis was once again under siege.

For nearly a year, the Saleucid king Antiochus III tried to force Sardis's ruler Achaeus from his fortress atop the great rock. For nearly a year he was unsuccessful. Perhaps that explains Achaeus's overconfidence. And his carelessness.

Repeating Hyeroeades's wiliness and exploiting a two-century-old mistake, a band of enemy soldiers climbed the steep cliffs and found the city unguarded.

And once again Sardis fell.[10]

But it didn't have to. Had Croesus and Achaeus simply posted a guard at the point of their weakness, Sardis might have continued to stand safely on its rocky citadel. But those rulers didn't. And I repeat their foolish mistake whenever I get lazy or complacent about the weak areas in my life.

I'm realizing that as long as I'm alive, as long as Flesh Woman remains my roommate, I will probably struggle with my need for approval. God has been so kind to heal me in many ways. His unconditional love and acceptance continue to fill the gap that runs through my soul. Yet I believe I will always be vulnerable to sin in this particular area. Not as vulnerable as I was before God revealed it to me, but vulnerable all the same.

That might sound like a lack of faith, but I prefer to call it wisdom. For even though I am far less needy than I used to be, I still have days where — as Brennan Manning puts it — "My ravenous insecurities [make] my sense of self-worth rise and fall like a sailboat on the winds of another's approval or disapproval."[11]

Being realistic about my weakness has prompted me to post a guard at that spot. With the Holy Spirit's help, I have recognized several warning signs that indicate the enemy is trying to exploit my weakness. Recognizing and responding appropriately to those warnings has protected me more times than I can count.

My own careless words, for example, have become a warning sign for me. Whenever I begin to tout my opinions as gospel truth, I know trouble isn't far away. I've also learned to watch out for self-pity. In my case, "poor me" thoughts are a one-way ticket to depression as well as a sign that I don't trust God's provision in my life. And my tendency toward self-promotion is a real red flag. Whenever I make "me" and my accomplishments the topic of a conversation, I know I'm treading on dangerous ground. I'm much better off making others my focus.

Hebrews 12:13 promotes this kind of healthy awareness of our weaknesses. "Make level paths for your feet," it says, "so that the lame may not be disabled, but rather healed."

You don't hear many sermons on this verse. But I find its message helpful because sometimes we do need to make special provision for our known weaknesses. If we want to stay safe, for instance, there are some places, some situations, where we simply cannot go. Let me illustrate.

Growing up, I used to love going down to the creek near our house. Walking across the rocks was a favorite pastime of mine. Except when I had a sprained ankle. Then this activity was nothing but foolishness. Weak ankles need flat places to walk, not rugged creek banks.

So how do we make level paths for our feet? It may mean steering clear of activities and experiences that put pressure on our fault lines. If you struggle with lust, for instance, bodice-ripping romances may not be the best reading material for you. If discontentment haunts your marriage, *Desperate Housewives* may be a dangerous viewing choice. If your weak spot is envy, perusing lifestyles-of-the-rich-and-famous magazines may feed your inability to enjoy what you have.

I've also found it helpful to do a motivation check before I step out on potentially rocky ground. So, on a regular basis, I ask myself why I do the things I do: *Am I doing this for the Lord or so people will like me?* I might ask about a particular activity. *What insecurity in my life is causing me to need affirmation or to be the center of attention?*

Your specific struggle and weak spot may require different kinds of questions:

- *Why do I feel the need to own this particular item?* Do I genuinely need what I yearn for, or am I really yearning for prestige or acceptance?
- *Why did I assume it was the other person's fault?* What makes it hard for me to take responsibility for my part of the situation?
- *Why was I less than honest in that last conversation?* Is it because I'm afraid people might reject me or because I really don't know who I am?

147

- *Why am I avoiding this phone call or difficult conversation?* Does this habit indicate passive-aggressive rebellion or a type of fear?

You may have to wrestle with these issues a little — asking the Holy Spirit to help you overcome denial, self-deception, and rationalization. Journaling your thoughts and prayers about these issues may also help — it's certainly helped me. (See Appendix D for suggestions on "Journaling Your Transformation.") But keep in mind that the point isn't so much to find "right answers," as it is to get honest before the Lord. Because until we recognize our weaknesses and ask for God's help with them, we will continually stumble. As long as we live on earth, we'll need God's help and protection for the vulnerable spots in our souls.

CAN FAULT LINES BE HEALED?

In a sense, we who follow Jesus live out our lives in the Land of In-Between, caught in the middle of a now and a not-yet reality. Because of what Christ did on the cross — and because of His ongoing redemptive work in our lives — we are being made new. Healed. Transformed. Right now, even as I write this line. Yet because we live as human beings in a fallen, sinful world, our complete transformation is still to come.

That's why I must constantly bring my life under the spotlight of heaven. I must continuously ask the Holy Spirit to make me aware of the snares created by my human weaknesses and my own deceitful desires.

Aware. But not anxious or worried. Because the best thing I can do with any of my fatal flaws is to place them in God's hands. My fault lines and imperfections do not hinder Him — and neither do yours. For He is the flawless onc. He sees what we are — defects and all — but He also sees what we can be.

What used to make us stumble, God can use to make us stand.

What once made us bow our heads in shame, He can use for His glory.

Because when I put my trust in Christ rather than in Sardis to keep me safe, I choose an unshakeable fortress. Rather than trusting my own strength, wisdom, and ability, I put my hope in the One who "is able to do immeasurably more than all we ask or imagine, according to his power that is at work within us" (Ephesians 3:20).

Earthquakes and invaders may come. In fact, they *will* come. Satan will do everything in his power to exploit my vulnerabilities.

And Flesh Woman will continue to revel in the places where I hurt the most.

But all will be well because my true home is no longer a citadel built on a fault line. My home is built on the solid Rock of Jesus Christ.

And if I put my trust in Him, even though the world around me shakes and trembles and even slides into the sea — no matter what happens, "I will not be shaken" (Psalm 62:6).

6
DYING TO LIVE

If anyone would come after me,
he must deny himself
and take up his cross daily and follow me.
LUKE 9:23

Having acknowledged the existence of Flesh Woman, I'm finding that she is becoming more and more real to me. Perhaps too real. This afternoon, for instance, as I pondered how to open this chapter, an idea suddenly came to me in high-definition color. A big-budget blockbuster film complete with soundtrack, closeups, and highly entertaining trailers. (I told you she might be getting a little too real.)

The lights go down, and the title appears on the screen: *Flesh Woman Crucified*.

Then the subtitle: *And You Thought Getting Your Weight Under Control Was Hard . . .*

The film opens with Flesh Woman slowly making her way through a crowd on the way to her cross. A 683-pound sumo-wrestler chick squeezed into a purple-sequined evening gown. Her flushed but carefully made-up face framed by a cloud of feather boa. Pausing now and then as the background music swells, she waves to all her fans lining the path. Black-mascara tears course down her cheeks as Frank Sinatra sings "I did it my way."

"Wish you didn't have to go!" Gluttony calls from the crowd. Laziness and Procrastination agree, weeping in each other's arms. "Yeah, it hasn't been the same since you left the throne. (Sob!) We're having a tough time getting a break."

"I know, dahlings. I know. But, as they say, all good things must end." Flesh Woman throws her final kisses to her dearest friends. But she's overcome when she sees the crossbeam lying at my feet and the hammer I'm holding in my hand.

"Really, my pet," she says, reaching to stroke my arm. "Is all this necessary?"

"I'm afraid so," I reply, firm in my resolve and anxious to have it done and over. "Please lie down. It's time."

"But . . . but . . . but . . . ," she sputters as I pull her toward her demise. "We need to talk."

She puts up quite a fight, but I'm determined. I know I will never have any peace until I obey. "Those who belong to Christ Jesus have crucified the sinful nature with its passions and desires," Paul said in Galatians 5:24. He made it sound so easy. I wonder if Paul had to brawl with a sparkling eggplant in his fight against sin.

With a knee on her chest and one arm pinned to the cross, I attempt to fasten her down. "Think of all you'll miss," she says, struggling to get up.

I try to ignore her, to concentrate on what I must do.

"All the things I do for you!" she adds with a pout.

But I grit my teeth and begin to hum, "Have thine own way, Lord. Have thine own way . . ."[1] And suddenly He is there.

Having problems? Christ asks.

"Quite a few," I admit. "But I'm willing, Lord. I want You to rule and reign in my life."

"What are you talking about?" Flesh Woman screams, flailing wildly at the sight of my Master. "I give you everything you want! I make sure you get your own way! Nobody loves you like I do!" she wails.

"Here, Lord," I say, stepping back and handing Him the hammer. "I guess it's more than I can do on my own." Christ takes the heavy mallet and kneels down beside my thrashing, frantic flesh.

Be silent, He says (Zechariah 2:13, KJV). And Flesh Woman obeys. For all flesh falls silent before the Lord. The music stops; all is still.

Flesh Woman glares at Jesus. Then, subdued but not yet conquered, she turns to look at me. "Don't you know?" she asks, her eyes narrow and cold. She draws out her words in an effort to draw me in.

"Don't you know? When you kill me, you die too."

The camera closes in on my face. I turn to look at Jesus, then I look back at the pitiful woman I once adored.

"Yeah, I know," I smile. "In fact, that's the whole point."

And the screen goes black. Curtain. The end. *Finito*.

At least for today.

FLESH WOMAN MUST DIE

Okay. I know. That was a bit over the top. But I wonder . . .

If our spiritual eyes could somehow be opened — if we could see our daily struggles with the flesh as heaven sees them, if we could glimpse the battle that takes place between the Spirit of God and Satan over our souls — well, I think the scene described above might seem more like a documentary than a chick flick.

For whether we realize it or not, there's a war going on. And Flesh Woman — well, she's a double agent.

"Satan's only real hope to control my life is *me,*" author Mark Rutland writes in *Holiness*. "We often labor under the misguided notion that Satan wants us to do *his* will. Satan has no will in our lives. He only wants us to do *our* will. We have met the enemy, and he is us."[2]

Or, to be more precise, the enemy is Flesh Woman. And while Flesh Woman *is* us to a certain extent, she's also not the real us. No matter what she claims and no matter how enthusiastically Satan backs her up, she's not who God created us to be.

That is why Scripture holds little sympathy for our lower nature. For God knows that Flesh Woman lives in direct opposition to Him. There really is no middle ground. We are told to "make no provision for the flesh" (Romans 13:14, NKJV) and that "those who are in the flesh cannot please God" (Romans 8:8, NKJV). While it's important to remove Flesh Woman from the throne of our hearts, our holy makeover won't be complete until she's actually been put to death.

As you work through this book, you may discover, as I have, a number of thoughts and ideas in Scripture that seem to contradict one another. For instance, Paul teaches that salvation comes solely by faith (Romans 3:22–26). Yet James said that faith without works is dead (2:17). Paul tells us that our flesh has been crucified with Christ — past tense! But then he urges us to "put to death the deeds of the body" (Romans 8:13, NKJV) on an ongoing basis.

So which one is it? you may ask. *Which is true? Which one do I do?*

The answer, I believe, is often . . . both. Both are true. And we must do both.

If you're even more confused now, here's an explanation that may help.

In eastern Montana, farmers and ranchers often plant trees as windbreaks. But in order for a young tree to survive the winter blasts as well as the summer heat of the prairie wind, the farmer has to stake off the tree. So he ties four strings to the trunk and then drives stakes deep in the ground at four corners — east, west, north, and south. Then the wind can howl, but the little tree, held secure by the tension between the four strings, won't fall.

I believe God has built the same kind of four-cornered "holy tension" into His Word. Because we humans tend toward extremes, swinging too far in one direction and then veering way too far in the other, God wrote balance points into Scripture. Principles that appear contradictory at first glance, but — when followed — help us grow straight and tall, strong and deep. As I continue to live the mystery of these scriptural paradoxes, I'm beginning to find they make perfect sense. More important, the very contradictions that stretch my mind are the ones that change me most deeply.

And isn't change the whole point?

But God has revealed it to us by his Spirit. The Spirit searches all things, even the deep things of God.

1 CORINTHIANS 2:10

And this is where it all gets a bit complicated. Because the Bible says this work has already been done. The moment Jesus died on the cross, Flesh Woman died as well.

"For we know that our old self was crucified with him," Paul writes in Romans 6:6–7, "so that the body of sin might be done away with, that we should no longer be slaves to sin — because anyone who has died has been freed from sin."

Because of the Cross, I am no longer a slave to sin. No longer controlled by the spirit of this world. No longer held captive by the fault lines in my soul. And no longer under the dominion and sway of Flesh Woman . . . seductive and relentless though she may still appear to be.

Does that sound confusing? I must admit it kind of confuses me. How can Flesh Woman be dead when I seem to wrestle her every day? And where is the victory over sin when I consistently feel trapped by its power?

Here's an analogy that has helped me.

THE PUPPET MASTER

Of the forty-five times the word *sin* appears in Romans, it is used as a noun in every instance except one. This has radical implications for my life — and yours. Too often we think of sin as something we do — wrong thoughts, wrong attitudes, wrong behavior. But according to Romans 5–8, sin is an active entity, a force at work within us. An unholy spirit, if you will. And this active entity — sin "at work in the members of my body" (Romans 7:23) — manipulates me, as well as my flesh, to do the wrong things.

Before I met Christ, sin was fully in charge. It pulled my strings like an evil puppet master, causing me to dance like a helpless marionette. Enslaved by his dark choreography, I flopped here and there, going through the motions of life. On the outside I appeared to be in control, but in reality I was a powerless captive. A slave. Addicted to self-love, pain avoidance, and pleasure, I did sin's bidding — beating myself up for my failures and slapping myself on the back for my accomplishments. I was a one-person Punch-and-Judy show.

Then Jesus came. When I said yes to Him, He cut the strings that tied my soul to sin, the Puppet Master, and allowed me to truly live. I was no longer a wooden Pinocchio wishing and longing to be real. Christ breathed His breath of life into me and set me free to be all I was created to be.

Free to live.

Free to move.

And free to remain in bondage if I wished.

For it is possible for me to belong to Christ and still act as if I'm controlled by sin. To actually believe I'm controlled by sin, although the strings — that is, the bonds of sin — have been severed by Jesus's death and resurrection.

I call it muscle memory.

Muscle memory is a term used by pianists and others who perform tasks requiring specific physical skills. It refers to the experience when muscles seem to perform almost automatically, without conscious thought. It's a physical pattern developed by many years of practice.

Habitual sin can have the same effect on our bodies and souls. Though we are no longer tied to sin's pull, too often the patterns of sin remain. It's as though we've played sin's melody so many times, it comes naturally to our fingers.

Teacher and author Anabel Gillham explains it like this: "The patterns in your life become so deeply entrenched that you perform them habitually — not even recognizing that you are exhibiting un-Christlike behavior . . . or that you have a choice to resist."

"That's just the way I am," we tell ourselves.

No, Anabel says, "that's just the way you've learned."[3]

Where does Flesh Woman come into all this? We'll look more closely at her alive-but-dead status a little later. But for now just remember that she's our lower nature, still controlled by the puppet master's strings. Though our innermost spirit has been changed by salvation, Flesh Woman keeps dancing to sin's unholy tune. And because she's connected to us, we tend to go through the motions of sin right along with her.

But we don't have to. Our strings have been cut. That's the whole point of Romans 6:14: "For sin shall not be your master, because you are not under law, but under grace."

So how do we change these entrenched muscle-memory patterns that keep us fighting sin and the flesh even after we've been set free from their influence? The apostle Paul suggests two things we must do.

First, we must *reckon ourselves dead to sin* — choosing to rest our faith completely in what Christ has done for us. Then we must continue to *put to death* the residue of our earthly nature which remains even after Flesh Woman has been crucified (Romans 6:11, NKJV; Romans 8:13, NKJV).

But how do we do that?
And what does it look like?

DOING THE MATH

Growing up, I loved watching that old television western *Bonanza*. If you are a little, ahem, younger than I am . . . maybe you've seen it on Nickelodeon. A family of men — father Ben and brothers Hoss, Adam, and Little Joe — all lived on a big ranch called the Ponderosa.

It was a fun show to watch. Not only because Little Joe (played by Michael Landon) was gorgeous, but I got a kick out of good ol' Hoss. "Waell, Pa," he'd say, tipping his ten-gallon hat to scratch his balding brow, "I *reckon* I best get them horses rounded up."

"Yup," Ben Cartwright would reply, hitching up his trousers. "I *reckon* you should."

Every week one of the boys — usually Little Joe — would fall in love. "I *reckon* you're the prettiest gal I ever saw," the youngest Cartwright would say as he rode up beside her on his paint pony. "Won't you marry me?"

"Of course," she and I would say together, batting our long eyelashes. But just when Little Joe had finally convinced our overly protective father of his good intentions and had our new log cabin nearly built, we'd up and die from some terrible disease.

And every week I'd weep. Not only because Little Joe's true love had died, but also because Michael Landon was old enough to be my father. "I *reckon* I'll never be loved like that," I'd sob into my popcorn. At least not by someone so handsome — by anyone's *reckoning.*

But then my very own movie-star-gorgeous John came along and proved me wrong. This year we'll celebrate twenty-five years of a happy marriage. And while we may not own the Ponderosa, at least I — unlike most of the *Bonanza* stars — am still alive.

In fact, I *reckon* I'm the most blessed girl in the world.

Reckon. To me, it's always been Old West slang for "seems to me" or "I suppose." Simply an expression of personal opinion. But in the Bible the Greek word translated *reckon* is an accounting term. *Vine's Expository Dictionary* defines *logizomai* as "properly used of a numerical calculation."[4]

When Paul writes in Romans 6:11, "Likewise you also, reckon yourselves to be dead indeed to sin, but alive to God in Christ Jesus our Lord" (NKJV), he's not asking us to suppose anything. He's just telling us to do the math. Stop making things difficult.

163

Just add it up!

Because of all that Jesus did, the debt you owed was cancelled — "Paid in full!" Sin no longer owns you. You are no longer obligated to obey its commands. Puppet Master has lost his "punch" as well as his Judy.

When we reckon our account in the light of Jesus's sacrifice rather than by adding together our clumsy attempts to earn the Lord's love, we come up with a sum so amazing, so remarkable — yet so logical and indisputable. It's the bottom line we can take to the bank.

We are not forgiven because we feel bad. We are not forgiven because deep down we're really good people and God knows that so He grants us pardon. We are not even forgiven because of God's amazing love. The only reason we're forgiven is because Jesus Christ died on the cross. Period.

But we must *appropriate* what He did. We must do the math, make the reckoning. We must choose to *believe* that the work of the Cross was enough to purchase freedom from sin for us.

That so many of us miss the great riches of righteousness available to us in Christ is the greatest tragedy of the church today. To settle for so little when Jesus provided so much is like having a billion dollars sitting in a bank account under our name and at our disposal, yet never going to the bank to make a withdrawal.

What Christ has done for you and me through His death and resurrection is essentially make a huge deposit in our account. His righteousness, according to Romans 4:11 (NKJV), has been "imputed" to us — that is, put under our name. We have been sanctified — set apart and made holy. Jesus's right standing before God and His power for right living are now ours.

For the asking.

For the taking.

But ask we must, and take we should.

Otherwise everything Christ has provided for us sits in the bank while we wander the streets of life, begging for bread, looking for meaning, trying to tell others about the goodness of God while we ourselves are starving, wretched, naked, and cold.

But how, practically speaking, do we make withdrawals from our account of righteousness?

That's where faith comes in. We do it by believing.

FAITH IS OUR WITHDRAWAL SLIP

As a young man, Martin Luther was a tortured soul. He wanted to please God. Desperately. So he joined a monastery at age twenty-two and dedicated his entire life to becoming holy, no matter the cost. Fastidious about sin, he was constantly going to his confessor to repent of his wrongdoing. The kind prelate tried to direct him to God's love, but Luther's failings haunted him continually. The young man would pace his cell screaming at himself, trying to battle the sin that seemed so dominant, so overpowering, so unrelenting in his life.

It wasn't until God showed Luther the meaning of the words in Romans 1:17 that he finally found peace. "For in the gospel a righteousness from God is revealed," the verse says, "a righteousness that is by faith from first to last, just as it is written: 'The righteous will live by faith.'"

Suddenly Luther realized that God was not demanding that he be holy in and of himself. Instead, God offered the very thing this tired monk had spent so many years striving for — not just right living, but the righteousness of God Himself. A righteousness offered as a free gift — to be received by faith alone. "At this I felt myself straightway born afresh and to have entered through the open gates into paradise itself," Luther writes.[5]

I love how the movie *Luther* portrays this moment.

"Look to Christ," his father confessor tells the young monk as he presses a crucifix into Luther's hand. "Bind yourself to Christ. Say to him, 'I am Yours. Save me.' "

Sitting on the cold stone floor of his cell, Luther stares at the cross, then wraps his hand around it. "I am Yours," he whispers to Jesus. "Save me."[6] And at the moment he decides to trust, he is finally set free. No longer in torment, Luther is a man at peace.

As are we . . . when we give up striving and choose rather to draw from the rich storehouse of grace Christ purchased for us on the cross.

I love the picture Hannah Whitall Smith paints in her classic book *The Christian's Secret to a Happy Life.* It is a portrait of a weary Christian much like Martin Luther. Much like you and I at times.

A lot of Christians, she notes, are like the man who was carrying a heavy burden down a country road. The driver of a passing wagon offered him a ride, and he joyfully accepted. But even after climbing aboard, the traveler kept his pack on his shoulders. He rode along still hunched over under his heavy load.

"Why do you not lay down your burden?" the driver asked.

"Oh, I feel that is almost too much to ask

Crucifying Flesh Woman means I have to take a good honest look at myself — but only to a point. I've been known to self-examine myself sick. Prodding and poking at dead areas I hope are still dead, picking off scabs of things almost healed. Apart from the Holy Spirit's work, Hannah Whitall Smith says, self-examination can actually breathe life into the flesh we are trying to put to death.

> Self is always determined to secure attention and would rather be thought badly of than not to be thought of at all. And self-examination, with all its miseries, often gives a sort of morbid satisfaction to the self-life in us and *even* deludes self into thinking it is a very pious sort of self after all. . . .

you to carry me," the man said. "I could not think of letting you carry my burden too."[8]

Like the man in the story, many of us continue to trudge beneath the accumulated weight this world puts on our shoulders. When, all along, Jesus has been waiting to bear our load.

We grow like what we look at, and if we spend our lives looking at our hateful selves, we shall become more and more hateful. Do we not find as a fact that self-examination, instead of making us better, always seems to make us worse?

The only healthy type of self-examination, according to Smith: "For one look at self, take ten looks at Christ."[7]

This then is . . . how we set our hearts at rest in his presence whenever our hearts condemn us. For God is greater than our hearts, and he knows everything.

1 JOHN 3:19–20

"In laying off your burdens," Hannah Whitall Smith observed, "the first one you must get rid of is yourself."[9] Your temptations as well as your temperament. Your feelings as well as your fears.

"Just as truly as [Christ] came to bear your sins for you, has He come to live His

169

life in you," Smith continues. "You are as utterly powerless in the one case as in the other. You could as easily have got yourself rid of your own sins, as you could now accomplish for yourself practical righteousness. Christ, and Christ only, must do both for you, and your part in both cases is simply to give the thing to Him to do, and then believe that He does it."[10]

Faith. It really makes all the difference in my ability to live as a free woman. Believing that what Christ did on the cross was enough. Enough for me. For my life. For my situation. Enough for everyone who will simply come to Him and ask . . . and believe . . . and then receive.

For faith alone is our withdrawal slip.

It is the debit card that accesses our account.

Faith makes it possible to put Flesh Woman to death and move on with the process of being made new from the inside out.

KA-CHING!

One of the most life-changing Bible studies I've ever been a part of is Beth Moore's *Believing God* video series. Each week throughout the study, Beth had us repeat a little exercise. Raising one finger at a time to emphasize each point, we'd recite the following five basic statements of faith:

1. God is who He says He is.
2. God can do what He says He can do.
3. I am who God says I am.
4. I can do all things through Christ who strengthens me.
5. God's Word is alive and living in me.[11]

After each statement, she had us point at ourselves, then at our heads, and then at God, saying, "I'm . . . believing . . . God."

Interesting exercise. Clever memory device. And that's all it would have been. Except that somewhere in the course of repeatedly declaring God's identity and mine in Him, I began to experience a divine shift in my understanding of faith. In my learning there suddenly came a knowing — a filtering down of head knowledge to heart knowledge. As though the pieces of a giant puzzle had come together and I saw what had been floating before me all the time:

God *is* who He says He is.

And I *can* be who He says I am.

Because "I *can* do all things through Christ!" (Philippians 4:13, NKJV, emphasis mine).

I'd been saying the words. Now I was starting to really believe them, to appropriate them for my life.

One week, as Beth talked about Abraham and how his belief in God was credited (that is, reckoned) to him as righteousness (Romans 4:3), the Holy Spirit began to take me on a spiritual side trip. In between Beth's words, God reminded me how I've lived with a set of scales in my heart — scales that measured my worth by my performance. I was always trying to make the good outweigh the bad. But no matter how hard I tried, the smallest of failures easily displaced any success.

Using the accounting metaphor from Romans 4, Beth quoted the eighth verse: "Blessed is the man whose sin the Lord will never count against him."

Suddenly that truth converged with the reality of Isaiah 64:6, which says that "all our righteous acts are like filthy rags" — absolutely worthless, weighing nothing in our favor. Placed beside my sin on the scale in my mind, I realized my good deeds just don't count. But, because of Jesus's death on the cross, neither do the bad things I do.

I don't think I can fully explain what this insight did in my spirit. But let me try. Truth, like a scroll unfolding, began to fill my heart. *If my sins don't count and my good deeds don't count, then what does?*

Faith. That's the only thing that counts in God's mathematics.

Abraham believed God, and his belief was credited to him as righteousness. Because he chose to trust God in the face of impossibilities, a deposit of holiness was made in his spiritual bank: ka-ching!

But the kind of faith that pleases God, that tilts the reckoning in our favor, is not passive. It's not nodding our heads to an idea and saying, "I guess that sounds all right." Far from it.

True faith requires obedience. It requires being willing to stake everything on God's love and faithfulness — and then doing what He asks.

Even when we don't understand.

Even when He demands that we give up the things we love the most.

That's the kind of faith Abraham showed when he packed up his son and a load of firewood and headed for Mount Moriah (Genesis 22). If you'd been there listening, I think you might have heard "Ka-ching!"

And had you been there when Abraham raised his knife and blessed his God, fully intending to obey and yet fully believing God would still fulfill His promise (Hebrews 11:19), I believe you would have heard something besides a voice from heaven telling him to stop and the rustling of a sacrificial ram caught in the thicket. I can almost hear it now: "ka-ching!"

For though God had promised Abraham that "through Isaac . . . your offspring will be reckoned" (Genesis 21:12), the greatest act of Abraham's faith was leaving the reckoning up to God. And it is the same for us.

When we stop trying to manhandle our circumstances and start giving them to God, something incredible happens. God takes everything we give Him and begins to work on our behalf. Because we've chosen to believe and trust rather than doubt and fear, He makes all of it — the good and the bad — count *for* us rather than against us. And that's when we start laying up serious treasure in heaven. And treasure on earth.

Ka-ching! Faith is credited to us as righteousness — and that righteousness comes in the form of Christlikeness. For when I believe that Jesus is not only able to save me but also to make me holy, I make deposits in my righteousness bank. Ka-ching, ka-ching, ka-ching!

And every time I do, by any reckoning, I end up looking more like Jesus and less like me.

KILLING WHAT'S ALREADY DEAD

The problem, of course, is that there are still so many times when I don't look like Jesus at all. So many days when I look at myself and wince at my failures and stubborn sins. So many areas of my life where it seems Flesh Woman still rules and Puppet Master pulls my strings.

Which brings us back to some tricky questions: If Flesh Woman really is dead, if she truly was crucified with Christ, why does she still seem so alive? And why am I told to put to death something Scripture says is already dead? For that matter, if Flesh Woman is powerless, how can she affect so much of my living?

I'm afraid I don't have definitive answers to these questions. Spiritual truths lived out in the confines of our flesh and this natural world often seem to contradict themselves. And, yet I'm discovering that the deepest truths often lie somewhere in the space between what appear to be contradictions.

Paul knew that. In his epistles, he often highlighted the clash of concepts instead of ignoring them. In Romans 7 and 8, for example, he points directly to the paradox that while sin has lost its power and we're truly free, we still must deal with its effects as long as we live.

Martin Luther acknowledges that paradox as well. "Faith doesn't so free us from sin that we can be idle, lazy and self-assured, as though there were no more sin in us," Luther writes in his *Preface to Romans*. "Sin is there. . . . Therefore we have in our own selves a lifetime of work cut out for us; we have to tame our body, kill its lusts, force its members to obey the spirit and not the lusts."[12]

While I may not fully understand the theological implications of this continuing war between sin and my spirit, I definitely feel it. Though sin's power has been broken in my life and Flesh Woman is doomed, I still must participate in the fight against sin and the flesh. If I want that holy makeover we've talked about, there's still a lot of work for me to do.

Whenever I find my mind confused by this paradox, it helps me to remember the giant tree that used to grow in the front yard of our church. A towering poplar, it offered wonderful shade, but it was also infested with bugs. Every summer it dropped deformed leaves with huge knotty growths all over the ground. When the growths broke open, annoying gnatlike creatures would fly up and fill the yard. My kids liked to open them prematurely so they could see the larvae. The whole thing was disgusting. Truly disgusting.

Finally, we decided the tree had to go. Out came the chain saws and down it came, piece by piece, until all that was left was an immense stump, probably six feet across, sticking up from the ground. We added a few flowerpots to adorn its new flattop and assumed that was the end of the problem.

But it wasn't long before we realized the tree was far from gone. Yes, we had cut it down. But the entire next spring and summer we fought shoots like *Invasion of the Body Snatchers*. They sprang up everywhere. Anywhere. You'd cut them off, but they'd reappear. You'd pull them up by the root, only to drag a ragged line of torn grass that led right back to — you guessed it! — the original tree.

After fighting that unpopular poplar for several summers, we finally rented a special machine and ground the tree down to its taproot. It wasn't enough to chop it down. We had to dig it out.

The same is true of Flesh Woman. Christ's death and resurrection most definitely ended her reign. The Cross toppled her proud figure, and she no longer towers over the yard of our lives. She has no power to make us sin as she once did, but she still manages to make her presence felt. And the process of digging her out will continue for quite a while.

The shoots — those annoying deeds of the

flesh that pop up when we least expect it — are what Paul said we must put to death daily. We will spend the rest of this book learning how to do just that. But never forget, this uprooting is a work that must be done in the power of the Holy Spirit and not on our own.

THE GREAT EXCHANGE

I spent much of my early Christian life like a young Martin Luther. Though I didn't live in a dark cell, I hated myself and constantly obsessed about my sins and failures. Thinking I had to "buffet my body" as Paul instructed in 1 Corinthians 9:27 (ASV), I routinely beat myself up in order to kill off Flesh Woman. Unfortunately, the discipline Paul meant by "buffet" didn't correspond to the all-you-can-eat *buffet* Flesh Woman kept sneaking out to enjoy.

Trying to crucify my natural self so Christ could live through me was a noble pursuit. Unfortunately, I kept failing. Even on my most disciplined days, the best I could manage was a mock funeral with an empty casket. Lots of flowers and tears, but little spiritual effect.

In *Beyond Our Selves* writer Catherine Marshall, describes the problem and impossibility of spiritually renovating ourselves:

178

Our nature might be compared to an apple shot through with brown specks of imperfection. There is no way to cut out every brown speck and save the apple; the doom of decay is on the fruit. . . . Each of us is tinctured with self-will; with self-ambitions; with the desire to be pampered, cushioned, and admired; with overcriticalness of everyone else and oversensitiveness about ourselves; with a drive to enlarge the self with an accumulation of things. Thus, try as we may to separate these self-centered qualities from the unselfish ones, the self keeps cropping up again and again, tripping us every time.[13]

The only solution, Marshall concludes, is that of making Jesus truly our Lord and letting Him handle Flesh Woman's demise entirely. Which requires "the painful, all-out . . . handing over to Him all of our natural self to be destroyed (the good parts of the apple along with the brown specks) so that Christ can give us a new self, one born from above, one in which He will live at the center of our being."[14]

Much of our inner wrestling with Flesh Woman would be eliminated if we would just choose to do that. But handing her over for destruction isn't easy either. That's partly

Oswald Chambers writes: No one enters into the experience of entire sanctification without going through a "white funeral" — the burial of the old life. If there has never been this crisis of death, sanctification is nothing more than a vision. There must be . . . a resurrection into the life of Jesus Christ. Nothing can upset such a life, it is one with God for one purpose, to be a witness to Him.

Have you come to your last days really? You have come to them often in sentiment, but have you come to them *really?* . . . Death means you stop being. Do you agree with God that you stop being the striving, earnest kind of Christian you have been? We skirt the cemetery and all the time refuse to go to death. . . .

Is there a place in your life marked as the

because, if we're honest, we're not so sure we want her to die.

Flesh Woman is like a "conjoined twin," my friend Barb says. "She looks like me, feels like me. It's hard to imagine that I need to get rid of her because, deep down, I think she is me."

last day, a place to which the memory goes back with a chastened and extraordinarily grateful remembrance — "Yes, it was then, at that 'white funeral,' that I made an agreement with God."

. . . Are you willing to go through that "white funeral" now? Do you agree with Him that this is your last day on earth? The moment of agreement depends upon you.[16]

— *My Utmost For His Highest*

No one takes [my life] from me, but I lay it down of my own accord. I have authority to lay it down and authority to take it up again. This command I received from my Father.

JOHN 10:18

I must confess I've harbored hopes that my own Flesh Woman might be redeemed. That, given enough time and spiritual rehabilitation, she could be convinced to come around to Christ's way of thinking. But Scripture doesn't point to any such reconciliation of the flesh. Instead, it points cate-

181

gorically to its annihilation: Flesh Woman must die. But what we receive in return for her death is what makes the whole messy process worthwhile.

C. S. Lewis puts it this way: "Christ says, 'Give me *all*. I don't want so much of your money and so much of your work — I want *you*. I have not come to torment your natural self, but to kill it. No half-measures are any good. . . . I will give you a new self instead. In fact I will give you myself, my own will shall become yours.' "[15]

It's the great exchange. Christ's life for mine.

The original holy makeover.

7

A WILLING SPIRIT

"I am the Lord's servant," Mary answered.
"May it be to me as you have said."
LUKE 1:38

I wonder what it must have been like.

Did it happen as she walked to the well for water or as she straightened her room? Was she overlooking the rolling hills around Nazareth or helping around the house? Did she awaken that morning with an intuitive sense of expectancy that told her this day would be like no other?

We don't know when and where she received the message that her life was about to change. The Bible doesn't give many details. It only says that God sent the angel Gabriel to a young virgin named Mary living in a village called Nazareth (Luke 1:26–27).

"Greetings, you who are highly favored!" the angel said (verse 28). "The

Lord is with you."

And in that instant Mary's life changed forever.

FOOLISH THINGS TO CONFOUND THE WISE

God has always seemed to use the most unlikely people in the most unusual ways to perform His most perfect will. A risky practice, I think. After all, we humans have so many ways of messing things up. Procrastination. Pride. Not to mention our tendency to add a few things or skip a few steps in order to "enhance" God's plans.

Even the archangel must have wondered what God was up to, entrusting His grand plan to this unassuming young person. Frederick Buechner writes in his book *Peculiar Treasures:*

She struck the angel Gabriel as hardly old enough to have a child at all, let alone this child, but he'd been entrusted with a message to give her, and he gave it. He told her what the child was to be named, who he was to be, and something about the mystery that was to come upon her. "You mustn't be afraid, Mary," he said. As he said it, he only hoped she wouldn't notice that beneath the great golden wings, he himself was trembling with fear to think that the whole future of Creation hung on the answer of a girl.[1]

So why, out of all the Jewish young women who'd ever lived, did God choose Mary?

Certainly, it might have been that she was in the right place at the right time. After all, she was a resident of Nazareth and pledged to be married to a descendant of David, a man who would soon be called by a Roman census to return to Bethlehem, the City of David — all of which set the stage for the fulfillment of several prophecies. But to choose the woman who would bear His own Son? Surely there must have been something more on God's wish list than a pedigree, an address, and her availability for a road trip.

I believe there was. For Mary was no ordinary teenage girl, as we will discover. She was a woman willing to say yes to God — to lay down her own hopes and dreams so that His plans and purposes could come to pass.

Mary was the kind of woman God still looks for today.

Because, for some mysterious yet marvelous reason, God willingly links His hopes and dreams to fickle, failing humans like you and me. And in that divine insanity, I see three amazing implications:

185

- God must really love us.
- He must be up to something bigger and more wonderful than we know.
- He must want us to join Him in the adventure.

Oh, how the angels must tremble to realize these truths. How they must lean over the portals of heaven, waiting to see, listening to hear. Dumbfounded to think that the whole future of Christianity hangs, again and again, on your answer and mine — on our willingness to say yes to what God asks. To rearrange our lives in order to accomplish His plans.

A WILLING SPIRIT

Gladys Aylward was born in London in 1904. When she was a young woman, she dedicated her life to Jesus Christ and became convinced that she was called to preach in China. Unfortunately, she failed her mission-board exam. But Gladys wasn't the kind of person to give up. When she heard of an elderly missionary looking for someone to carry on her work, Gladys wrote and received word that if she could get to China, she would have a place to serve the Lord.

Just a poor parlor maid, Gladys didn't have enough money for ship fare, but she was able to scrape together enough for a train ticket. So in October of 1930, with only her passport, her Bible, and two pounds, nine pence to her name, Gladys Aylward left England and made her way to China by the Trans-Siberian Railway. And so began a ministry that would make her one of the most famous missionaries of the twentieth century. All because she was willing. All because she said yes to God.

It's amazing what God can do with a heart surrendered to Him. A heart that says yes in spite of the cost.

A Mary heart linked with a Mary spirit.

I can only imagine what must have gone through the mind of Jesus's mother-to-be when Gabriel appeared to her. Angelic visitations were not common in Israel in those days. In fact, the four hundred years leading up to Christ's birth had been strangely devoid of God's manifest presence. "The days are coming," God had warned his people in Amos 8:11, "when I will send a famine through the land — not a famine of food or a thirst for water, but a famine of hearing the words of the LORD." And that prophecy had come to pass. Because of the hardness of Israel's heart, God had stopped sending signs to His people. No pillars of cloud. No columns of smoke. Not even one prophetic

Donna Otto writes: As far as I can tell, once Mary had said yes to the angel, she kept on saying yes to whatever God was doing in her life and her home. She said, "Yes, I'll go to Bethlehem with my husband even though I'm very pregnant." She said, "Yes, I'll settle for a stable" and "Yes, I'll agree to let all those grungy shepherds see my newborn." Much later she said, "Yes, I'll let my Son leave home to be an itinerant preacher." And "Yes, I'll be with Him no matter what — even at the foot of a cross."

The life of Mary shows that great things, important things, always begin with someone saying yes to God, and then moving along one yes at a time. When you keep in mind that your whole life is holy ground, you keep yourself open to the wonderful opportunities He has planned for you. . . .

There will be sacrifices as well as surprises when you choose to say yes to God

voice. And certainly no angels.

But now, in the village of Nazareth, Yahweh chose to speak once again. Not to a priest or a king, but to a frightened teenage girl. Luke

— sacrifices of your time, of your plans, and sometimes of your dearly held dreams. . . .

But . . . God's intention overall is to bless you — in your life as a woman and in your life at home. He has already blessed you. . . . He has . . . promised to dwell in you just as you dwell in Him. And He has indeed favored you among women by giving you a vital part in the process of bringing about His kingdom on earth.

Once you say yes to the Lord, you won't know exactly where you end up, but you can know you'll always find your way home.[2]

— *Finding Your Purpose As a Mom*

If you are willing and obedient, you will eat the best from the land.

ISAIAH 1:19

1:28–37 tells the story:

The angel went to her and said, "Greetings, you who are highly favored! The

189

Lord is with you."

Mary was greatly troubled at his words and wondered what kind of greeting this might be. But the angel said to her, "Do not be afraid, Mary, you have found favor with God. You will be with child and give birth to a son, and you are to give him the name Jesus. He will be great and will be called the Son of the Most High. The Lord God will give him the throne of his father David, and he will reign over the house of Jacob forever; his kingdom will never end."

"How will this be," Mary asked the angel, "since I am a virgin?"

The angel answered, "The Holy Spirit will come upon you, and the power of the Most High will overshadow you. So the holy one to be born will be called the Son of God. Even Elizabeth your relative is going to have a child in her old age, and she who was said to be barren is in her sixth month. For nothing is impossible with God."

Don't you love how thorough the Lord is! Look at His attention to Mary's needs, telling her, in effect: "In case you think this might be too hard, Mary, remember Elizabeth? Your relative who is, um, well . . . old?

She's going to have a baby too. Just think! You won't be alone. You can even share maternity clothes!"

But I'm sure finding something to wear was the least of Mary's concerns once she heard the angel's announcement. This God-planned pregnancy had deep ramifications for her. *What about Joseph?* she must have wondered. *What about our upcoming marriage?*

And — worst of all — *What will people say?*

Mary must have known she would be considered an adulterous woman and that Joseph would likely end their betrothal with a divorce. According to Jewish law, she could even be stoned. Such severe punishment was rarely carried out. All the same, Mary knew the cost of this unplanned pregnancy would be high.

But God's call was higher. So Mary answered the angel: "I am the Lord's servant. . . . May it be to me as you have said" (verse 38).

SAYING YES TO GOD

I must confess I have a hard time relating to Mary. She's everything I'm not — at least in the natural. Quiet. Submissive. Willing to trust God.

Had an angel appeared to me telling me I'd

been chosen to carry the Son of God in my womb, I would have asked for a lot more details before I said, "May it be to me as you have said." And chances are, a praise song would not have been the first thing out of my mouth (Luke 1:46–55). And instead of pondering these things in my heart, as Mary did, I would probably have raced out the door to buy a maternity shirt with the word *MESSIAH* printed on the belly and *HIGHLY FAVORED OF GOD* on the back.

But oh, how I want a willing spirit like the mother of Jesus had. I want to be able to say yes to the Lord without asking why and where and how. Unfortunately, I understand all too well what Richard Foster writes about in *Prayer: Finding the Heart's True Home:* "To applaud the will of God, to do the will of God, even to fight for the will of God is not difficult . . . until it comes at cross-purposes with our will. Then the lines are drawn, the debate begins, and self-deception takes over."[3]

It is one thing to want God's will and quite another to do it. As we've seen, the human heart has a huge capacity for self-deception, and our flesh is contrary to His ways. So even when I'm nodding yes to Him, too often my actions are saying no.

That's why I keep returning to King

David's prayer in Psalm 51: "Create in me a clean heart, O God; and renew a right spirit within me" (verse 10, ASV). However, it is the last phrase of this prayer I've come to appreciate in a special way: "and grant me a willing spirit, to sustain me" (verse 12, NIV).

A willing spirit — that's what I need. A heart and a mind that say yes to God and a will and a body that set that yes in motion. Philippians 2:13 tells us that the Holy Spirit is more than able to help us both "to will and to act according to his good purpose." Without this help, I don't know that I could ever manage to do what God wants me to do.

What has God been asking of you lately? Does it feel impossible? Does it feel like perhaps He chose the wrong person for the task? Do you find yourself listing the reasons you can't rather than the ways He can?

If so, let me share with you a little lesson I've been learning lately. A lesson Mary has been teaching me.

You see, it's not our job to accomplish God's will. That responsibility belongs to Him alone. Our job is simply to say yes to whatever specific tasks He puts before us. Then to follow through, one request at a time, with our lives as well as with our mouths: "May it be to me as you have said."

Obeying then simply believing that God

will do what He says He will do.

Even when it doesn't seem to make sense.

BELIEVING GOD

It would be a busy season for the angel Gabriel. He had to tell Mary and then Joseph the good news they were about to be God's parents. Earlier he had the delightful duty of shocking an old priest in Jerusalem as he burned incense before the Lord.

Imagine what that day must have been like for Zechariah! He hadn't expected to be chosen for the yearly honor of sacrificing to the Lord. To actually be in Jerusalem and on duty in the temple was one thing. To be chosen to enter the Holy of Holies — that was quite another. Hundreds of priests lived and died without experiencing such a tremendous privilege.

But then to have an angel appear just as he was about to light the incense — that in itself was enough to give an old man a heart attack.

"Do not be afraid, Zechariah," the angel said, "your prayer has been heard. Your wife Elizabeth will bear you a son, and you are to give him the name John" (Luke 1:13).

Of everything one might expect an angel to say, this must have been the last thing Zechariah expected to hear. In fact, he demanded proof. "How can I be sure of this? I am an old man and my wife is well along in years" (verse 18).

While I am touched by Zechariah's careful wording concerning his wife's age, Gabriel wasn't impressed by his answer at all. Who was Zechariah to question God's ability — *and* demand a sign?

"Now you will be silent and not able to speak until the day this happens," Gabriel told the priest, "because you did not believe my words" (verse 20).

"You want a sign, Zechariah?" he was saying. "We'll give you a sign."

Bam! For the next nine months, the priest was literally speechless. Unable to communicate except in writing. Completely mute.

You see, when we doubt God's ability to fulfill His promises to us and through us, no amount of explanations on His part, no signs and wonders performed for our benefit, will ever satisfy us. And God knows that. So sometimes instead of putting up with all the questions, the cynicism, and the theological debate, He simply puts His hand over our mouth and shuts us up — though not quite as literally as He did with Zechariah.

"Shh . . . just wait," He tells us. "You'll see."

Which raises a point. Mary had questioned God too, remember? Why didn't God silence her?

One possibility is that she wasn't asking *if* God could accomplish what He had promised. Her question was an innocent inquiry about *how* God would bring it to pass — and the angel answered her reassuringly (Luke 1:35–37). But I think the real difference between Mary's response and Zechariah's is found in the prophetic words Mary's cousin Elizabeth used to greet her when she came to visit. Luke 1:42–45 (emphasis mine) tells the story:

> Blessed are you among women, and blessed is the child you will bear! But why am I so favored, that the mother of my Lord should come to me? As soon as the sound of your greeting reached my ears, the baby in my womb leaped for joy. Blessed is she who has *believed* that what the Lord has said to her will be accomplished!

"Blessed is she who has believed" — that's the key. Believing God is who He says He is and that He can and will do what He says He will do. That kind of faith releases the impossible. It gives God permission to work uninterrupted and unhindered in our lives. Best of all, that kind of faith releases blessing. And the wonder of this all made Mary sing! Luke 1 records her famous Magnificat, or song of praise, a testimony of God's love sung from a heart filled with gratitude and humble awe:

> My soul glorifies the Lord
>   and my spirit rejoices in God my Savior,
> for he has been mindful
>   of the humble state of his servant.
> From now on all generations will call me blessed,
>   for the Mighty One has done great things
>   for me —
> holy is his name. (Luke 1:46–49)

DON'T MISS THE BLESSING

Zechariah doubted. But — and this amazes me — God still worked. God's plans and purposes were nevertheless accomplished. The sad part is that Zechariah, a man who truly loved the Lord, missed the joy of cooperating, of willingly stepping back and letting God have His way. Zechariah saw the miraculous, but he was unable to sing the song.

Until the day he agreed with God.

When Elizabeth finally gave birth to their long-awaited son, the entire village rejoiced with the priest and his wife. Surely God was good to show such mercy after so many years. Eight days later, when it came time to circumcise the baby boy, everyone was ready to call him by his father's name.

"No! He is to be called John," Elizabeth insisted, wanting to be obedient to the angel's instructions (Luke 1:60).

A murmur probably ran through the crowd, and a few eyebrows probably lifted. There was no one in the family by that name. What could that possibly mean?

But when the neighbors and relatives went to Zechariah, the old man took out a tablet and firmly wrote, "His name is John" (verse 63).

And when he did, Zechariah's angel-imposed silence immediately ended. His "mouth was opened and his tongue was loosed, and he began to speak, praising God" (verse 64).

See the progression here?

With Zechariah's obedience to God's instruction came deliverance. And with deliverance came a song. A blessing.

So, filled with the Holy Spirit, Zechariah began to prophesy:

Praise be to the Lord, the God of Israel,
   because he has come and has re-

deemed his people. . . .
And you, my child, will be called a prophet
　of the Most High;
　for you will go on before the Lord to pre-
　　pare the way for him,
to give his people the knowledge of salva-
　tion
　through the forgiveness of their sins.
　(Luke 1:68, 76–77)

Mary willingly said yes to the extraordinary, even though she didn't fully understand it. As a result, I believe she spent her nine months cradled in God's tender hand. Zechariah's practicality and the age on his driver's license demanded a flow chart and a thought-out business plan. So he spent his nine months cloaked in silence, shut up, forced to wait and wonder as God's perfect plan unfolded.

It's a lesson we should take to heart. When God comes to us, when He asks us to join His great plan of salvation and redemption, we may doubt and we may question. But if we persist in unbelief, we will miss the blessing.

So I say this to myself as well as to you: Don't let your chronic attachment to facts and rationality cause you to miss the miraculous things God wants to do in your life.

Don't be so addicted to details that you miss the opportunity to join God on great adventures.

When His Spirit speaks to you, say yes.

Choose to believe God will accomplish what He's promised.

Rejoice in it.

Then trust God to handle the rest.

THE ART OF PONDERING

Tradition tells us that when some ancient artisans portrayed Mary in stained glass, they used clear material. No dyes, no colors, just transparent-as-water glass. The reason was that, when Mary offered herself to God, she offered herself unreservedly and completely. "There was nothing of her to affect the light that came through," says pastor and author Ben Patterson. "She could not advance herself and advance the work of God."[4]

Mary was that rare kind of woman who knew her part and did it without trying to do anything more. She had a submitted, trusting spirit. She let God call the shots and then went along for the ride.

When the shepherds came to worship Jesus, telling Mary and Joseph what the angels had said, the Bible tells us that "Mary treasured up all these things and pondered them in her heart" (Luke 2:19).

Do you get that? Instead of talking about what was happening, Mary pondered. She thought about it. She held the events in her heart rather than blabbing them at the well or in the village marketplace.

I've already told you, that's so not me. Had I been in Mary's place, I'm afraid I would have been tempted to interrupt, tell of my own angelic encounter, and force my husband to share his story as well. After all, the shepherds were already spreading the news to anyone who would listen. Adding our stories to the mix would only substantiate what they were saying. *Dateline, 60 Minutes, Live with Larry King* — they'd all be begging us for an interview. With such a spectacular mix of advance publicity, our baby could be crowned king of Israel within the week!

But Mary refused to pander to the public. Instead, she pondered in private. And I wonder if we wouldn't be smart to follow her example. For, too often, when God invites us to join Him in His work, we run ahead trying to help Him out. Rather than allowing the Lord to work out His plan in His own time, we pull out our penknives and try to force open the bud before it was meant to blossom.

And whenever we do, we cause trouble.

Just ask Joseph. Not Mary's husband

We tend to think that saying yes to God's call on our lives involves the big issues — the dramatic "Here am I, Lord! Send me" events. But being available to be used by God can often be seen best in our willingness to do the small things — the little yesses that may seem unimportant at the moment but make a big difference. Helping others but, more importantly, changing us.

- Saying yes to inconvenience so someone else might be blessed.
- Saying yes to a backseat role though we're fully qualified to drive.
- Saying yes to doing the unseen, the unnoticed, and the underappreciated.
- Saying yes to overlooking faults and inconsiderate slights.
- Saying yes to patient listening though there's much to do and more to say.
- Saying yes to chores others should rightfully do.
- Saying yes when we'd rather say no.

Whoever can be trusted with very little can also be trusted with much.

LUKE 16:10

Joseph, but Jacob's son in the Old Testament. Had he pondered and treasured his dreams rather than parading them in front of his brothers, his journey to Pharaoh's palace might not have required a side trip to the pit and thirteen years in the slammer.

Just ask Jacob's mother, Rebekah. Had she trusted God to keep His promise rather than tricking her husband, Isaac, into blessing their younger son, she would have spared the entire family a great deal of pain.

While I know that God used Joseph's slavery and Rebekah's trickery to accomplish His purposes, I can't help but wonder what would have happened had they chosen to wait and ponder instead of rushing ahead. My own experience as a recovering Martha has taught me that a submitted heart says yes to God, but it doesn't demand a time frame or a money-back guarantee. After all, sometimes agreeing to God's will means saying no to the right to make it happen as we'd like and saying yes to trials and hardships, heartache and suffering, terrible loss and great pain.

Just ask Mary. Thirty-three years after the prophet Simeon held her baby son in his arms, blessed Him, and prophesied over Him, she learned that the old man's prophecy had been right on the mark (Luke

2:35). For with every blow of the hammer that drove spikes into the body of her precious firstborn, a sword pierced Mary's soul. Breaking her heart as she watched Jesus die on the dark hill of Golgotha.

The truth is that saying yes to God brings blessing, but it can also bring pain. That's why we need a submitted heart that keeps on believing . . . even when it hurts.

TRUSTING HIS HEART

Why do we secretly believe that following Jesus should always be easy? I know we don't say it out loud. Instead, out loud we talk about the price of obedience and the cost of discipleship. But when it gets right down to it and the going gets tough, haven't we all wondered if we somehow misunderstood God's instructions? If perhaps, we missed God's will when, like Bugs Bunny, we took that left turn at Albuquerque? If we were really walking in obedience to God's plan, we reason, things shouldn't be so difficult.

Mary must have had all those thoughts and others when she heard what was going on with her oldest son early in His ministry. She hadn't seen Jesus since He'd left home three years before. She missed Him so much that it sometimes took her breath away.

"Did you not know that I must be about

My Father's business?" Jesus had told her and Joseph almost twenty years earlier after their frantic search finally led them to their twelve-year-old teaching in the temple (Luke 2:49, NKJV). And it was His Father's business that kept Him away from her now. Most of the time Mary was okay with that. But as news of miracles and healings gave way to reports of Sanhedrin meetings and attempts to capture her Son, she must have wondered if she'd misinterpreted all the events that surrounded His birth.

Maybe she shouldn't have asked Jesus to intervene in the wedding at Cana. After all, He'd said clearly, "My time has not yet come" (John 2:4). She hadn't pressed Him, only instructed the servants to "do whatever he tells you" (verse 5). But now, in light of all the controversy swirling around Jesus, Mary couldn't help but wonder. *Did I miss something? Did I mess everything up?*

Her mother-heart must have hurt as she remembered the day she and Jesus's brothers traveled to where He was speaking in hopes of bringing Him home. There had been threats even then — riots and attempted stonings. The entire family had been concerned about Jesus's health — both mental and physical. But instead of coming out to greet them, instead of explaining what

He was up to and putting their hearts at ease, Jesus's only response to the news of their coming had been a not-so-veiled rebuke: "Whoever does God's will is my brother and sister and mother" (Mark 3:35).

Mary must have been grieved at the turn of events that seemed to be leading her Son toward the Cross rather than a crown. And so are we when all our grand plans to do something important for God go up in smoke and our high-flying hopes come crashing down.

At times like these, we need to remind ourselves that God knows what He's doing.

When we can't trace His hand, we must trust His heart.

Dark Days — Glorious Beginnings

"I can still believe that a day comes for all of us," Arthur Christopher Bacon writes, "however far off it may be, when we shall understand; when these tragedies that now blacken and darken the very air of heaven for us will sink into their places in a scheme so august, so magnificent, so joyful, that we shall laugh for wonder and delight."[5]

That's the future reality we must cling to during those times when the high cost of saying yes to God weighs heavily on our hearts.

For God always sees a bigger picture than we do. And although He loves us with tender passion, He will use whatever method is needed to make us more like His Son.

Even though it hurts.

Even when we struggle to understand.

My favorite scene in *The Passion of the Christ* comes as Jesus struggles up the road to Calvary. Though He's bloody, beaten, and nearly dead on His feet, the soldiers whip Him to get Him to go on. Trying to reach her Son, Mary fights through the crowd, but she can't get to Him. Then, somehow, just as Jesus crumples under the weight of the cross, their paths meet, and for a moment they seem entirely alone.

As blood mixed with the sweat of exhaustion drips from His body, Jesus lifts His face and looks at His mother. Then, with an intensity that still reverberates in my heart today, He speaks these words: "Behold, I make all things new."[6]

"Don't look at what you see," Jesus tells her. "Remember what you know. Remember what the angel said. Remember the prophecies. Don't forget that I was born to die. For I am the final sacrifice. I lay the path to eternal life upon this road to death. And because I die, you — and all who come afterward — will live. I make all things new.

And that includes you."

God's ways rarely make sense to our finite human minds. And if we aren't careful, we will spend most of our life arguing with God rather than embracing His ways.

Doubting His promises rather than trusting His power.

Resisting His love rather than resting in His arms.

A PATTERN TO FOLLOW

Though she wasn't perfect, Mary did many things right. Therefore, as a godly woman and a faithful mother, she set an example for us all to follow.

An obedience and willingness to say yes to God.

May it be to me as you have said (Luke 1:38).

A heart that believed the impossible and responded with praise.

My soul glorifies the Lord and my spirit rejoices in God my Savior (verses 46–47).

A submission to God's will and His timing.

She treasured up all these things and pondered them in her heart (2:19).

A heart that made requests but refused to make demands.

Do whatever He tells you to do (John 2:5).

Most of all, she exemplifies a heart of love

that followed Christ to the cross and died to itself so that it might live with Him.

Yet for Mary, Jesus's death was not the end. In a very real sense, it was a new beginning. After her Son's resurrection and ascension into heaven, Mary joined the disciples in the Upper Room as they waited for the promised coming of the Holy Spirit (Acts 1:14).

But after the birth of the church on the Day of Pentecost, the mother of Jesus disappeared into biblical anonymity. And perhaps that is best. For while she was an incredible woman, a tender mother, and a faithful disciple, I believe Mary would want us to focus on Jesus. For He is the true treasure. Christ is the One we should ponder, worship, and adore.

And yet I want to learn from His mother as well.

I want my life to be a Bethlehem. I want to be a portal through which Christ may come into my world.

I want my heart to be a womb in which Jesus is not only birthed, but also a throne from which He rules and reigns.

I want to have a Mary spirit.

For I believe God is still looking for willing people through whom He can work His purposes and perform His plans. People who say yes instead of asking how. People willing to sell all they possess in order to buy an ordinary field that just might hold the pearl of great price (Matthew 13:45–46).

Mary was that kind of person. And so was Gladys Aylward.

The young woman missionary had no idea what lay before her when she said yes to the call of God to go to China. She had no way of knowing that, because of her willingness to be spent for the Lord, China's heart would be turned to God. So marvelous was the story of Gladys Aylward's life that it was eventually made into a movie.[7] And though she dined with kings and queens, the most notable thing about Gladys was her simple willingness to say yes, to be available to God.

Gladys once said, "I wasn't God's first choice for what I've done for China. . . . I don't know who it was. . . . It must have been a man . . . a well-educated man. I don't know what happened. Perhaps he died. Perhaps he wasn't willing. . . . And God looked down . . . and saw Gladys Aylward . . . And God said — 'Well, she's willing.' "[8]

I wonder, what God could do through you and me if we stop questioning His plan, stop trying to understand, and simply say yes. What new, miraculous work could God accomplish in our world if just one or two of us said, "May it be to me as you have said" (Luke 1:38)?

I don't know about you, but I want to find out.

"Here am I. Send me" (Isaiah 6:8).

8
MIND CONTROL

For as he thinks within himself, so he is.
PROVERBS 23:7, NASB

It doesn't look like much just lying there. Weighing less than three pounds, the wrinkled grayish white blob is unimpressive, to say the least. With the texture of soft Jell-O and made up of 80 percent water,[1] it wouldn't stand a chance in the outside world. But housed in a compartment of bone and hooked up to the neurology of the human body, it is a supercomputer beyond anything the world has ever known.

In fact, it has been estimated that the Cray supercomputer — the world's largest processor at one time, which was capable of making four hundred million calculations a second — would have to work nearly one hundred years to equal what the human brain can do in a minute.[2]

As the command center of life, the brain

uses a 30,000-mile network of nerves to relay information at a speed of up to 220 miles per hour or 323 feet per second.[3] Commands to walk, to talk, to laugh, to cry — all the information for life is sent by small electrical impulses firing over tiny gaps called "synapses" between the one hundred billion neurons (nerve cells) that make up our brains. With each brain cell connected to as many as forty thousand others, the human mind has the ability to make as many synaptic connections as there are stars in the universe.[4]

Truly, we are fearfully and wonderfully made.

BEAUTIFUL AND DANGEROUS

Although we are amazing creatures living in an incredible world, most scientists would like us to believe that all of this is just a cosmic accident. Fortunate, perhaps, but entirely unplanned. The same scientists say that you and I are really nothing special since we share 90 percent of our DNA with chimpanzees. But since I recently heard that we also share 50 percent of our DNA with yeast, the chimpanzee fact fails to impress me. I have to believe there's something beyond my genetic makeup that sets me apart from George of the Jungle and a loaf of Eddy's Bread.

And there is. Some call it a divine spark.

God calls it His image.

In Genesis 1:26, the Lord said, "Let us make man in our image, in our likeness." So God formed man from the dust of the earth and "breathed into his nostrils the breath of life, and the man became a living being" (Genesis 2:7). Not quite animal. Not quite God. A strange mixture of dirt and divinity brought together in a remarkable creation called human.

With His breath and His life, God gave men and women the amazing ability to reason, to make choices, and to know Him and love Him. Unlike the rest of Earth's creatures, we are not enslaved to animal instincts and primal urges. We are not salmon, driven mindlessly upstream to our birthplace to spawn and die. This life we've been given is much richer and more complex than that.

To think that this life-changing, decision-making power resides primarily in a three-pound gelatinous mass no bigger than two clenched fists — amazing! There is no part of our body more important than the brain. And no aspect of our personhood more vulnerable than the human mind.

No wonder the Bible warns us about an ongoing conflict in each of us. For as we've already read in Romans 7:23, "There is another law at work within me that is at war with my mind" (NLT).

It is a raging battle, and it has eternal consequences.

WHICH WAY TO THE FRONT?

To be honest, I've always pictured the battlefield of my mind like an old John Wayne war movie — with plenty of tanks and platoons, machine guns, and exploding mortar shells. The forces of evil marching against the forces of good in a cloud of dust and sweat and really ugly khaki. Or perhaps a celestial *Star Wars* epic — with Darth Vader and Luke Skywalker duking it out for my soul using light sabers and special effects. The kind of battle where the only practical response is to stand back and hope the good guys win.

But I'm coming to realize that, though it may feel like an all-out nuclear showdown, the battle for my mind is really more of a chess match. Still a dangerous game, but one of subtle moves and intense strategy, much like what C. S. Lewis describes in his well-known book *The Screwtape Letters.*

Using a fictional framework of letters exchanged between an older, more experienced demon named Screwtape and Wormwood, his young nephew, Lewis offers an inside peek at Satan's secret battle plan. The letters reveal the diabolical yet deceptively simple methods the enemy uses in the war for our minds. (Keep in mind that when Screwtape writes "the Enemy" he is talking about God.)

In his first letter, for example, Uncle Screwtape writes:

I once had a patient, a sound atheist, who used to read in the British Museum. One day, as he sat reading, I saw a train of thought in his mind beginning to go the wrong way. The Enemy, of course, was at his elbow in a moment. Before I knew where I was I saw my twenty years' work beginning to totter. . . . I struck instantly at the part of the man which I had best under my control, and suggested that it was just about time he had some lunch. The Enemy presumably made the counter-suggestion (you know how one can never *quite* over-hear what He says to them?) that this was more important than lunch. At least I think that must have been His line, for when I said, "Quite. In fact much *too* important to tackle at the end of a morning," the patient brightened up considerably; and by the time I had added "Much better come back after lunch and go into it with a fresh mind," he was already halfway to the door. Once he was in the street the battle was won. . . . He is now safe in Our Father's house.[5]

Why are such petty distractions such an important battle strategy for the enemy of our souls? Because he's absolutely intent on keeping our minds from working the way God wants them to work and doing what God wants them to do. Above all, Satan wants to keep us from knowing and loving our heavenly Father.

You see, we serve a God who longs to know and be known by us. A God who has gone out of His way to reveal Himself as well as His love to humanity. Romans 1:20 tells us that "since the creation of the world God's invisible qualities — his eternal power and divine nature — have been clearly seen."

One of the reasons God made Himself known, Acts 17:27 tells us, is "so that men would seek him and perhaps reach out for him and find him, though he is not far from each one of us." And one of the important tools God gives us for searching and connecting is the mind.

Using the physical faculties of the body God gave us, we are able to see and enjoy His creation, sending our brain both information and emotional feedback in the form of chemical reactions. If the process stopped there, we would be no different than the thousands of other species that inhabit the earth. But we humans, remember, are more than a set of chain reactions easily charted on a cardboard junior-high science fair project. We have souls and spirits as well as higher-functioning brains. That means we are able to think and to reason, to know God, and — most important — to make choices about our lives.

All of which explains why Screwtape was so intent on disrupting the subject with the white noise of life. He wants our thoughts totally focused on fleshly concerns, our emotions conflicted and confused, and our wills weakened by indecision and preoccupied with self.

Because a mind focused on "earthly things" has a tendency to fight the call to follow Jesus. But a mind set "on things above" (Colossians 3:2) is a mind that chooses obedience without waiting to feel the inclination.

And that is a dangerous mind indeed. One that not only rattles Uncle Screwtape, but also shakes the dark recesses of hell.

SATAN'S DIRTY SECRET

Writing never comes easily to me. But I must tell you, I've never experienced the kind of inner opposition I did as I was trying to write this particular chapter.

Over the last few weeks, I tried every trick in the book to get something on paper. I attempted outlining and brainstorming, walking away and pressing through. But whenever I sat down to the keyboard, my mind went empty. Despite much intercession, blank spots and dead ends seemed to be the best I could manage.

The worst part was the overwhelming fear that threatened to sweep me away like an emotional tsunami, pulling me under to drown in doubt and despair.

Where did this fear attack? Where was the battle waged?

In my mind, of course.

I suppose I shouldn't be surprised. Writing about the battlefield of the mind increases the chances you might see a little action. In fact, I've discovered that you usually have to live a book in order to write it. (That's why I've decided my next publishing endeavor will be: *How to Be a Beautiful Brilliant Billionaire!* Look for it in a Wal-Mart near you.)

Though I didn't expect such a full-scale assault, I'm glad it happened. Because I'm coming to realize that this topic may be the most important thing we discuss in the entire book.

You see, Satan obviously doesn't want us in the know. He'd much rather keep us in the dark, wandering aimlessly in ignorance. Untrained, undisciplined, unordered. Mentally unproductive and absolutely no threat to him and his devious schemes.

The devil knows that a mind controlled by the Holy Spirit of God and operated by a wide-awake, fully aware follower of Christ literally means his doom. For whoever controls the mind and the will controls the person.

That has been Satan's dirty little secret all along. We will continually lose this deadly, dangerous game if we don't wake up to the fact that we must engage as players, not as pawns.

THE POWER OF THE WILL

One of the myths we Christians must get rid of is the false belief that we are helpless. That we are, as I mentioned in an earlier chapter, just puppets on Puppet Master's string — helpless, hapless marionettes.

God has made us to be so much more than that. Locked up within each one of us lies unbelievable power and potential — power that is accessed through the portal of our mind by the key of our will.

What do I mean by the will? It's the part of

our souls that makes choices and decides what we are going to do. Though closely tied to our reasoning capacity and our emotions, the will also operates independently. That means we can actually make choices about how we think and what we feel. And though our thoughts and feelings may push us toward certain actions, we can choose by exercising our will not to proceed.

Even people who haven't surrendered their lives to Christ have this power of free will. Sin may influence their minds or emotions, making them *think* or *feel* powerless in the face of their circumstances or habits. But every day thousands of them make positive as well as negative choices. Alcoholics stop drinking. Smokers stop smoking. Gamblers stop gambling. By the sheer force of the will God placed within them at birth, they decide to stop, and they do stop — at least for a while.

I realize some people may think it heresy to say that unbelievers can make good moral choices. But I want us to consider reality — the reality of what is ours in Christ. If unbelievers can use their free will to make choices that better their lives — and I believe they can — how much more decision-making power do you and I have when it comes to changing our behavior? For once we open our lives to the work of the Spirit, we also begin the process of transforming our souls — that is, our thoughts, our feelings, and our wills. And as we do, our behavior will also change.

The Bible confirms this. Philippians 2:13 says that God Himself is at work in us "to will and to act according to his good purpose." Ephesians 1:19–20 says the same "incomparably great power" that raised Christ from the dead is also at work "for us who believe."

I could go on and on and on. Scores of scriptures outline the glorious riches and supernatural enabling available to us in Jesus Christ.

But as I've said before, we must partner with Him in the process. For when we choose to exercise our wills, our wills begin to shape our minds.

My choice to *accept* Christ as Savior was a single decision I made the day I gave my life to God. But my decision to *follow* Christ as Lord is made up of hundreds of smaller choices I make every day. How will I act? How will I react? What will I think about? Whom will I obey?

Every time I choose to answer those questions in the light of God's Word and deliberately obey Him, all the power of heaven is released to help me follow through. As Oswald Chambers puts it, God "will tax the remotest star and the last grain of sand to assist us with all His almighty power."[6] For He has invested all that He is and all that He has to help you and me live more like Christ and less like the world.

Imagine what would happen if we actually took back the helm of our minds and made conscious choices about what we set our focus on rather than allowing our thoughts and feelings to wander unrestrained.

I don't know about you, but I can almost sense hell's gates trembling right now. "Quick, Wormwood!" hollers Uncle Screwtape. "Where did you put that tsunami?"

Ah . . . too bad, so sad. I think you're too late.

CHANGING OUR MINDS

"For most of my life," Joyce Meyer writes in *Battlefield of the Mind,* "I didn't think about what I was thinking about. I simply thought whatever fell into my head. I had no revelation that Satan could inject thoughts into my mind. Much of what was in my head was either lies that Satan was telling me or just plain nonsense, things that really were not worth spending my time thinking about. The devil was controlling my life because he was

Emotions are a gift from God, but they were meant to enhance life, not rule it. Whenever your feelings get the best of you, when what you feel threatens to block out what you know, it helps to go back to the truth of Scripture:

When I feel afraid . . .
  "The LORD is my light and my salvation — whom shall I fear?" (Psalm 27:1).
When I feel overwhelmed . . .
  "My grace is sufficient for you, for my power is made perfect in weakness" (2 Corinthians 12:9).
When I feel like running away . . .
  "And he will stand, for the Lord is able to make him stand" (Romans 14:4).
When I feel threatened . . .
  "O LORD my God, I take refuge in you; save and deliver me from all who pursue me" (Psalm 7:1).
When I feel betrayed . . .
  "Be strong and courageous. . . . For the LORD your God goes with you; he will never leave you nor forsake you" (Deuteronomy 31:6).

When I feel confused . . .

"If any of you lacks wisdom, he should ask God, who gives generously to all without finding fault, and it will be given to him" (James 1:5).

When I feel angry . . .

"Everyone should be quick to listen, slow to speak and slow to become angry, for man's anger does not bring about the righteous life that God desires" (James 1:19–20).

When I feel depressed . . .

"He lifted me out of the pit of despair, out of the mud and the mire. He set my feet on solid ground and steadied me as I walked along" (Psalm 40:2, NLT).

When I feel unloved . . .

"I have loved you with an everlasting love; I have drawn you with loving-kindness. I will build you up again and you will be rebuilt" (Jeremiah 31:3–4).

Whatever is true . . . whatever is right . . . if anything is excellent or praiseworthy — think about such things.

PHILIPPIANS 4:8

controlling my thoughts."[7]

God has recently been convicting me of such careless thinking. Of allowing thoughts to come and go much like cars crossing the Oklahoma-Arkansas border. No roadblocks. No checkpoints. No sin-sniffing dogs. No discipline of the will.

Careless thinking is a dangerous habit. For as our thoughts go, so go our emotions. And as our emotions go, so often goes our faith. If the enemy can get me confused, he can get me discouraged. If he can get me discouraged, he can cause me to doubt. If he can make me doubt, he can distract my mind — and that's just a step away from dividing my heart.

I'm learning that if I let her, Flesh Woman will pull my mind away from the things of God with very little effort. A hankering for a Frappuccino can sidetrack Bible study. Remembering I forgot to turn on the dryer can pull my heart from prayer.

No wonder God says our transformation must involve what Romans 12:2 calls "the renewing of your mind." We need a mental makeover that heals our faulty assumptions and twisted thinking; our knee-jerk and often inappropriate emotional responses; our skewed and selfish decision making: and even the way we talk to ourselves. For nothing is more destructive than the self-talk tapes that Flesh Woman incessantly plays in our heads.

THE PERILS OF SELF-TALK

Studies have shown that when we speak normally, we speak at the rate of about 120 words a minute. But psychologists tell us that when we self-talk — that is, carry on a conversation with ourselves inside our heads — we talk at a rate of about thirteen hundred words a minute![8]

Imagine the impact of this constant self-talk. Thirteen hundred words a minute equals seventy-eight thousand words an hour, which comes to 1,248,000 words a day (not including the eight hours we sleep). And the bad news, according to author Tim Hansel, "is that 70 percent or so of our self-talk normally is negative. That means that you and I spend quite a bit of time saying such things as *Oh no, I shouldn't have done that,* or *Oh, what a jerk I am,* and other similar, self-defeating phrases."[9]

The impact of such self-talk is really destructive. Not only in its negativity but also in its unrelenting nature. For if Tim Hansel is right, we listen to well over a million pieces of degrading, God-forgetting self-talk per day.

And, to make matters worse, it may not always be me who is talking to me.

"Satan is just as capable of using the personal pronouns *I, you,* and *me* as we are," explains Anabel Gillham.[10] In her book *The Confident Woman* she writes:

These thoughts will correlate perfectly with your unique version of the flesh (your old ways, your old habit patterns) and will be disguised as the way you have *always thought,* the way your [mental] computer has been programmed. His success comes when you, because the thoughts are so familiar, so "like you," *accept* these thoughts. Then he has you, and you wind up doing the very thing you don't want to do.[11]

How well I understand this sort of self-talk. It often slips into my mind before I even have time to think. Satan disguises lies as personal assessment and plays and replays the demeaning statements inside my head like a never-ending song:

- "There's no use in starting this project — I'll never finish it."
- "I can't believe I forgot to do that! I'm such a flake."
- "I'm a domestic nightmare — even the dog won't eat my cooking."

Your self-talk tapes may be different from mine, of course. They are shaped by your own experiences and misconceptions about life (with a little help from the enemy of your soul). As a result, as Anabel Gillham points out, they're beautifully adapted to your specific core issues. That's why they'rc so hard to see — and so hard to change.

But change *is* possible. That's the whole point of renewing the mind. With the help of the Holy Spirit, we can learn to recognize the lies. We can learn to push *stop* on the constant playback of these mind tapes, to eject the "if only" videos that replay our failures and the "what if" software that exploits our fears.

We'll need diligence to do it, though. For we must patrol our mental borders in order to catch our faulty thinking as soon as it appears.

CAPTIVE THOUGHTS

It's right there in 2 Corinthians 10:5. We are directed to "demolish arguments and every pretension that sets itself up against the knowledge of God, and . . . take captive every thought."

While I may not be able to keep every negative idea from coming to mind, I must take responsibility for what I allow to stay. Taking

What do you do when an ungodly thought pops into your head? (It happens to all of us.) We can't keep them from coming, but how we deal with those thoughts makes all the difference. In *The Confident Woman,* Anabel Gillham suggests these "five Rs" for handling sinful thoughts prudently:

1. ***Recognize*** the thought as sin. Recognize it as defamatory, as selfish, condemning, attacking your character, accusing or confusing you. Recognize it as what it is: the Deceiver's tool, a lie, a destructive thought.
2. ***Refuse*** to accept the thought as yours, and don't dwell on it. You know where it's coming from.
3. ***Reckon*** yourself dead to the power of sin (Romans 6:7; Colossians 3:5). Just as though you were a dead person, do not respond to the power of sin's suggestion.
4. ***Rest*** in knowing that you are *in* Christ and He is *in* you. And when

you fail, when you fall, don't spend the rest of the day receiving thoughts about how you hate yourself, allowing the power of sin to do instant replays, going over and over what you should have done but didn't do.

5. **Remind** yourself of who you are in Christ, dust yourself off, confess that you listened to the Deceiver and actually believed his lies. Tell God you're sorry, learn from your mistake, realize how you were deceived, and go on about life — walking with the poise and confidence of a woman who knows she is deeply loved, totally forgiven, and completely able to live life. *All because of Christ Jesus.*[12]

You will keep in perfect peace all who trust in you, whose thoughts are fixed on you!

ISAIAH 26:3, NLT

thoughts captive means catching them as they occur and dealing promptly with those that are wrong or inappropriate. As the old saying goes, I can't keep the birds from flying over my head, but I can keep them from nesting in my hair.

However, it isn't enough to take the thoughts captive. According to 2 Corinthians 10:5, I must also bring them into obedience to Christ. Which means that, after exposing the lies with truth, I need to promptly hand them over to Jesus.

This is especially important for me, because I tend to place my thoughts under the microscope of self-introspection and study them so intently that I become captivated by the very thoughts I've captured. I over-analyze and overscrutinize to the point that the thoughts I once imprisoned imprison me.

Which shows how messed up my thinking can become! Better to take my captive thoughts to the Lord and let Him deal with them. For He's always right there, fighting for me in this ongoing battle for my mind.

"The weapons we fight with are not the weapons of the world," 2 Corinthians 10:4 reminds us. "On the contrary, they have divine power to demolish strongholds." And we have that very power too, for the Holy

Spirit lives within us. Providing the weapons we need to strengthen our flabby thinking. Helping us set up mental checkpoints to weed out the enemy's lies. And most important of all, showing us how to replace the negative tapes inside our heads with the promises of God's Word.

THE POWER OF GOD'S WORD

I'll never forget coming home late after church one Sunday evening when the kids were little. The night was dark. No moon. No stars. I held John Michael's hand as we left the car and walked toward the house.

Suddenly the deep-pitched barking of a very large dog broke the stillness. It sounded as if it were right behind us. Startled, we both tensed and squeezed hands. I was about to reassure him that the dog was several houses away. But before I could, in a quivery little voice, my four-year-old son began to quote, "The Lord is my helper; I will not be afraid. What can man do to me?" (Hebrews 13:6).

I'm so glad that Colleen, John Michael's Space Cub teacher, didn't think three- and four-year-olds were too young to hide God's Word in their hearts. As a result of her dedication and the fact that we practiced his verses as we drove in the car, my little boy knew fourteen scriptures by the time he was five. And it wasn't just head knowledge or rote memorization because the Holy Spirit brought it to his heart whenever he needed it.

When it was dark and danger barked loudly behind him, John Michael didn't look to me. He knew to look to God.

I'm learning to do that more and more myself. For there is nothing more powerful than the Word of God when it comes to shattering Satan's lies and disarming his devices. Especially when we are able to call Scripture to mind.

In John 14:26, Jesus tells us the Holy Spirit will help us remember everything we have learned from Him. And it's true. In those moments that frighten, confuse, and frustrate us, God is faithful to bring scriptural truths to our hearts and minds that both comfort and direct us.

Unfortunately, if we haven't memorized or actively studied those promises, the comfort can feel a bit diluted. We *think* there is something in the Bible about God never leaving us nor forsaking us, but we're not certain where. Perhaps it was just a sermon we heard . . . or something from Shakespeare . . . or our mother. And while the thought is reassuring, we hesitate to place our trust in human opinion. At moments like these, we don't need comforting sentiments. We need the Word of God.

Author and speaker Mike Quarles agrees. In *One Day at a Time,* Quarles and his fellow authors categorically states that filling our minds with "the crystal-clear Word of God" is the only effective way for us to have victory over Satan's lies and devices.

Merely trying to stop bad thoughts won't work. Should we rebuke all those tempting, accusing and deceiving thoughts? No. If we attempted to win the war for our minds that way we would be doing nothing but rebuking thoughts every waking moment for the rest of our lives.

It would be like telling a man in the middle of a lake to keep 12 corks submerged by hitting them with a small hammer. He would spend his entire life treading water and bopping down corks. What should he do? He should ignore the stupid corks and swim to shore. We are not called to dispel the darkness. We are called to turn on the light. We overcome the father of lies by choosing the truth![13]

As we fill our minds with the clarity of God's Word, Christ uses it to make us holy, "cleansing [us — his church] by the washing with water through the word" (Ephesians 5:26). And as our natural minds are being cleansed, something wonderful happens. New synaptic patterns are formed both in the natural and the supernatural realms, and we begin to think — and act — differently. As the New Living Translation of Romans 12:2 puts it, we "don't copy the behavior and customs of this world" because we've "let God transform [us] into a new person by changing the way [we] think."

Though it may take time, we are being changed — all because of the incredible mind-cleansing power of God's Word. (For more on memorizing Scripture, see Appendix E.)

A WHOLE NEW MIND

"You Christians are all brainwashed!" the angry talk-show host shot across the airwaves as he hung up on a contrary caller and continued his diatribe against the religious right. It was an ugly exchange, so I turned off the radio. But his words stayed with me: "You're all brainwashed."

He'd meant that phrase as a barb, a criticism. But the more I considered what he'd said, I began to pray that he was right. For in a sense, a brainwashing is exactly what you and I need. Not manipulation or mind control, of course. But a thorough mind scrubbing. An all-out erasing of destructive self-talk. A cleansing of old thought patterns and false beliefs. A complete reprogramming of our mental circuits by the Holy Spirit of God so we can "be made new in the attitude of [our] minds" (Ephesians 4:23).

God's Word promises all of that — and something even better. According to 1 Corinthians 2:16, "We have the mind of Christ."

I don't completely understand what that means, and I'm certain I haven't fully attained it yet. But this verse seems to say that you and I can experience the wisdom, power, and insight of Christ Himself. His thought processes, reasoning, and decision-making power — all at work within us.

This is our inheritance. And because of Jesus's death and resurrection, we can claim it here and now. The mind of Christ. For me. For you.

But how do we obtain this treasure, you ask?

Tim Hansel tells the story of a class he attended in which a brilliant Bible scholar asked the group what word was most important in the New Testament. "We all took stabs at it," Hansel writes. "Was it love? faith? hope? sanctification? grace?"

"No," the scholar answered. "It's the little word *let*. L-E-T."

Let.

As in "let the word of Christ dwell in you richly in all wisdom" (Colossians 3:16, NKJV).

And "let this mind be in you which was also in Christ Jesus" (Philippians 2:5, NKJV).

And "let your light shine before men" (Matthew 5:16).

"*Let* is a word of transforming faith, with encyclopedias of meaning poured into it," Hansel observed. "*Let* assumes the total love and power of the Creator. It assumes that heaven is crammed with good gifts the Father wants to give his children. The profoundly simple word *let* is the gate that opens to that power. It gives God permission to work his might in us."[14]

Let. Allow. Choose. Give me permission, Christ promises, and it is yours. My mind for yours — a holy exchange.

Perhaps it's silly, but I'm visual. So I've started taking this promise from God's Word and claiming it through a simple exercise. Sometimes in my mind, but sometimes (on especially difficult days) with an actual poke to my chest, I push an imaginary button.

Then, by faith, I envision my mind dropping out of sight while the mind of Christ rises to take its place.

After all, there are situations and circumstances in my life when a sparkling, washed-by-the-Word mind is simply not enough. Times when I need my thoughts and feelings and will to be Christ's very own.

According to the Bible, I can have both.

The natural made new; the supernatural made mine.

My mind bound to His.

Three pounds of Jell-O. Filled with His power.

9
GUARDING THE WELLSPRING

Above all else, guard your heart,
for it is the wellspring of life.
PROVERBS 4:23

The quaint little village lay nestled high in the Austrian Alps. Surrounded by emerald forests and alpine peaks, it had become a favorite of tourists wanting to escape city life. Located in the center of town was a glistening pond fed by a stream that wound down from the mountains high above. Each summer, beautiful white swans floated across its sparkling depths as townsfolk and visitors sat on its grassy banks. The whole place was paradise, some said. Absolute paradise.

But one evening, as the town council met to review its budget, one member pointed to an expense no one had noticed before.

"Keeper of the Spring," the line read.

"What's that?" he asked.

"Just an old man who lives up the mountain," another answered. "Not quite sure what he does. Something to do with the spring and the city's water supply."

Perhaps this was an area where they could save money, they reasoned. And so they sent word that the old man's services would no longer be needed.

At first, nothing seemed to change. The pond was not quite as clear as it had been, but no one really noticed. But by the following spring, when the swans didn't return, several commented. Others wondered about the yellowish brown tint of the water and the odor that wafted up when the weather was just right. Tourist reservations lagged, and the town council contemplated a national ad campaign. But no one thought anything about the old man on the mountain — until the day a curious few hiked up to the source of the spring.

Along the way, they noticed rocks and debris blocking the water's flow, but the real problem lay at the spring itself. Its once bubbling depths were now still and dark, clogged with rotting leaves and forest litter — the very things the old man had spent his summers working so faithfully to remove.

And that's when everyone realized.

No one was more important to the town than the Keeper of the Spring.[1]

THE PROBLEM WITH COMPROMISE

"Above all else, guard your heart," King Solomon wrote in Proverbs 4:23, "for it is the wellspring of life." Intended as advice to his son, this was a lesson Solomon himself should have heeded. For although he started out as the wisest man who ever lived, Solomon ended his life in disgrace and ruin. All because he didn't guard his heart.

From the beginning of his reign, Solomon began to compromise God's principles. At first it was small things like worshiping the Lord on high places — a practice Yahweh had clearly forbidden (see 1 Kings 3:3 and Numbers 33:51–52). But that seemingly insignificant compromise led to larger concessions. By the end of his life, Solomon had not only built temples to his wives' pagan gods, but he had bowed down and worshiped them himself (1 Kings 11:3–6).

This mixing and mingling of the holy with the unholy is a temptation God's followers still face today. It didn't work then, and it won't work now. Not because God is unreasonable in His demands, but because He knows such compromise will eventually destroy not only us, but everything He wants to do through us. For even a little sin in our wellspring has the power to pollute and corrupt the very essence of who we are.

If King Solomon were here today, I think he would warn us: Guard your heart! Whatever you allow into your life will eventually be revealed — both the good and the bad.

SIN MATTERS

Jesus rcinforced that truth in Matthew 12:34–35: "For out of the overflow of the heart the mouth speaks. The good man brings good things out of the good stored up in him, and the evil man brings evil things out of the evil stored up in him."

Unfortunately, because of the Fall, it's quite possible for the wellspring of a Christian's life to give forth both bitter and sweet water, salt and fresh. Because Flesh Woman still influences our lives, sin still trips us up.

And sin always matters.

Please don't forget that bedrock truth in the glorious light of God's grace. Because Christ is so quick to forgive us when we confess our sins, we can mistakenly believe that what we do doesn't make any difference. So confident of God's forgiveness and willingness to give us a new beginning, we continue to sin. We never think that if we're always returning to the starting block, we never arrive where we were meant to be — the finish line.

Too many of us live like a kid in our youth group years ago who came to Sunday school with an obvious hangover. He told us, "Yeah, I went to a beer kegger last night. But I asked God to forgive me before I went." As if that somehow canceled out any guilt on his part.

Many of us might shake our heads at such a statement, but that's only because we're not so silly as to ask for forgiveness beforehand. No, we carry out our plans with full malice aforethought. Knowing we'll feel ashamed Sunday morning, we have our fun Saturday night. We embrace our sin, then fling ourselves on God's mercy. As if God will somehow not guess that we knew what we were doing all along. And fooling ourselves that our sin won't make much of a difference in the long run.

Every time we do, we harden our hearts a little more to the voice of the Spirit, causing our consciences to become "seared as with a hot iron" (1 Timothy 4:2). Eventually moral scar tissue forms, and our hearts become indifferent to the fact that we're displeasing the Lord.

The truth of the matter is, the more we see of sin, the less it bothers us. And the less it bothers us, the more likely we'll let it into our lives.

Unfortunately, our world is so steeped in sin you don't have to work very hard to pollute your wellspring. Just turn on the television indiscriminately. Read a questionable novel. Spend an afternoon eavesdropping at a beauty salon. You'll hear sin. You'll see sin. And before you know it, the fresh water of your heart will take on the aftertaste of the world.

EARS THAT CAN'T HEAR

"Therefore," James 1:21 tells us, "get rid of all moral filth and the evil that is so prevalent and humbly accept the word planted in you, which can save you."

James was writing to a scattered church surrounded by decadence and compromise. He saw firsthand the effects of sin infiltrating the heart of a Christian. Perhaps that's why he used the Greek word *ruparia* — translated "moral filth" — when he wrote the verse above. New Testament scholar William Barclay says *ruparia* comes from the root word used for earwax.[3]

Have you noticed, as I have, that things which used to bother you as a Christian don't grieve you anymore? That attitudes you once avoided have become second nature and behaviors which once hurt your heart as much as they hurt God's now seem almost normal?

That's what *ruparia* does. Like collected

245

In *Beyond Our Selves,* Catherine Marshall quoted a preacher friend's explanation of why sin, especially unconfessed sin, is so deadly in our spiritual lives:

- "Our sins come between us and God and make it difficult to feel His presence. They are like mud and dirt thrown up on a windowpane, shutting out the sunlight."
- "Even small sins narrow down the channel by which life and vitality flow to us, thus choking off creativity. But often we don't understand the connection between our lack of productivity and sin."
- "Sin divides us on the inside, splits us asunder. It separates conscious

earwax, it muffles the voice of the Spirit in our lives, making it difficult to discern right and wrong. As a result, we begin living by the world's philosophy rather than God's truth. We tread dangerously upon the "way that seems right" to us, not realizing we are actually walking along a road that "leads to death" (Proverbs 14:12).

mind from subconscious, so that we are a personality in conflict with our-selves."

- "Our wrongdoings cut us off from other human beings. God reaches down to hold my hand. With my other hand I touch the lives of fellow human beings. Only as both connec-tions are made can the power flow. And sin will break the connection every time."[2]

Then, after desire has conceived, it gives birth to sin; and sin, when it is full-grown, gives birth to death.

JAMES 1:15

A HARDHEARTED HARVEST

"When a person first sins," Chip Ingram writes in *Holy Transformation,* "there may be a short-lived thrill, but there also enters into the heart remorse and regret. But if the per-son continues in sin, there comes a time when he loses all sensation and can do the most shameful things without any feeling at all. His conscience has become petrified."[4]

After excusing one sin, in other words, we find it that much easier to commit others. For sin's nature is to reproduce itself in every area of our lives, causing us to do things we previously would have found unimaginable.

I once had lunch with a friend who had recently left her husband and children to move in with another man. Rather than being embarrassed by the situation, she bubbled with excitement over her newfound love. I was stunned. She'd been raised in a strong Christian home with strong Christian values. Yet now, in the heat of the affair, she seemed to have lost all moral grounding.

"Oh, Joanna!" she effused. "You don't understand. We *pray* together before we make love!"

This woman sincerely felt she had God's blessing on her sin — though the Bible is abundantly clear about adultery. She wasn't argumentative or defensive, but any mention of such principles was quickly met with dismissals of why those particular scriptures didn't apply to her.

While I'm grateful to report that my friend eventually repented and her marriage was restored, the cost of the sin was high. It always is. For sin matters.

"Don't be misled," Paul wrote in Galatians

6:7–8. "Remember that you can't ignore God and get away with it. You will always reap what you sow! Those who live only to satisfy their own sinful desires will harvest the consequences of decay and death. But those who live to please the Spirit will harvest everlasting life from the Spirit" (NLT).

This law of the harvest declares that there are logical consequences for everything we do. You don't plant a kumquat tree and hope for lemons. You don't seed your garden with radishes and expect soybeans. Yet, as someone has said, we tend to sow our wild oats and then pray for a crop failure!

The truth is, many of us are already living with the consequences Paul wrote about. We've made poor decisions in the past. We've alienated people. We've refused to forgive. We've compromised our values or even outright rebelled. We've chosen poorly. We've loved badly. We've also been hurt by the words and actions of others. We know what the decay and death of sin feel like. We live with its stench every day.

For while the Lord *forgives* sin, He doesn't necessarily remove the *results* of that sin. Spiritually speaking, forgiveness means our sins will never be brought against us again. But in the natural realm, many of us find ourselves living in the wild cucumber patch of our own choices and those of others. Entangled with vines. Caught in a pickle. Wondering if our pain will ever end.

SOWING FOR THE FUTURE

If that's true for you today, may I offer a word of encouragement? While you can't go back and undo the past or avoid its consequences, you can make choices today that will improve your future. Even if you are living out consequences not entirely of your own making.

When my friend Lauraine[5] went through a terrible divorce, she spent a long time feeling as though she were being punished for her husband's sin. After all, it was his unfaithfulness that destroyed their marriage. The bitterness and hurt that wrapped around her heart threatened to choke out any hope of a happy future. She found herself becoming an angry, hard woman.

"I hate what this is doing to me," she told me one day. "But all I can think about is what he stole from me."

"You're definitely reaping the consequences of his actions," I agreed. My heart broke as I listened to all the things my friend had to face — her children's pain, the struggle with her finances, an uncertain future. It seemed so unfair, and I found myself growing angry along with her. But then God interrupted my sympathy with a profound thought.

"What are you planting today, Lauraine?" I asked my friend. "Because what we plant today determines what we harvest tomorrow."

We both began to cry as we allowed God to heal our perspective. For it really isn't what has been done to us or even what we have done that matters. It is what we let those events do to our hearts. And so we both prayed, "Lord, change me."

Because sin — both the act and our response to the act — really does matter.

Yes, God forgives. And He brings healing and restoration to all of us who surrender our failed attempts and shattered dreams to Him.

But in light of sin's painful consequences — hardened hearts, spiritual deafness, and shattered lives — doesn't it make sense to do whatever we can to avoid sin as much as possible?

Isn't it easier to guard the wellsprings of our hearts today rather than sorting out a messed-up life later on?

A BALANCED GRACE

Perhaps the most important step we can take in guarding our hearts is to allow God to establish boundaries and borders in our lives: deciding ahead of time what we'll allow ourselves to see, hear, and do.

For when we allow God to help us establish personal convictions based not on popular opinion or what everyone else is doing but on His Word, we will not only begin to *think* biblically, but we will also *live* biblically.

"If I want to fully experience the love of Jesus," John Ortberg writes in *Love Beyond Reason,* "I must receive one of the most important gifts he sends me — his teaching. . . . I must trust that he is right — about everything. And that therefore where I disagree with him" — and, may I add, where the world disagrees with Him — "I must either be wrong or not yet understand what it was he was saying. I must allow Jesus to teach me how to live."[6]

Allowing Scripture to prescribe personal life limits is not a popular idea today, even in the church. Somehow we've allowed the world's propaganda to infiltrate our thinking, to the point that we've labeled the very idea of having scruples — that is, strong moral or ethical beliefs that affect behavior — as intolerant or legalistic.

"Well, it might be wrong for you," we say, "but don't tell me it's wrong for me."

I'm the first to applaud the fact that we're

no longer bound by the legalistic rules that marked much of the last hundred years of evangelical Christianity. I'm thrilled with the newer emphasis on grace that sets us free. But I'm a bit concerned that we may carry this idea of personal freedom to such an extreme that it becomes something entirely different from what God intended it to be.

The apostle Paul spoke directly to that concern when he wrote, in 1 Corinthians 6:12, " 'Everything is permissible for me,' — but not everything is beneficial. 'Everything

---

OTHERS MAY — YOU CANNOT

If God has called you to be like Christ, He may draw you into a life of crucifixion and humility, and put on you such demands of obedience that He will not allow you to follow other Christians, and in many ways He will seem to let other good people do things which He will not let you do.

Other Christians, who seem very religious and useful may push themselves, pull wires, and work schemes to carry out their plans, but you cannot do it; and if you attempt it you will meet with such failure and rebuke from the Lord as to make you sorely penitent.

Others may boast of themselves, of their work, of their success, of their writing, but the Holy Spirit will not allow you to do any such things, and if you begin it He will lead you into some deep mortification, that will make you despise yourself and all your good works.

Others will be allowed to succeed in making money . . . but it is likely God will keep you poor, because He wants you to have something far better than gold, and that is a helpless dependence on Him, that He may have the privilege of supplying your needs day by day out of an unseen treasury.

The Lord will let others be honored and put forward, and keep you hid away in obscurity because He wants to produce some choice fragrant fruit for His coming glory.

He will let others be great, but keep you small. He will let others do a work for Him, and get the credit for it, but He will make you work and toil without knowing how much you are doing.

The Holy Spirit will put a strict watch over you . . . rebuking you for little words and feelings, or for wasting time.

God is an Infinite Sovereign; He has the right to do as He pleases with His own.

Settle it forever, then, that you are to deal directly with the Lord Jesus — that He is to have the privilege of tying your tongue, chaining your hand or closing your eyes in ways that He does not deal with others.

Then, you will have found the vestibule of heaven.

Others may. You cannot.[7]

— G. D. Watson

I once thought all these things were so very important, but now I consider them worthless . . . compared with the priceless gain of knowing Christ Jesus my Lord.

Philippians 3:7–8, NLT

is permissible for me' — but I will not be mastered by anything."

In other words, even good things can enslave us if we're not careful, ruling over us like masters instead of God. And it is possible to distort our freedom in Christ to such a point that we do whatever we want — including flat-out sin — just to prove we can. That's the heresy Paul, the great defender of grace, encountered in the church at Galatia: "You, my brothers, were called to be free. But do not use your freedom to indulge the sinful nature" (Galatians 5:13).

One of the reasons we get confused about this, I believe, is that we misunderstand the relationship between legalism and grace. We tend to think of them as opposites. But I've come to believe that the opposite of legalism isn't grace, but licentiousness — defined by Lockyer's *Illustrated Dictionary of the Bible* as "undisciplined and unrestrained behavior" and "outrageous conduct" that "goes beyond sin to include a disregard for what is right."[8]

Grace, on the other hand, is the central place where God's love and forgiveness balance His absolute holiness and sense of justice. It is a space of safety carved out by the Cross, a gift that enables us not only to approach a Holy God, but to be accepted as

His very own. Anytime we swing too far toward either license or legalism, we take ourselves away from that perfect balance — and into error. (See illustration below.)

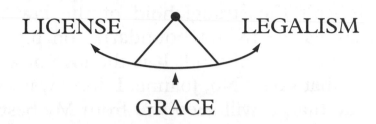

LICENSE   LEGALISM

GRACE

We are pendulum people,[9] spending most of our time swinging between such extremes. And extreme sports are Satan's favorite pastime. He loves to piggyback on conviction as well as complacency, causing his unholy weight to swing us beyond what is good. Causing us to obsess and torment ourselves about spiritual perfection as well as making us so comfortable in our assumptions of grace that we forget how to care about sin. One way or another is fine with him. Just as long as we are out of balance.

That is why we so desperately need a Savior. For we were created to live in the balanced realm of grace — free from law but compelled to holiness by love. The realm Paul wrote about in his letter to Titus: "For the grace of God that brings salvation has appeared to all men. It teaches us to say 'No' to ungodliness and worldly passions, and to live self-controlled, upright and godly lives in this present age . . . [becoming] a people that are [Christ's] very own, eager to do what is good" (Titus 2:11–12, 14).

It isn't the stranglehold of the law that prompts me to put boundaries on my life, but the grace of God. It is the love of a Father that says, "No, Joanna. I don't want you to do that. It will keep you from My best."

Sticking to personal convictions — that is, learning how to say no to ungodliness and worldly passions — doesn't thwart or harm me. It sets me free! As I walk in obedience, my heart is purified, and I am drawn closer to the Lord. Closer than I ever dreamed. For it is the "pure in heart," Jesus promised in Matthew 5:8, who "will see God."

A DAILY CLEANSING

I'm thankful for parents who created boundaries in my life. Parents who remained unswayed in their convictions and refused to allow certain activities even though I assured them everyone else was doing those things. My mom and dad guarded my wellspring diligently throughout my childhood and teenage years.

And while, as an adult, I attempt to do the same, sin still tends to find me — and I find sin. While my transgressions may not be overtly obvious, they are quite real. Iniquitous thoughts that twist and play with the truth to cast me in a favorable light. Envious thoughts that begrudge others their blessings. Impatience that tends to flare into anger when things or people move too slowly. And there are more, so many more.

Sin — all of it. Dark, rotting garbage that, if not removed, leaves my heart looking (and smelling!) more like a sewer than a wellspring.

That's why I so desperately need a Savior. For He is the true Keeper of the Spring. Because of His death on the cross, you and I can be truly clean, actually pure. Today, and then again, tomorrow. For as long as we live in this sin-riddled flesh.

That realization came to me anew several years ago when my eyes were drawn to a hand-hewn cross that sits on the right side of our church stage. About nine feet tall, it is a constant reminder of all that Christ has done for us. But one night during our annual week of prayer, it became a living object lesson of the ongoing power of Christ's shed blood in my life.

I was struggling once again with my continued inadequacies. It had been a tough week, and my responses had been far from godly — angry words, sullen moods, knee-jerk reactions.

"Will I ever change?" I asked God. "Will I ever be what You want me to be?"

There was no audible answer, but as I confessed my sins, I felt the gentle reassurance of His love settle around my heart. And then a word picture came to my mind. Not a vision, but a visual thought. As though I could see a shower head attached to the top of the cross and, in the middle, a sign marked with the word *Repentance*.

How often do you shower, Joanna? the God-thought came softly to my heart.

Every day, my heart answered back. *Or at least every other day.*

Why is it, then, that you only find it necessary to come to the cross once in a while?

Wow. That stopped me in my tracks. Did I really think that the moment I gave my heart to Christ as a four-year-old was the only time I would need the cleansing power of His precious blood?

After all, I sensed the Spirit reason, *in the natural you shower every day because your body produces toxins and because life involves contact with things that make you dirty.*

The same is true in the spiritual realm. Your flesh is toxic by nature, and you will inevitably rub up against things in this fallen world that contaminate your heart.

Don't wait till sin builds up to a spiritual crisis, I sensed the Lord saying. *Deal with it daily. Come clean so I can make you clean. The cross made you My child, and it is the cross that will also make you holy. Not because of your striving, but because you daily take advantage of My forgiveness and love.*

"There is a fountain filled with blood," the old hymn says.[10] And when we go to its life-giving flow, it washes us white as snow. Changing us from the inside out. Cleansing us so thoroughly that we qualify to be vessels for living water.

The very thing God had in mind for us all along.

GOOD NEWS FOR THIRSTY PEOPLE

It was the last and greatest day of the Feast of Tabernacles. Jerusalem was filled with worshipers celebrating the harvest and giving thanks to God for His goodness. For the entire week, the Jews had commemorated their deliverance from Egypt by living in shelters made of willow branches. Each day a priest had taken a golden pitcher, drawn water from the Pool of Siloam, then marched back to the temple though the Water Gate while the people recited Isaiah 12:3 — "With joy you will draw water from the wells of salvation."

I don't know about you, but after a week of camping outdoors and celebrating in Jerusalem's dry and dusty streets, I might have secretly begrudged the cool water the priest poured out upon the altar. Wiping my sweaty brow, I'm sure I would have thought, *I could use some of that.* Especially on the final day, when the ritual required marching around the altar seven times before pouring out the water as a prayer for rain in the upcoming year and a thank offering to the Lord for all His blessings.

Scholars tell us that it may have been in this setting at the Water Gate, at the very moment the priest lifted up the pitcher to pour it out, that Jesus stood and said in a loud voice the words we read in John 7:37–38: "If anyone is thirsty, let him come to me and drink. Whoever believes in me, as the Scripture has said, streams of living water will flow from within him."[11]

Can you imagine how revolutionary Jesus's words must have sounded? A mere man offering what priests could only hint about? Interrupting ritual and religion, Jesus offered Himself as the source of life. With open arms, He invited thirsty, weary people to drink so deeply they would never thirst again.

It was the same offer of living water Jesus had made to the woman at the well. John 4:4–30 describes a side trip through Samaria that brought Jesus face to face with one of the thirstiest people He'd ever met. A woman who knew quite a lot about going to wells and coming up dry.

"Everyone who drinks this water will be thirsty again," Jesus told her, "but whoever drinks the water I give him will never thirst. Indeed, the water I give him will become in him a spring of water welling up to eternal life" (John 4:13–14).

Jesus makes the same offer to you and me today. If you're thirsty, if you can't seem to satisfy that longing in your soul . . . "Come to Me and drink," He says. If you've tried the well of religion and gone away empty, if you've looked to relationships for meaning but need something more . . . "Come to Me and drink."

But Jesus offers more than water to satisfy our thirst. He desires to create in us a well-spring of Himself — a bubbling surge of life that flows out of our innermost beings as John 4:14 says, satisfying our needs as well as the needs of others.

For we weren't created to be mud puddles for Jesus — or clogged, filthy wells. We were meant to be rushing rivers, pouring out His love and mercy to everyone around us. We were meant to be conduits of living water, the sweet and refreshing flow of the Holy Spirit coming in and flowing through and out of our lives.

Wow. I could use some of that.

And so could our world.

CLEAN AND POURED OUT

Our little Joshua has one favorite beverage. He doesn't like milk. He tolerates juice. But he loves water.

"Wa-wa." Because of some developmental delays, he still uses his earliest form of the word, and so I hear it a lot. Throughout the day and often at night.[12]

"Wa-wa, Mommy!" he says. "Wa-wa. Pweeeeze!"

And when he gets it, he drinks it down like a man lost in the Sahara Desert. You have never seen a kid enjoy something so much. His response reminds me of John Michael's from long ago. "Refreshering!" he would say, smacking his lips.

Wa-wa. It's all Joshua wants. It's what he needs.

It is staggering to realize that, every day, nearly four thousand children die around the world, simply because they don't have clean water to drink. Polluted water and a lack of basic sanitation is responsible for the death of 1.6 million children each year.[13] Unnecessary deaths which could be prevented by drilling wells and providing easy-to-use pump systems. Unfortunately, while the answer seems simple, the progress has been slow. Clean life-giving water has yet to be provided in most of the world.

Spiritually, I fear the situation is even more desperate. You and I live in a dry land filled with thirsty people. People who travel from well to well, dipping their battered cups down to get a drink, only to thirst again. Frantically searching for water in the earthly realm. Never realizing that what they really crave is Christ.

If the inner ears of our spirits were opened and the moral filth and complacency removed, I wonder if we wouldn't better hear the cry of our world: "Wa-wa . . . please can't someone give me wa-wa?"

For the world really could use some of that. And that is where you and I come in. God has chosen us to be vessels for His presence. As we dig our spiritual wells deep and rely on Him to help us keep them clean, as we daily prime the pumps of our spiritual hunger, Christ fills us with Himself. Then He places us strategically as living water drinking fountains in a drought-stricken land. Tall crystal goblets filled with His mercy, brimming over with His love. Lush oases where weary travelers come and taste and see that the Lord is good.

You and I have been cleansed — and filled — in order to be spilled.

A crystal-clear "refreshering" drink of Jesus Christ.

"Wa-wa" for the world.

10
A FEARLESS BEAUTY

For God has not given us a spirit of fear,
but of power and of love
and of a sound mind.

2 TIMOTHY 1:7, NKJV

Have you ever had God answer a prayer and not realize it? After you'd prayed for one thing, did He give you something entirely different? And only later did you realize He'd really given you both?

Part of my lifelong prayer for Christian perfection has involved having the quiet and gentle spirit Peter wrote about in 1 Peter 3:4. When I first shared this life goal with friends, their response was loud laughter and a few poorly disguised snickers. Because anyone who knows me well knows I'm not very gentle. And I'm definitely not quiet.

It isn't because I haven't tried. I really have! For years I've gone to social functions determined to be seen but not heard, only to come home beating myself up for my sanguine silliness. I've spent many restless nights overanalyzing conversations where I sounded much like I do in our home movies — obnoxious and loud. Driven to provide extensive commentary on every event in life.

In the natural, the quiet gene has little chance of swimming in my pool.

Perhaps that's why I've always found Peter's statement so appealing, so provocative. Something within me craves the kind of settled peace he describes.

And so I have continued to ask the Lord for a quiet and gentle spirit. For it not only appeals to me. It also pleases God.

GREAT WORTH TO GOD

When Peter wrote the letter that contains this verse, the church had been scattered by persecution to the far corners of the known world. Written from a pastor's heart to his flock, this particular passage targets the husband-wife relationship. But I believe it holds rich truth for every woman in every stage of life. For in it is the key to lasting beauty and the holy makeover we all long for:

Your beauty should not come from outward adornment, such as braided hair and the wearing of gold jewelry and fine clothes. Instead, it should be that of your inner self, the unfading beauty of a gentle and quiet spirit, which is of great worth in God's sight. For this is the way the holy women of the past who put their hope in God used to make themselves beautiful. (1 Peter 3:3–5)

I don't know about you, but I'm glad it was Peter who wrote these words. Coming from someone else (even our old friend Paul), the message might feel like a slam on women — a veiled comment that we need to stop being so shallow and, while we're at it, keep our big mouths shut.

But for everyone who has ever struggled to hold her tongue and failed, for everyone who has let great intentions be derailed by clumsy words and actions — Peter is our patron saint. Making bold statements of faith in one breath and denying the Lord the next. Seeing Jesus transfigured, talking to Moses and Elijah — standing on truly holy ground — only to destroy the moment by offering to pick up plywood at Home Depot so he could build the three of them shelters (Luke 9:28–33).

Shelters? As if the natural could ever hope to hold, let alone protect, such a manifestation of God's glory! I love the parenthetical explanation of Peter's suggestion that Luke

9:33 offers: "He did not know what he was saying."

I wonder how many times grace has had to add that particular footnote to the story of my life? "She meant well, but she had no idea what she was doing."

Mark 9:6 adds a little more information concerning Peter's statement: "He did not know what to say, they were so *frightened*" (emphasis mine).

I think that addition is crucial. Perhaps you've never thought of fear as a factor that makes people shallow and insecure, loud and obnoxious, pushy and anxious. I know I didn't. But Peter also mentions fear immediately after his passage about the quiet and gentle spirit:

> For this is the way the holy women of the past who put their hope in God used to make themselves beautiful. They were submissive to their own husbands, like Sarah, who obeyed Abraham and called him her master. You are her daughters if you do what is right and *do not give way to fear.* (1 Peter 3:5–6, emphasis mine)

It's fear that makes us do those slightly crazy, often inappropriate things. Fear that blurts out thoughtless, sometimes hurtful words. Because fear babbles. It freaks out. It searches frantically for explanations and solutions. It races around trying to fix things or, at the very least, figure things out. It fusses and fidgets, messes and obsesses. Fear sews together fig leaves to cover our inadequacies and paints bright smiles to hide our tears. It builds makeshift shelters and puts on far too much makeup. It forces us to hide behind facades simply because we don't know what else to do.

Perhaps that's why Peter instructs us to spend less time on outward adornment — on the building of ornate shelters to house our fragile egos — and to spend more time making our inner lives lovely. To become so secure in who we are in Christ that we have no trouble calling Him "Master" or trusting Him as Lord.

THE BEAUTY OF TRUSTING GOD

The revelation that God had answered my request for quiet gentleness came as I sat in the middle of a Bill Gothard Basic Life Principles seminar about sixteen years ago. There we were, about a thousand of us, scribbling down notes as Bill spoke to us from a giant video screen. When he mentioned 1 Peter 3:3–5, my ears perked up. What would he say? Could this be the answer to my prayer?

"A quiet and gentle spirit," Gothard said, "is a heart free from fear."[1]

Well, I couldn't help it! I had to shout "Hallelujah!" right there in the middle of the silence. Everyone looked at me strangely, but I didn't care. God had done exactly that over the previous year — He had delivered me from fear. It had never occurred to me that the quiet and gentle spirit I had been praying for was really a heart at rest. A mind free from anxiety. But when it finally came together and I saw what God had done — well, when the Holy Spirit changes you in such a deep, elemental way, you've just got to shout about it!

You see, when I prayed for a quiet and gentle spirit, I thought it would mean that the Holy Spirit would change my personality. That I would become one of those sweet, subdued women I admire so much. Women who know how to respond appropriately to any situation. Women who don't shout, "Hallelujah!" and disrupt otherwise quiet and gentle proceedings. Women who never lose their tempers or say things they later regret. Women who always look put together and never drop meatballs on their dresses at church potlucks. Angels, really — secret agents straight from heaven.

No wonder my friends doubted the likelihood of my prayer being answered. "God made you the way you are," they tried to reassure me as I mopped up the ranch dressing I'd dribbled on my shirt. "He's not going to make you stop being you."

And they were right. God is infinitely more creative than that. He is a God of diversity and not monotony. He's much more interested in taking our personalities, tempering and taming them by His Holy Spirit, and recruiting them for work in His kingdom than He is in churning out church-lady clones.

Well, after I had disturbed the crowd with my unladylike holler-lujah, everyone settled back and focused on the rest of Gothard's teaching. But I couldn't. My heart was too full of the realization that God had answered my request even though I hadn't fully understood what I was asking. Like Martha of Bethany, I'd spent most of my life "worried and upset about many things" (Luke 10:41). And, like Martha, I'd asked for what I thought I lacked — more help in the kitchen. Tools to live more effectively in this life. Something to make me . . . well, less like me.

But God in His wisdom had given me what I needed and what Martha needed as well — freedom from fear.

He hadn't changed my personality. He'd changed me.

He hadn't made me quiet. He'd quieted my soul.

WILL YOU TRUST ME?

For nearly all of my twenties, I awoke every morning with a sense of impending doom. As though something terrible was about to happen. And with that sense had come an urgent need to run faster, to work harder, to somehow stay ahead of the darkness that stalked my soul. It was as though a black cloud hovered over my life, squelching any glimmer of hope or ray of happiness.

Oh, I laughed. I lived. I went through the motions and even experienced the emotions of a victorious Christian. But at night, though it was quiet, my heart still clamored with anxiety. I finally admitted to my husband, "I can't remember having a moment of pure joy." Every event or celebration seemed tainted by fear of the future, regret from the past, or frustration with the present.

Some would diagnose my condition as depression, and perhaps it was. But I believe my problem went deeper than that — all the way down to a flaw in my spiritual foundation. The same old false belief that my Christianity was up to me. That God was up there somewhere with a holy fly swatter just waiting for me to fail.

However, somewhere around my twenty-eighth birthday, all that began to change. And it started with a rebuke.

You don't trust Me, God whispered to my heart one day during my quiet time.

"Of course I trust You," I argued. "I love You."

But you don't trust Me, God countered. Then He began showing me "all" the little ways I looked to myself rather than to Him — the times I got tired of praying and waiting and decided to act on my own. The Holy Spirit especially put His finger on the area of my marriage and my difficulty in submitting to my husband.

I was having a tough time right about then. John and I were both overwhelmed in our ministry positions, and Flesh Woman was flexing her muscles. My core issue of approval and need for success meant I couldn't bear the thought of failure. And my self-deception painted it all as my husband's fault.

If John would just do this . . . If John would just do that . . . From my lofty position as all-knowing wife, I could see exactly what he needed to do. We'd both do much better if he'd only listen to his helpmate, his gift from God, his very own personal Holy Spirit living right there next to him in the flesh.

Well, I was in the flesh all right! And that was the problem.

Anxiety had distorted my thinking and twisted any help I might have offered my hard-working husband. While I may have been right in some of my judgments, I was far from righteous. And I had let my frustration and perfectionism eat away at the fabric of our marriage until it was in tatters, shredded by the never-ending blast of my opinions and the cold wind of my disrespect.

"But, God . . . ," I sputtered as He pointed all this out to me. "If John would just . . ."

Joanna, the problem isn't with John — the problem is with you. You don't trust John because you don't trust Me.

Then the Lord reminded me of Ephesians 5:22 — "Wives, submit to your husbands as to the Lord." (The same command is implied in 1 Peter 3:5.)

Ouch. Suddenly I saw what God was getting at. In my eagerness to *do* everything right so everything could *be* all right, I had usurped both John's role — and God's. When I attempted to manipulate my husband rather than submitting to his God-given role as head of our home, I was essentially telling God He had set things up all wrong.

"But what if my husband isn't doing what he ought to do?" I asked.

Unfortunately, God wasn't in the mood for my arguments. He wasn't impressed by my list of spiritual achievements or by the details of my husband's spiritual faults. When I looked closely at Ephesians 5:22, I saw that it didn't read as I had previously supposed.

It didn't say, "Wives, submit to your husbands *if* they are really wise and practically perfect."

It didn't say, "Wives, submit to your husbands *if* they are really godly, spend three hours a day in the Word, and have regular family devotions."

It didn't even say, "Wives, submit to your husbands *if* they are Christians."

It only said, "Wives, submit to your husbands" and then referred me back to God: "as unto the Lord."

The choice was simple, if not easy.

"All right, Lord," I finally prayed. "I do trust you. Or at least I want to. But you're going to have to help me. A lot."

That one little prayer of willingness marked the beginning of something new in my life. For as I focused on trusting the Lord by submitting to John — offering my opinions when asked but then supporting his decisions and trusting his judgment — some interesting things began to happen.

For one thing, our marriage began to heal.

But even more important was the transformation happening in my heart.

Gradually, almost imperceptibly, my capacity for faith grew. With this growing faith came a new understanding of grace. And, amazingly, as I began to trust God's heart and His plan for my life, I grew less and less afraid. It was just as John Newton's famous hymn says: " 'Twas grace that taught my heart to fear and grace my fears relieved."[2]

The more I began to rest in the Father's perfect love, the more freedom I felt from my chronic anxiety and frantic fear.

FALLING BACKWARD INTO LOVE

The "beloved disciple" John made this connection between love and fear in 1 John 4:16–18:

> And so we know and rely on the love God has for us.
>
> God is love. Whoever lives in love lives in God, and God in him. In this way, love is made complete among us so that we will have confidence on the day of judgment, because in this world we are like him. There is no fear in love. But perfect love drives out fear, because fear has to do with punishment. The one who fears is not made perfect in love.

I must admit, I haven't always appreciated the "perfect love" part of this verse. To me, it only accentuated my failure. Because I feared, I wasn't perfect — and I certainly wasn't handing out anything resembling perfect love.

But when I read the verse that way, I was entirely missing the meaning! For it is *Christ's* perfect love, not ours, that banishes fear . . . by making us right with God. Apart from Christ's sacrifice, the only thing we deserve is punishment. Even on our best days, the most perfect one of us could never approach the purity of divinity. In ourselves, we are eternally inadequate, perpetually vulnerable. No wonder fear and anxiety stalk our lives.

But that's why Jesus came. That's why the black clouds are gone! That's why we no longer have to live in fear of torment and under the brutal tyranny of sin.

Perfect love has come. The power of fear in our lives has been destroyed. All we have to do is receive the gift. But because we humans tend to forget, we may have to remind ourselves that we've received God's perfect love.

How do we do that? Well, this may sound kind of silly, but one way I do it is by falling backward onto my bed. Let me explain.

Fearing the Lord is one of the most important principles of Scripture. But in order to understand what it is, we must know what it isn't. According to author Joy Dawson in her book *Intimate Friendship with God,* fearing God doesn't mean being afraid of Him.

Instead, fearing God involves (1) having God's attitude toward sin, which is to hate it (Proverbs 8:13) and (2) showing proper respect for God's holiness, His power, and His sufficiency to meet our needs (Psalm 33:8–9, NKJV).[3]

When we fear the Lord in those ways, we no longer need to fear anything else. For we are

- ***Protected:*** "The angel of the LORD encamps around those who fear him, and he delivers them" (Psalm 34:7).
- ***Given wisdom:*** "Who are those who fear the LORD? He will show them

On those difficult, overwhelming days when I'm struggling with fear — when the heat waves of my failure obliterate my aware-

the path they should choose" (Psalm 25:12, NLT).

- *A friend of God:* "Friendship with the LORD is reserved for those who fear him. With them he shares the secrets of his covenant" (Psalm 25:14, NLT).
- *Secure in God's love:* "For as high as the heavens are above the earth, so great is his love for those who fear him" (Psalm 103:11).
- *Provided for by God:* "Fear the LORD, you his saints, for those who fear him lack nothing" (Psalm 34:9).
- *Satisfied:* "The fear of the LORD leads to life, and he who has it will abide in satisfaction; he will not be visited with evil" (Proverbs 19:23, NKJV).

Blessed is the man who fears the LORD, who finds great delight in his commands.

PSALM 112:1

ness of God's perfect love — I make a conscious choice to both repent and then believe I am forgiven in spite of what I feel.

281

And not just forgiven, but cherished. Beloved. Protected. Held close with a love that far surpasses anything we could ever experience here on earth.

"And so we *know* and *rely* on the love God has for us," I say, repeating 1 John 4:16 with the italicized emphasis, throwing open my arms, and falling back on my bed. There I lie — safe and received, welcomed into the forgiving arms of my heavenly Daddy. When I get up, I purposely take with me that delicious sense of being loved and cared for. And fear loses its grip on my heart as my mind delights in God's grace.

"In this way, love is made complete among us," 1 John 4:17 says, "so that we will have *confidence* on the day of judgment" (emphasis mine). The only way to experience the perfect, dread-banishing love that casts out fear is to know and rely on what God tells us He's already given.

For when we trust His love — when we take the plunge and fall backward into joy — we no longer give way to anxiety. We are "made perfect in love" simply by resting in the One whose perfect love drives out fear.

FEAR OR FAITH?

God knew we would struggle with anxiety. He knew that insecurities within and troubles without would press constantly upon our souls, drawing us away from Him and into fear. That is why, over and over in the Bible, we hear the words, "Fear not! Be of good courage."

In this world we will have trouble. Jesus said so Himself in John 16:33. There will be hundreds and thousands of reasons to fear throughout our lives, (not to mention next week) for fear is an integral part of living in the world. What will we eat? What will we wear? Where will we live? Will there be enough money to pay the bills? Are we saving enough for retirement? Will our marriage survive? Will the diagnosis be wrong? Will our kids rebel?

In the natural, life is terminally unstable, and fear is inevitable.

And yet, when you think about it, the conditions that inspire fear are often the very same conditions needed to inspire faith. Any life challenge presents us with a basic choice: fear or faith?

For you see, difficulties can't separate us from God — only fear can. And fear in its purest form is really unbelief, the false conviction that "God can't, God won't . . . so I must."

Faith, on the other hand, chooses to believe that "God can, God wants to, and God will . . . so I choose to trust Him with my life."

Can fear and faith coexist in one person? Of course they can . . . and they do. As long as we live on earth, flesh-fed fear retains an influence. But the more we persist in faith, obeying God and opening our hearts to His love, the weaker fear becomes.

Because, in the end, faith and fear are mutually exclusive.

Only one can rule our hearts.

And only faith offers us the gift of quietness and rest.

No More Need to Run

One of my favorite verses is found in Isaiah 30. It was the verse my husband, John, kept bringing me back to during that dark time of sabotaged relationships. And it is the verse that the Lord still uses to center me when my heart wants to chase after fear.

"In repentance and rest is your salvation," God said to the people of Israel through the prophet. "In quietness and trust is your strength" (verse 15).

"Return to me," the Lord said, offering sweet shelter. But Israel refused, choosing instead, to run — to "flee away" (verse 17) from her enemies.

And so, very often, do we.

I believe that women are especially prone to run away in response to fear — or at least we'd like to. When we're weary and overwhelmed, our first thought is escape. We look desperately for ways to be anywhere but where we are.

Not that we actually "flee on horses" the way Isaiah's people did. But we run away by avoiding conflict, by losing ourselves in books or movies, the Internet or shopping, overmedicating or eating to anesthetize our pain. We may even attempt to distract ourselves with good, important work. And while many of those things are fine in moderation, escapism can become a nasty habit. When we choose to run away rather than turn to God, we experience the same fate God promised the people of Israel when Isaiah warned them, "Your pursuers will be swift!" (verse 16).

You see, fear avoidance doesn't work because when we run, our fears pursue us. They hunt us down and devour us, for that is the nature of anxiety. Fleeing only makes things worse. Just when we think we've succeeded in outrunning fear, we run straight into its arms.

But not all running is fleeing *away*. Sometimes we're the pursuers. For fear makes us doubt God's love and his ability to provide

1. **Turn On the Light.** Tell a godly friend about your struggle, speak your fear out loud, then together give it to God. The bogeyman under the bed isn't nearly as big and scary in the light as he is in the dark. Not when you invite God into the room.

2. **Interrogate Fear.** Stop fear at the door to your heart and ask, "Is the danger I fear real or imagined? a current reality or an exaggerated possibility? Is there something I can do about it? If so, what?" If the situation is out of your hands, place it in God's.

3. **Speak God's Truth Out Loud.** Replace Satan's haunts and taunts with Scripture. When fear knocks on the

for us. So we decide to take care of ourselves, running for all we're worth to chase down our wants and our desires.

If I could only be there, if I could only have that, we think, *then I would be happy.* Satan dangles our "if onlys" in front of our faces like a carrot in front of an old, worn-out nag. And we respond, galloping after our dreams

door, open your Bible and speak the words out loud. Declare what you know, not what you feel. Fear flourishes in silence — the spoken Word breaks its power.

4. **Follow Fear to Its End.** Ask, "What's the worst thing that could happen if this fear came true?" Then look for signs of God in your worst-case scenario. Remember He loves you and has good plans for you. Inform fear that, no matter what happens, you'll serve God.

I sought the LORD, and he answered me; he delivered me from all my fears.

PSALM 34:4

day and night, only to find when we get there that "there" has moved — and happiness and fulfillment remain out of reach.

God's kingdom is not like that. He doesn't tempt and tease, nor does He ruthlessly hunt us down. Instead, He simply asks us to trust Him, and He provides. "The LORD longs to be gracious to you; he rises to show you compassion," Isaiah 30:18 promises. "Blessed are all who wait for him!"

What a difference. Running from our fears and chasing our dreams bring us nothing but anxiety and frustrated hopes. But waiting on the Lord not only renews our strength (Isaiah 40:31, NKJV); it also brings us everything we need.

It may not happen according to our timetable, but God will come through. In fact, according to Deuteronomy 28:2, "All these blessings shall come upon you and overtake you, because you obey the voice of the LORD your God" (NKJV).

Did you catch that? Instead of your pursuing blessings — blessings will pursue you! Now that's an amazing promise. For as you choose faith over fear, you'll experience a holy makeover that not only removes your worry lines, but refreshes your heart and meets your needs.

An inner beauty treatment that goes far beyond skin-deep.

KEEP ME SWEET!

"You don't just wake up a sweet old lady," my friend Rosemarie Kowalski reminded me not long ago. "It has to start now. My auntie is proof of that."

Disabled and bedridden by a stroke, Rosemarie's Aunt Amalia still radiates with the joy of the Lord. Though her once-active lifestyle is now behind her and there are plenty of reasons to murmur, Rosemarie's uncle says, "I've never once heard her complain."

Now that's a far cry from my prop-me-up-on-the-couch-and-listen-to-me-whine approach to suffering. If I have the sniffles or my back aches, everyone knows about it. I want Jell-O and tapioca pudding served on a tray just like Grandma used to bring when I was little and out of sorts. Stroke my hair and rub my back. And don't forget a glass of 7-Up for my upset tummy.

Suffer in silence? Not me. My misery loves company — and a large audience as well.

Needless to say, my family is not looking forward to my old age. And neither am I. It's miserable being miserable.

"Keep me sweet, Lord!" has become my after-forty prayer. I don't want to be a contentious, demanding, fearful old woman. But that means I've got to stop being a contentious, demanding, fearful younger woman. And that means I must get serious about living according to what I *know* rather than what I *feel*.

"Blessed is the man who trusts in the LORD, whose confidence is in him," God promises in Jeremiah 17:7–8. "He will be like a tree planted by the water that sends out its roots by the stream. It does not fear when heat comes; its leaves are always green. It has no worries in a year of drought and never fails to bear fruit."

I want to be like that! I want to be so rooted and secure in the Lord that even in times of burning stress and lonely drought, I have no worries. I want my response to difficulties to be full of faith, not fear. Instead of griping and groaning, I want to produce peace and joy.

Hudson Taylor, the famous nineteenth-century missionary to China, lived a life like that — one so vibrant with faith and hope that a friend wrote these words after his death:

He was an object lesson in quietness. He drew from the Bank of Heaven every far-thing of his daily income — "My peace I give unto you." Whatever did not agitate the Saviour, or ruffle His spirit was not to agitate him. The serenity of the Lord Jesus concerning any matter and at its most critical moment, this was his ideal and practical possession. He knew nothing of rush or hurry, of quivering nerves or vexation of spirit. He knew there was a peace passing all understanding, and that he could not do without it.[4]

The longer I live, the more I realize how deeply I need that peace. And I'm learning, as Hudson Taylor clearly did, that such peace is mine for the taking. I don't have to run. I don't have to fret. I don't have to fuss and primp to make myself acceptable. I don't have to jump up and down to get attention or search for ways to escape blame by making my problems someone else's fault.

Instead, I can trust my heavenly Father, whose perfect love is the answer for all my anxieties. As I come to Him in faith, He blesses me.

For under His protection, I have nothing to fear.

In His loving arms, I find quietness and rest.

And the gentle beauty "which is of great worth in God's sight."

11
Rooting Out Bitterness

*See to it that no one misses the grace
of God and that no bitter root
grows up to cause trouble and defile many.*
HEBREWS 12:15

I love gardening. As soon as the Montana snow melts and the grass starts turning green, I get the itch to be outside working in the yard. Turning over the dark rich earth in my flower beds, I prepare the soil for the bright petunias, cosmos, and marigolds I will plant after the threat of frost is gone. When it is finally time, I scout all the garden centers, picking out the colors and varieties that will combine in a burst of lush beauty.

To hear me tell it, you might assume I'm a dedicated gardener. And I am — until about June. After that, my flowers are more or less on their own. Because while I love gardening, I hate upkeep. So I'll water, but I rarely weed. I figure I've given the flowers a head start — the rest is up to them.

Unfortunately, we have a wild area in our acre of land whose primary crop is Russian thistles. You know the kind. Thick, sturdy stalks with flesh-piercing spikes. Purple flowers that go to seed, germinate, and seem to grow Jack-and-the-Beanstalk tall overnight. Choking my cosmos. Massacring my marigolds. Pulverizing my petunias.

We've tried chemical herbicides and burning the wild area to keep it from seeding into the yard. But each year the purple-headed monsters find their way back to my flower beds.

As a last resort, I've even tried weeding. But thistles are stubborn plants. You can't chop off the top and hope they die. You have to dig them out by the root. The whole root. Every little piece. Forget about a rototiller. If, in a moment of insanity, you pull out the John Deere and let 'em have it, I can tell you from experience they will rise again to haunt you, with every chunk growing into yet another plant.

Those thistles are invasive. They are tenacious and relentless. They have no place in my garden.

Just as bitterness and unforgiveness should have no place in my life.

Every single one of us will be hurt. It's a fact of life. Live around people long enough, and you'll be disappointed. You will be ignored and forgotten. Your needs will be disregarded and your feelings trampled upon. You will be slandered and betrayed — sometimes innocently, sometimes on purpose. And not because you are overly deserving of pain, but simply because you are a human living with other humans in an imperfect world. Because ever since the Fall, these three things have been true:

- Life is unfair.
- People will hurt us and let us down.
- We won't always understand why.

Taken together, those three realities are a recipe for pain. Worse, they can lead to destruction. Because hurt and disappointment left to fester will eventually become resentment. Resentment unchecked will harden into bitterness. And bitterness destroys. As someone once put it, "Bitterness is like drinking poison and waiting for the other person to die."

Perhaps that is why Jesus placed such a high premium on forgiveness. He knew from personal experience that people do indeed let you down. They say one thing and do another. They kiss you on the cheek and stab you in the heart . . . or promise undying allegiance at the seashore but deny you at the fire. They bow down and hail you "King!" one day — and cry "Crucify!" the next.

Like you and me, Jesus was hurt by His fellow human beings. The Bible assures us He was "tempted in every way" (Hebrews 4:15) — which surely means He was tempted to hurl back insults. Tempted to plot revenge. Tempted to withdraw from people in order to avoid being hurt.

No wonder Christ made such a point of teaching forgiveness. For although He completely understood our natural response to pain, He also knew what unforgiveness does — that it not only destroys human relationships, but it also separates us from God (see Matthew 6:14–15). So while unforgiveness may have tempted Christ, He resisted. He forgave even those who put Him to death. By doing so, He introduced God's mercy to the world. Rather than giving His enemies what they deserved, Jesus put aside His right to vengeance and gave up His life instead.

And we are called to do the same.

Unfortunately, forgiveness is completely foreign to our human nature. It feels wrong, unjust, unfair. "What about them?" we ask pointing our fingers. "What about what they've done?"

One of the most amazing discoveries I've made as I've studied God's Word is how very personal its instruction is. Almost always, it's about my response. Focusing on what *I'm* supposed to do regardless of what the other person may be doing. When someone slaps me on the cheek — whether that person is right or wrong — I'm to offer the other side of my face for more punishment. When someone steals my coat, I'm to give my sweater as well (Luke 6:29). Rather than overcoming evil by getting even, I'm told to overcome evil by doing good (Romans 12:21). And when someone hurts me or lets me down in any way, I'm called to give up my right to be avenged or even justified.

Ouch!

Christianity is a radical, radical lifestyle! And nowhere is it more radical than in this sweeping command to forgive unconditionally.

THE COST OF UNFORGIVENESS

In his excellent book *Total Forgiveness,* R. T. Kendall tells how God challenged him personally in this area of Christlike forgiveness. Reeling from the hurt of an unexpected injustice, he shared the details of his situation with a Romanian pastor far removed from the situation. But instead of the sympathy he'd hoped for, Kendall received firm instructions from his godly friend.

"You must totally forgive them," Josif said.

"I can't," Kendall replied.

"You can — and you must," the man insisted.

It wasn't easy advice to hear or follow. Kendall writes:

Astonishingly, before the reprimand from my friend, my unforgiving spirit had not bothered me all that much. . . . I assumed that since nobody is perfect and we all sin in some measure every day, the bitterness in my heart was no worse than any other person's transgression. Moreover, I thought, God fully understood and sympathized with my particular circumstances. . . . But mercifully, the Holy Spirit spoke to me that day through Josif's words. At first, I was angry; I felt hemmed in. But it was a pivotal moment for me, and it changed my life. I was never the same again.[1]

Why are we given such unequivocal orders to forgive? Surely it has something to do with the way unforgiveness works in our lives.

Refusing to forgive people is like setting ourselves up as God over their lives. We take the role of judge, jury, and executioner. After a brief trial — one-sided, of course! — we march them down to the dark caverns of our hearts and lock them in the dungeon of our resentment. We slam the door shut and rattle it for good measure so they know just how imprisoned they are. Then we clip the key to our belt, pull up a chair, and settle in for a long, long wait.

For you see, it is impossible to keep people jailed in unforgiveness without being enslaved to it ourselves.

The sad part about all of this, of course, is that most of the people who've caused us pain are completely oblivious to the fact that they are imprisoned. They may never feel one lash of our inquisitor whip or lose any sleep tossing and turning on the straw mat we've laid for them on the cold, concrete floor of our heart. They won't grow weak and pale from the constant diet of angry gruel and bitter mush.

But there's a good chance we will. According to a recent *Newsweek* article, scientists are finding that unforgiveness is linked to all kinds of physical problems ranging from increased blood pressure and cardiovascular disease to hormonal changes, immune suppression, and possibly impaired neurological function and memory.[2]

The spiritual and emotional fallout of unforgiveness can be just as damaging. The stronger our resentment and the longer we hold on to it, the less joy we're apt to experience. Even more tragic, we may become frozen — emotionally paralyzed — at the point of our pain. On the outside we appear to live and move and even grow, but inside we're like the needle on an old record player, stuck in the deep groove of the injustice done to us. Repeating the same story to anyone who'll listen. Playing the same sad song for ourselves over and over again, year after year.

The frightening reality is, even as Christians, we don't *have* to forgive. God never forces forgiveness on us. When you and I insist on living in our dungeons, He'll respect our choices.

But while God won't force us to forgive, we shouldn't fool ourselves into thinking He'll somehow bless our refusal or protect us from its consequences. For our grudges cost us dearly. If we could only see how distorted and twisted our lives are made by our refusal to forgive and how deeply our resentment affects the lives around us, perhaps then we'd choose to let it go.

Author Paul Borthwick identifies two types of people: "enlarged souls" who live life with faith-filled optimism and "shriveled souls" who let themselves become embittered and withered by life's hardships. His nine suggestions for avoiding the "shriveled soul syndrome" are also keys to rooting out bitterness in our lives.

1. **Avoid Gossip**. . . . Gossip shrinks our souls because we are living at the expense of others. We build our identity by tearing others down.
2. **Release Bitterness.** Bitter people shrivel spiritually as they walk through life under the weight of "apologies owed me." . . .
3. **Take Risks**. . . . Expanded souls step out in faith. Shriveled souls run when no one is pursuing. Expanded souls believe God and take risks. Shriveled souls . . . live in fear of what might happen.
4. **Trust.** Living a life of worry guarantees a shrinking soul. When we try to be God by grabbing control, we

shrivel because we cannot bear the weight. Enlarged souls live comfortably with the unknown because they choose to trust God.

5. **Don't Live for "Stuff."** Keep materialism in check in your life. Those who live for the accumulation of things — either by purchasing or by constantly longing for what they cannot afford — degenerate into shriveled souls.

6. **Master Your Appetites.** People controlled by cravings will shrink their spiritual capacity because food, lust, or other unchecked desires will take over. . . .

7. **Grow Deep.** Enlarged souls think about the meaning of life. They look for purpose . . . based on a philosophical and theological foundation. Shriveled souls get preoccupied with drivel . . . and then they find their conversations filled with superficiality.

8. **Be Generous.** Stinginess might enlarge our bank accounts, but it shrinks the soul. Celebrate the past,

embrace the present, and anticipate the future. . . .

9. **Think Globally.** Enlarged souls follow the Lord of the universe. Shriveled souls want a village God who attends to their whims. . . . Enlarged souls see their role in serving the world. Shriveled souls make *their* world the whole world.[3]

I shall run the way of Your commandments, for You shall enlarge my heart.

PSALM 119:32 (NASB)

For the toxic root of bitterness poisons every area of our lives, leaving our hearts small and shriveled. Unable to give or receive love because we've chosen to hold on to our pain rather than give it to God.

THE BITTER ROOT

"Make every effort to live in peace with all men and to be holy; without holiness no one will see the Lord," Hebrews 12:14–15 says. "See to it that no one misses the grace of

God and that no bitter root grows up to cause trouble and defile many."

"See to it that no one misses the grace of God." I've so appreciated Bill Gothard's teaching on this passage of Scripture. Suppose I say something careless that hurts you — or do something much worse. When that happens, you have two choices. You can either forgive me or refuse to forgive me.

However, the moment I offend you, Gothard says, grace is released in two ways: grace to you to forgive. And grace to me to repent. We are both given the "grace of God" to do the right thing, right there.[4]

But too often we let the moment pass, or we accelerate it into a full knock-down-drag-out fight. I'm too stubborn to admit I'm wrong. You're too hurt to let it go. So we both withdraw in resentment — having missed the grace that was available to us at that moment.

That's when the "bitter root" begins to grow. The longer we let the situation go unresolved, the bigger and stronger the offense grows. And though grace is still available to us for reconciliation, it may become harder and harder to access.

"Resentment is when you let your hurt become hate," Max Lucado writes in *The Applause of Heaven*. "Resentment is when you allow what is eating you to eat you up. Resentment is when you poke, stoke, feed, and fan the fire, stirring the flames and reliving the pain. . . . Resentment is the deliberate decision to nurse the offense until it becomes a black, furry, growling grudge."[5]

I must warn you, bitterness is far more than a one-time, one-relationship problem. Bitterness, unchecked, will grow and spread like Russian thistles. It won't stop until it has infected every part of your life — even your relationship with Christ. For it is impossible, the Bible tells us, to be estranged from people and not be estranged from God. As 1 John 4:20 says, "If anyone says, 'I love God,' yet hates his brother, he is a liar." When we build walls against people, in reality, we build walls against God.

No wonder Hebrews 12:15 says that missing grace and refusing to forgive cause trouble. The bitter root that grows as a result doesn't defile only one relationship. It defiles many.

If we let it, it can choke out our joy and peace as well as the life Christ came to give.

How to Forgive

A Brazil-nut tree is majestic both in size and strength — a true giant of the Amazon rain forest. However, it has one enemy — the strangler fig. When a strangler-fig seed lands on the Brazil-nut branches, its vinelike roots snake down along the tree trunk to the ground, then spread out and fuse together until they totally encase the tree. Overhead, the fig's canopy of leaves blocks sunlight as the fig's grip on the tree increases. The vine-encased tree slowly dies and then disintegrates within the shell of twisting vines. Its shape remains, outlined by the fig's latticed root structure. But inside the shell there is nothing; the tree has disappeared.[6]

I was surprised by how quickly bitterness crept up around my heart during the conflict with my friends — and how quickly it began to stifle my joy and growth. No matter how I tried to make sense of our situation, it absolutely baffled me. My friends' reactions to my careless remarks seemed so unreasonable — at least to me. Though I'd made a myriad of mistakes before, the things I was being charged with didn't seem to fit my crime. Meanwhile, my friends felt as falsely accused and judged as I did.

I'm convinced that nothing is harder to deal with than a perceived injustice. When we know we're wrong, we may attempt to bluff our way out, but most of us eventually own up to what we've done (or we should!). But when we feel wrongly accused or have something senseless happen to us — that's where radical forgiveness really begins. Such total pardon is a work only the Holy Spirit can do in our hearts.

But as with all other aspects of my holy makeover, we must cooperate with His leading. In my own struggle with bitterness and unforgiveness, the Lord has revealed several important steps I need to take.

STEP #1: MAKE THE CHOICE

Choosing to forgive is an act of the will. It is a decision made completely apart from the person or people who hurt us. It doesn't depend on whether we feel like forgiving or whether the person or people ever repent or deserve our forgiveness. It is a gift we give out of obedience to God. Forgiveness is "for giving."

But more than that, forgiveness is a love offering we pour out before the Lord — an act of gratitude. Because He forgave us, we forgive others (Ephesians 4:32). Because He first loved us, we choose to love others (1 John 4:19).

Therefore one of the first things we must do on this journey of forgiveness is to get rid of the scripts we've written in our minds — the screenplays where people who have hurt us finally come to their senses, drop to their knees, and beg for forgiveness. In the first place, that kind of scene probably won't happen. But, more important, forgiveness with the expectation of return is nothing like the unconditional forgiveness we've been called to as children of God. Rather than healing a relationship, such scripts usually end in disappointment, which causes an even bigger rift.

In a sense, the best kind of forgiveness is done in private after initially being processed between us and God. As humans — and especially as women! — we tend to want closure with people. We want to kiss and make up and get on with the happily-ever-after. But often what we want even more is to have our offenders agree that they were wrong and we were right.

Total forgiveness relinquishes the right to such childish behavior. Forgiving isn't about being proven right. It's about being made righteous. And that requires absolute surrender of a self-gratifying conclusion to our dilemma. R. T. Kendall writes about it this way:

> I [had to make] a daily commitment to forgive those who hurt me, and to forgive them totally. I therefore let them utterly off the hook and resigned myself to this knowledge:
> • They won't get caught or found out.

- Nobody will ever know what they did.
- They will prosper and be blessed as if they had done no wrong.[7]

This may seem like a lot to swallow. But when we pray the Lord's Prayer and ask God to "forgive us our trespasses as we forgive those who trespass against us," this is basically what we are praying. We are asking God to forgive others the way we want Him to forgive us — covering our sin, prospering and blessing us as if we'd done nothing wrong. We ask for His mercy toward those who have wronged us because we so desperately need His mercy ourselves.

In a sense, to totally forgive means we list all offenses against us, then write across the list in red, "Canceled! Paid in full! With love, Jesus." Then we witness and affirm the transaction by signing our own name.

"Whatever you loose on earth will be loosed in heaven," Jesus told the disciples in Matthew 18:18 as He spoke to them about forgiveness.

Because it is only as we let go of the resentments that bind us that things begin to change.

STEP #2: FIND A FAITHFUL FRIEND
God was so good to give me a friend who

loved and counseled me during my friendship difficulties. Rather than telling me everything I wanted to hear — which was essentially how wrong they were and how right I was — she listened and she loved us all. Patty refused to pick up my offense, but instead she kept pointing me to Jesus. Even when it meant confronting my suspicious resentment and paranoid judgments and calling them sin.

When we are hurting, we too often look for people who will help us nurse our pain — baby-sitters for our black, furry, growling grudges. Unfortunately, when we do that, we cause our friends to feel offended with us. To take our side as if we were still schoolgirls playing childish games complete with cold shoulders, icy glares, nasty notes, and messed-up lockers.

Some of us actually work the phone and troll the gossip grapevine, hoping to validate ourselves by the number of women who agree that we've been treated horribly. At the very least, we'd like to gather enough people on our side to make the other person look foolish. Churches have been split and friendships forever severed because of such junior-high games. But, worse, godly women have been ensnared and ministries toppled on both sides, all because an offended person wanted (and received) comfort rather than correction from a friend.

So I'm very grateful for Patty's wise approach to friendship: she offered support without enabling bitterness. And for my husband, who refused to wallow with me in my self-pity. Both of them loved me best by gently calling me toward forgiveness and reconciliation with my other friends.

I must add a note of gratitude to those special ladies. Despite their own hurt, they chose to handle our conflict in a godly manner. As Scripture instructs (Matthew 18:15–17), they kept the circle of contention small, going first to me, then seeking out a godly mediator, and then, finally and privately, asking help from our church leadership.

Because they resisted the urge to line up allies, they not only spared our church a lot of hurt, they also left room for us to — thank You, Lord! — forgive one another totally and be restored to right relationship.

STEP #3: BLESS, DON'T CURSE

As my friends and I have looked back at what happened between us, we've been able to point to lessons God taught us on our path to healing.

For me, one of the most important was

practicing the art of blessing. When we're hurt, the last thing we want to do is bless the one who hurt us. Yet the Bible tells us over and over that this is part of our calling as Christians.

"Do not repay evil with evil or insult with insult," 1 Peter 3:9 says, "but with blessing, because to this you were called so that you may inherit a blessing." Just as our being forgiven is linked to our willingness to forgive others, the blessing upon our lives is linked to our willingness to bless those who harm us.

For me, the practical application of this truth was a daily necessity. Usually somewhere in the course of my day, I had to drive past the home of one of the friends I felt had wronged me. At first I couldn't even look in the direction of her house. The hurt was so deep it startled me. I'd never experienced such a tangible unwillingness to forgive.

I want you to bless her, I sensed the Lord saying.

"But, God . . ." I argued.

Bless her. Don't curse her.

"I haven't cursed her," I protested.

No, not with your mouth. But your unwillingness to bless is just as much a curse.

All right. I couldn't argue with that. So I began the practice of consciously blessing

I will greet this day with a forgiving spirit. I will forgive even those who do not ask for forgiveness.

Many are the times when I have seethed in anger at a word or deed thrown into my life by an unthinking or uncaring person. I have wasted valuable hours imagining revenge or confrontation. . . . I will now and forevermore silently offer my forgiveness even to those who do not see that they need it. By the act of forgiving, I am no longer consumed by unproductive thoughts. I give up my bitterness. I am content in my soul and effective again with my fellowman.

I will greet this day with a forgiving spirit. I will forgive those who criticize me unjustly.

Knowing that slavery in any form is wrong, I also know that the person who lives a life according to the opinion of others is a slave. I am not a slave. I have chosen my counsel. . . . I now know that criticism is part of the price paid for leaping past mediocrity.

I will greet this day with a forgiving spirit. I will forgive myself.

For many years, my greatest enemy has been myself. Every mistake, every miscalculation, every stumble I made has been replayed again and again in my mind. Every broken promise, every day wasted, every goal not reached has compounded the disgust I feel for the lack of achievement in my life. . . .

I realize today that it is impossible to fight an enemy living in my head. By forgiving myself, I erase the doubts, fears, and frustration that have kept my past in the present. From this day forward, my history will cease to control my destiny. I have forgiven myself. My life has just begun.[8]

— Andy Andrews, from
The Traveler's Gift

Jesus said, "Father, forgive them, for they do not know what they are doing." And they divided up his clothes by casting lots.

LUKE 23:34

my friend and her family as I drove by. With my eyes on the road, I said out loud the words "Bless her." As I continued to do this, I gradually felt the knot in my heart slowly loosen. Before long, I was able to genuinely pray for this friend, to sense the depth of her pain and to intercede for her.

I felt pretty good about my progress. But then God told me I actually had to look at her house.

"Look at her house?" I fumed. Wasn't it enough just to say the words? With that I realized there was still bitterness in my heart. If I were truly walking in forgiveness, what would it matter where God asked me to look?

So then discipline of blessing her continued — day by day, week by week — until the sting truly was gone. Until I could look not only at my friend's house, but also at my friend, without feeling the deep pain of what had happened between us.

"How I know I have forgiven someone," author and speaker Karyl Huntley says, "is that he or she has harmless passage in my mind."[9]

Isn't that beautiful? True forgiveness provides harmless passage. No accusing arrows. No passive attempts at revenge. The person's name is safe on my tongue — and I'm kept safe from the poison of my own resentment.

That's exactly what the act of blessing did for me.

STEP #4: KEEP NO RECORDS OF WRONGS

I once heard a story about a missionary who was teaching a group of women how to be more like Jesus. When she taught 1 Corinthians 13, the "Love Chapter" — how love is patient and kind and "keeps no record of wrongs" — she wasn't sure if her students really understood what she was trying to say. Until the next day, when one of the women knocked on her door and handed her a large notebook.

With tears in her eyes, the woman explained that, for years, she had meticulously recorded every instance her husband failed her or let her down. Every sin that he had committed against her had gone into that book. Thumbing through the pages, the missionary saw it was almost completely full of scribbled accusations.

"No more record of wrongs," the woman said in broken English as she pressed the book into the missionary's arms and turned to go. "No more record of wrongs."

It seems unlikely that any of us have kept an actual written record of our hurts and disappointments as this woman had. But, then, most women I know don't need to.

We're perfectly capable of keeping it all on our mental hard drives.

Let our husbands fail to tell us they'll be late for dinner, and by the time they (finally) walk in the door, we have drafted a six-page warrant for their arrest — complete with a detailed listing of prior offenses and parole violations. And if the silly man tries to put up a fight or offer any explanation in his defense, we're capable of pulling up every other marital felony he's committed, no matter how distant and unrelated they might be.

"Love keeps no record of wrongs." Paul's words sound just as revolutionary to our modern ears as they must have sounded to those village women. But if we want to be like Jesus, if we want to truly follow the way of love, we have no choice. We must forgive. We must give to the Lord our right to be treated fairly — and, more than that, we must surrender our mental (and written!) records of the times when we weren't.

Am I saying it's actually possible to "forgive and forget"? Well, yes and no.

We don't always have control over the recollections that arise in our minds. But we do have control over whether we will dwell on those memories and allow them to grow into a bitter root of lingering resentment.

God Himself doesn't actually forgive and

forget. According to Hebrews 8:12, God forgives and chooses not to remember. And so must we. When twinges of old hurt reappear and pain from the past bobs to the surface as if it had all happened just yesterday, we must do what we learned to do with our thoughts. We need to bring them to Jesus. Commit the issue to Him once again and leave it there.

It's not quite "forgive and forget," but it's the next best thing. For as we relinquish the situation once again to God, He takes our books of remembrance so we don't have to carry them with us anymore.

STEP #5: BRING IT ALL TO GOD

Have you ever stopped to think that some of your lingering resentment may actually stem from anger toward God? R. T. Kendall thinks that's the root of much of our bitterness "because deep in our hearts we believe that He is the one who allowed bad things to happen in our lives. Since He is all-powerful and all-knowing, couldn't He have prevented tragedies and offenses from happening?"[10]

This attitude of unforgiveness against God is perhaps the most damaging of all — primarily because most of us don't see it, and if we do, most of us are afraid to admit it. *Who am I to be mad at God?* we tell ourselves. We hesitate to admit our anger and resentment toward others as well because we're sure that He won't approve.

So we continue to stand at a distance, an arm's-length from the love our hearts so desperately long for and the reassurance we so deeply need.

Please know that there is nothing you can tell your heavenly Father that He doesn't already know. Bringing your anger out in the open between the two of you won't destroy your relationship. In fact, it just might heal it. For when you hand Him your diary of wrongs done against you, that honesty opens the door to true relationship.

"Pour out your hearts to him," Psalm 62:8 encourages us, "for God is our refuge."

Our heavenly Father can handle our feelings even when we can't. And while He may not explain Himself or satisfy our curiosity as to why hurtful situations happen, I can assure you of this: His arms are open wide, and He is waiting for you to come back home to Him. His Holy Spirit stands ready to comfort you and show you the way to reconciliation and restoration . . . with God and with others.

CHOOSING NOT TO BE OFFENDED

It was a beautiful summer afternoon. The sun sparkled against the water as members of the youth group floated down the wide

318

lazy river. Laughter and splashing mixed with sprays from water guns and squeals from teenage girls. It was a perfect day. But it was irrevocably interrupted by the sound of a large motorboat rounding the blind corner ahead.

Within moments the youth pastor's life was changed forever as the boat sliced through his inner tube as well as his spine, leaving him paralyzed from the waist down.

A well-meaning saint of the church visited the young man later that week in the hospital. Wanting to comfort but struggling with what to say, he could only offer a low murmur accompanied by an awkward pat. "These things sure have a way of coloring our lives, don't they?" the older man said.

"Yeah, they sure do," the youth pastor agreed. Then, with a slow smile, he added, "But I get to choose the color."

Terrible things happen in this life. Good people do mean things. Not-so-good people do even worse. Life is hard, and we don't get to choose what will and won't happen to us. But one thing we do get to do . . . we get to choose the color. Our response to life's difficulties and to difficult people determines our path.

"I'm learning I don't have to be offended," my very wise husband told me several years ago. "It's my choice. It's what I do with what happens to me."

You and I don't have to be offended either — and that can be an incredible, life-changing, heart-freeing, bitter-root-blasting revelation! This story about Booker T. Washington, the famous African American educator, shows how beautifully that truth can work:

Shortly after he took over the presidency of Tuskegee Institute in Alabama, he was walking in an exclusive section of town when he was stopped by a wealthy white woman. Not knowing the famous Mr. Washington by sight, she asked if he would like to earn a few dollars by chopping wood for her. Because he had no pressing business at the moment, Professor Washington smiled, rolled up his sleeves, and proceeded to do the humble chore she had requested. When he was finished, he carried the logs into the house and stacked them by the fireplace.

A little girl recognized him and later revealed his identity to the lady. The next morning the embarrassed woman went to see Mr. Washington in his office at the Institute and apologized profusely. "It's perfectly all right, Madam," he replied. "Occasionally I enjoy a little manual labor. Besides, it's always a delight to do something for a friend."[11]

What grudge do you bear? What offense do you carry? Isn't it time to give your burden to the Lord? Jesus is willing to pick up anything you are willing to lay down. He will carry it to the Cross for you so you no longer bear it on your own. He'll help you pull up the bitter root of resentment so completely that it can't return to ruin your life. And He won't embarrass or chastise you when He does.

"It's perfectly all right," Jesus whispers as He lifts our weary, shame-drooped heads and smiles hope and forgiveness back into our hearts.

"It's always a delight to do something for a friend."

12
BROKEN AND BLESSED

*Humble yourselves, therefore,
under God's mighty hand,
that he may lift you up in due time.*
1 PETER 5:6

It was a perfect day. One of those "it doesn't get any better than this" kind of days. The sky was pure blue, the air so crisp it took my breath away as I schussed down the snow-covered slopes of Red Lodge, Montana. Living on the plains of eastern Montana made finding a spot to ski a bit difficult. But just three hundred miles away we had found this little resort nestled on the outskirts of Yellowstone Park, a great place to hold our annual youth ski retreat.

So there I was, trying to catch up to my then-youth-pastor husband and our guest speaker. Being total show-offs, they had raced halfway down the run and now stood

smugly leaning on their poles waiting —
yawn! — for me.

I stopped, surveyed the run before me, and
adjusted my ski mask with a determination
only scorned women can understand. I
could almost make out an announcer's
voice: "And the third racer out of the gate —
Joanna Weaver!" I could hear the fans going
wild, chanting my name as I skillfully hurled
my body down the mountain. Tucked into
precise Olympic form, I carved my way over
death-defying moguls, plunging this way and
that, throwing caution to the wind, living on
the edge. Okay, so maybe I snowplowed a
couple of times. But I looked good — I
mean, really good. Especially for an ad-
vanced beginner intermediate.

As I neared the spot where the guys stood
watching me, their mouths gaping in awe, I
concocted a brilliant plan. The moment of
a lifetime lay within my grasp. Payback
time. I would simply make a couple of
turns, then slide expertly to a stop, thereby
spraying the two egomaniacs with a blanket
of bone-chilling snow. *It's too perfect,* I
chuckled madly to myself. *Just one more
right turn, then a quick left.*

But then it happened. Some psychopath
on skis came careening out of nowhere, right
into my path of well-planned revenge. I saw

him out of the corner of my eye just as I approached my moment of glory. With razor-sharp reflexes, I avoided the murderous missile by correcting my left turn and veering sharply to the right.

I missed the crazed skier.

And then, dizzy with relief, I ran head-on into my unsuspecting husband.

We have always been close, but at that moment we experienced the fulfillment of Scripture at 267 miles per hour: "And the two shall become one flesh."

I remember lying there sprawled in the snow and gasping for air. The trees swirled above me in a taunting dance while the annoying little birds flying around in my head mocked me with that old television-sports slogan: "The thrill of victory, the agony of defeat . . . agony of defeat . . . the agony of defeat . . ."

My feet felt fine. My head, however, was killing me.[1]

And my ego . . . Well, that's what this chapter's all about.

THE GREAT DOWNFALL

"Pride cometh before a fall" isn't just a proverb. It's a law of nature. What goes up must come down, for pride will always fall victim to gravity. Jesus said it in Matthew

23:12 — "For whoever exalts himself will be humbled."

Thinking too highly of ourselves is dangerous. So is thinking too lowly of ourselves — that is pride as well. In fact, the whole haughty problem stems from a preoccupation with self, the habit of thinking entirely too much about us. Left unchecked, pride quickly grows into full-blown *I*-disease — a nearsightedness that leaves us unable to see other people and their needs because we can only see ourselves. "Me, me, me" becomes our unending vocal warmup to our self-centered repertoire.

"I am so beautiful . . . to me."

"Of all the me's I've loved before . . ."

You get the idea.

But pride is a liar. Rather than working for us, it works against us. Rather than looking out for our best interests, it pits us against a Father interested only in our greatest good. For inevitably, whenever we get too full of ourselves, we find ourselves in a boxing match, facing off against Almighty God.

When James wrote, "God resists the proud, but gives grace to the humble" (4:6, NKJV), the word he used for *resist* implies taking an active fighting stance. God puts on boxing gloves and meets the arrogant in the center ring. But to the humble, He multi-

Is pride a problem in your life? Pride is basically self-obsession, so the following comparison between self-centered and God-centered personalities may help you assess your own attitudes. As you consider the contrasting elements below, check which ones most often apply to you. Be as honest as you can, asking for the Holy Spirit's discernment. Remember that pride can masquerade as humility!

Self-centered	God-centered
"I want it my way."	"Your will be done."
Is easily swayed by others' opinions	Focuses on pleasing God
Is rigid and opinionated	Is flexible and open to other people's ideas
Gets huffy and defensive if criticized	Doesn't take criticism personally; listens and responds if appropriate

Hungers to be admired and praised — the center of attention	May enjoy praise but doesn't need it; can work behind scenes, lets others have limelight
Makes sure others notice good works; demands credit	Performs good deeds without advertising them
Has power issues; uses other people	Is always concerned about the common good
Indulges self; makes personal comfort a priority	Is willing to sacrifice personal comfort
Feels little need of God and is proud	Looks daily to God for help of self-sufficiency
Practices entitlement thinking: "I deserve this; I'm worth it."	Practices gratitude thinking: "I don't deserve this, but I'm thankful!"

Self-centered	God-centered
Easily offended, nurtures resentment	Forgives quickly and completely; gives ongoing hurts to God
Inflexible; finds it hard to spring back from disappointments	Resilient; able to rise above disappointments and use them creatively
Responds to problems with self-pity	Responds to problems with healthy perspective
Tends to excuse her own sin while condemning the sin of others	Acknowledges her sinful tendencies and those of others, but accepts and extends God's grace to herself and others

plies grace upon grace, filling us with everything we need from His great riches in glory.

You see, there are only two ways to live: God's way or our own. Either we bend our

Obsesses about her obvious failures	Accepts God's forgiveness and moves on
Resents responsibilities and the lack of peace that often accompanies them	Knows life's struggle will not allow her undisturbed peace
Loves people who love her	Feels God's heart toward all humanity; is able to love the unlovable[2]

You save the humble,
but your eyes are on the haughty
to bring them low.

2 SAMUEL 22:28

knees or we thumb our noses.

WORSHIP WHOM?

King Louis XIV ascended France's throne at

the age of five, when his father died of tuberculosis. For the seventy-two years he ruled, Louis expanded French borders and brought his country remarkable reform and prestige. He was unarguably one of France's greatest rulers.

Unfortunately, he knew it.

Referring to himself as the Sun King, he required all his nobles to meet in his bedroom every morning to "watch the Sun rise."[3] And though he built a beautiful chapel in his great palace at Versailles, he required all in attendance to kneel with their backs to the altar so they could look up at him. This way they would be "worshiping Louis worshiping God."[4]

Nauseating, isn't it? But that is what pride does in our lives. We may not have the power or the audacity to push it to Louis' extreme. Our pride may show itself in subtler, seemingly humbler ways. But still, in our hearts, pride causes us to mimic Satan and his great sin of exalting ourselves and our opinions above everyone else. Even above God. We make self the center of our universe. And Flesh Woman, in all her purple-sequined glory, sits on the throne and calls the shots, acting as if she knows better than the Almighty.

No wonder God is forced to take a fighting

stance against His people whenever they puff themselves up with pride. For our own sake and for the sake of His redemptive plan, God loves us enough to break us one way or another.

CONFOUNDED TO BE USED

When I was going through that black, difficult time with my friends, the word that most often came to mind to describe what was happening was the word *confound.* That in itself was strange because *confound* is not a word I normally use. Still, I couldn't shake the sense that God was using my circumstances to confound me. So I went to the dictionary and the Bible to find what it might mean.

The word *confound* means to confuse or perplex as well as to contradict or refute. An archaic meaning is to defeat or overthrow.

Unfortunately, the Bible seemed to concur with that last definition. Because the only people God confounded in Scripture were His enemies.

Thankfully, I knew that wasn't the case. In fact, God had constantly reminded me of His love and favor throughout this difficult time, reassuring me that this wasn't punishment, but a necessary pruning. But why this confounding? this pain? this frustrating confusion?

During the same period, God kept bringing my heart back to the quiet and gentle beauty 1 Peter 3:4 talks about. And the corresponding term *meekness* seemed to be popping up everywhere I went. As I shared with my friend Patty what God was teaching me, she asked what *meekness* means.

"Well, the most popular definition is 'strength under control,' " I told her. "You know, like a wild stallion that has been tamed."

Suddenly, like a lightning bolt in my mind, the two concepts that had been stirring in my soul seemed to transpose over each other, and I saw what God was up to.

"That's what it is!" I told Patty as I stared at her in wonder. "That's why God has been confounding me."

Then I tried to explain what I was only beginning to understand. How do you break a wild horse? You confound it. It wants to go right; you pull on the reins and make it go left. It wants to run; you pull it to a stop. It wants to stand; you make it run. You confuse and contradict and, in a sense, defeat it — by refusing to give the horse its way. You confound the horse because it needs to obey. For until it does the animal will be useless to its master.

Patty caught the analogy and took it further. "That must be what my friend was talking about," she said, leaning forward, her brown eyes sparkling with excitement. "She told me she purchased a new horse and said it has the softest mouth. It responds to her every move without being forced. She only has to suggest a turn with the rein or press with her knee, and the horse immediately goes where she wants it to go."

By then we were crying. To be loved so much by God that He would break us so we might be useful to Him. What an amazing privilege!

This awesome truth stayed with me through the day and into the night. "Give me a soft mouth like that, Lord," I prayed as I lay in the dark. "I want to be so in tune with what You want that I obey even before You ask. Do whatever it takes to break my stubborn will and awful pride.

"Confound me for as long as it takes to make me entirely Yours."

RESISTING THE BREAKING

I wish I could say that, having had that revelation, I've never again fallen back into pride or resisted being tamed by the Holy Spirit.

I wish I could say I've been broken once and for all and have lived ever since in useful, graceful humility.

Sadly, I can't say either. Even more sadly, I'm in good company. The entire history of the Old Testament is, in fact, the story of a loving God and a nation that repeatedly refused to be broken. Again and again, instead of humbling themselves before God, the people of Israel chose to break His covenant. And, in the process, they broke His heart.

"In his love and mercy he redeemed them; he lifted them up and carried them all the days of old," Isaiah 63:9–10 says. "Yet they rebelled and grieved his Holy Spirit. So he turned and became their enemy and he himself fought against them." As a result, the Lord says in Jeremiah 11:11, "I will bring on them a disaster they cannot escape. Although they cry out to me, I will not listen to them."

Sounds harsh, doesn't it? But this was the same God, remember, who had lovingly pursued Israel for centuries. Forgiving His people when they repented. Restoring them when they turned back to Him. Receiving them every time they returned. The Old Testament saga spans nearly four thousand years, a miraculous story of a tenacious God who kept reaching out to a humanity that repeatedly spurned His advances. For when they weren't prostituting themselves with other gods and other nations, they were waving Yahweh off, telling Him they didn't need Him.

No wonder God called them "stiff-necked." That Hebrew word, which crops up again and again from Exodus through Jeremiah, means stubborn, unyielding, arrogant, and proud. "The phrase *a stiff-necked people* is a figure of speech for rebellion and disobedience taken from stubborn domestic animals such as oxen that turn their shoulders away from the yoke and refuse to follow directions," according to Lockyer's *Illustrated Dictionary of the Bible*.[5]

Stiff-necked. Stubborn. Unbending. Refusing to follow directions. Little has changed today, I'm afraid.

One day during my devotions, I asked the Lord, "Why do we Christians have so much 'head' knowledge and so little 'heart' knowledge?" Immediately that word *stiff-necked* came to mind. In my spirit, I sensed the Lord saying, *It's because My people are unwilling to be broken. It is only as they allow Me to break their stiff-necked pride that the truth can filter down into their hearts.*

"Then break me, Lord," I prayed once again. "I want to know You — truly know You. Not by head, but by heart."

I'm so glad God answers prayer.

Even when He chooses to work in *mischievous* ways.

ATTITUDE ADJUSTMENT

Pride is mentioned over a hundred times in the Bible — and always as something the Father absolutely hates. A prideful attitude is really mutiny against our Maker because it assumes we're the ones in charge of the universe. Certain we're right. Determined to have our way. Stubbornly refusing to bend or bow to anyone, including God. Stiff-necked in every sense of the word.

Which, by the way, was exactly what I was after my near-fatal collision with my one and only. I was hurtin' for certain.

Though the youth group prayed for me that night, the next morning I woke up stiffer than stucco. But being the suffering saint that I am, I insisted on skiing with them the next day.

I bravely led one of our youth-group girls, a pitifully helpless novice, to the beginner hill. In spite of horrendous pain, I skied ahead of her, demonstrating my stiff but exquisite form. She'd watch, then follow my tracks down to where I waited.

We were near the end of the run when it happened. One minute I was standing still, calling out encouragement and instruction, and the next, I was falling.

Well, to make a short story long, when my head hit the ground, my neck cracked about a thousand times, and twinkling stars joined the mocking birdies. I felt humiliated falling like that, being a pro and all, so I quickly looked around to see if anyone was watching. That's when I noticed something amazing. My neck didn't hurt. Not one tiny bit.

Jesus had answered the youth group's prayers and given me a chiropractic adjustment right there on the bunny slope.

Not to mention a remarkably effective attitude adjustment.

We all need our attitudes adjusted now and then. Some of us suffer from whiplash — God said stop, but we kept going. Instead of repenting, we continue in our stiff-necked pride, making ourselves and everyone around us miserable. Instead of saying "I was wrong," we just go on being a big pain in the neck.

Whenever we act that way, we're asking for trouble. For God will do whatever it takes to make Flesh Woman abdicate the throne so He can rule and reign — even if it means arranging a little accident. And a painful adjustment of our stiff-necked attitudes.

Though it hurts, I'm glad the Lord deals with my pride. And I've learned it's a lot easier when I actually choose to be broken. Jesus alluded to that reality when He warned, "He who falls on this stone will be broken to pieces, but he on whom it falls will be crushed" (Matthew 21:44).When I willingly fall on the Rock and stay there, the Holy Spirit begins adjusting my hidden life so that my outer life lines up with God's Word. The process is uncomfortable and requires patience. But as each area of my life pops into its rightful place, I find relief . . . and victory.

Victory over the need to be perfect. Victory over the need to always be right. For there is a thrill of victory that only comes when we're willing to face the agony of defeat.

The Miracle of "I Was Wrong"

"Most of us fear being broken," Charles Stanley wrote in *The Blessing of Brokenness.* "Because of our natural instinct for self-preservation, we fight hard to stay intact. Brokenness usually involves pain, and we will do almost anything to avoid that."[6]

But the very thing we resist most is the place where humility must begin: with receiving rebuke. With being willing to admit to God, "I am a sinner. I made a mistake." And to others, "You were right. I was wrong. Please forgive me."

You may need to look in the mirror and practice these lines. They come hard to most of us. But they are important confessions. For if we hope to be fit for the kingdom of God, we must accept correction — just as Martha of Bethany did when Jesus rebuked her in Luke 10:38–42.

It must have hurt Martha to be told that she was too uptight and that her unhelpful sister was doing the right thing. Part of her heart must have rebelled when she heard Jesus's words. After all, she was only asking for help in the kitchen. Did He really have to humiliate her in front of guests?

But correction is not rejection. While we might fight it, might even resent it at times, the Lord's rebuke is always a gift to our souls. For in every check to our nature is a promise of change — if we will receive it. If we will repent.

Martha learned that lesson. I believe she chose to receive the Lord's rebuke with a humble Mary spirit. For after that encounter she really seemed to change.[7]

Aren't you glad God doesn't let us get away with our sin? Part of the Holy Spirit's work is conviction — making us feel both the wrongness of our attitudes and the separation from God that sin causes. We need that inner sense of turmoil that will not let us

My name is Pride. I am a cheater.
I cheat you of your God-given destiny . . .
because you demand
your own way.
I cheat you of contentment . . . because
you "deserve better than this."
I cheat you of knowledge . . . because
you already know it all.
I cheat you of healing . . . because you're
too full of me to forgive.
I cheat you of holiness . . . because you
refuse to admit when you're wrong.
I cheat you of vision . . . because you'd
rather look in the mirror
than out a window.
I cheat you of genuine friendship . . .
because nobody's going to know
the real you.
I cheat you of love . . . because real ro-
mance demands sacrifice.

rest, not let us rationalize our actions or our attitudes, but keeps drawing us back to repentance. Back to our God.

I don't know how it works with you, but for me when the Spirit of God brings a check to my heart concerning a particular sin, there is

*I cheat you of greatness in heaven . . .
because you refuse to wash another's
feet on earth.
I cheat you of God's glory . . . because I
convince you to seek your own.
My name is Pride. I am a cheater.
You like me because you think I'm always
looking out for you. Untrue.
I'm looking to make a fool of you.
God has so much for you, I admit, but
don't worry. . . .
If you stick with me
You'll never know.[8]*

— Beth Moore, from
Praying God's Word

*Pride goes before destruction, a haughty
spirit before a fall.*

PROVERBS 16:18

a knowing — though perhaps, at the time, not a complete understanding. While I might not consciously admit it to myself or to the Lord, I know He is right. A light has been turned on in my mind. And if I'm willing to look, I'm enabled to see.

As I repent and turn from the heart attitude that led to the sin, the Holy Spirit helps me respond and react in new ways — in Christlike ways. That doesn't mean I never stumble or struggle with that specific area again. But gradually, as I continue to cooperate with the Spirit's work in my life, my patterns begin to change.

Never underestimate the value God places on a teachable heart. Martha's sister, Mary, is famous for pouring out a container of very expensive perfume to anoint Jesus's feet — a truly precious offering (John 12:1–3). But so was the gift Martha presented to Jesus when she not only accepted His rebuke, but chose to change. The fragrance of humility released in her life was just as sweet, just as priceless, as the one that wafted up from Mary's extravagant gift.

Humility. Brokenness. We fight it. We avoid it. Yet it is something our heavenly Father values immensely. "The sacrifices of God are a broken spirit," Psalm 51:17 tells us, "a broken and contrite heart, O God, you will not despise."

We know that all heaven rejoices when one sinner comes home. But I'm beginning to realize there is just as much joy in heaven when one saint turns from stiff-necked pride, admits her fault, and chooses an attitude of humility.

PROUD TO BE HUMBLE

I must insert a warning here. As we learned in an earlier chapter, Satan loves to get us coming and going. Whenever we experience victory in our lives, Satan will look for ways to push us into error. And nowhere is that truer than in the area of pride. For Satan is quick to distort any thought of selfless living by turning it into an extreme.

Remember Uncle Screwtape? He writes again to his nephew Wormwood in C. S. Lewis's *Screwtape Letters,* instructing him how to handle a "patient" who has become humble:

> Catch him at the moment when he is really poor in spirit and smuggle into his mind the gratifying reflection, "By jove! I'm being humble," and almost immediately pride — pride at his own humility — will appear. If he awakes to the danger and tries to smother this new form of pride, make him proud of his attempt — and so on, through as many stages as you please. But don't try this too long, for fear you awake his sense of humor and proportion, in which case he will merely laugh at you and go to bed.[9]

343

One of Satan's most insidious tricks is to present humility as self-hatred or low self-esteem. "By this method," Screwtape advises, "thousands of humans have been brought to think that humility means pretty women trying to believe they are ugly and clever men trying to believe they are fools."[10]

This kind of self-hatred is not humble. It's really just another variation of "me, me, me."

And, I might add, a particularly obnoxious form of pride.

THE SNARE OF INSECURITY

"I can't do this, Lord! I'm so undisciplined," I complained to God not long ago as I shut my laptop and listed all the reasons He'd chosen the wrong person to write this book.

"I haven't written in six years; I get distracted. This topic is so big and I barely know what I'm talking about." And then I added the big one: "Besides, I have a three-year-old!!!"

The Lord was patient at first, bringing scripture after scripture to my heart, reminding me that He would help me. That the same power which raised Christ from the dead not only could, but would, strengthen me to accomplish what the Lord asked of me.

The Holy Spirit held my hand as I'd start,

then stutter . . . push forward, then pull back. But one day He finally got tired of my unending litany of reasons why I couldn't.

Let me get this straight, I felt God whisper to my heart. *Although I spoke the universe into existence and hung the stars in space . . . even though I promised to help you when you said yes to My call . . . and even though you've cleared your life and made time to write this book . . . you still keep saying you can't do it.*

Well, that hit home. I started to squirm, but I could tell He was just warming up.

What you're really telling Me, the Lord said, *is that you're the omnipotent one around here. Because no matter how much I help you, no matter how willing I am to give you the words and the ability to write . . . you just know you'll find some way to mess it all up!*

Well, yes. That was pretty much what I was saying. Only it sounded so ugly and prideful the way He put it. Not nearly as humble and desperately pious as I felt.

It's unbelief, Joanna, the Lord concluded. *It is blasphemy. And it breaks My heart.*

And with that rebuke there finally came a deep inner breaking. A sorrow for my sin, but also a freedom in my heart. Satan's lie had been exposed. And in the revealing came the healing and the start of deliverance from its power.

Rather than humbling myself, I had actually been exalting myself against God. Telling the Almighty what He could and could not do. Daring Him to change me. Refusing to let Him help me. Focusing on my inadequacies rather than on His all-sufficiency and power.

No wonder God was offended.

No wonder the Holy Spirit had to bring a rebuke.

For when we refuse to give the Lord what we have — by dismissing it as unimportant or by hoarding it as too precious to give — we miss the opportunity to see what He can do with whatever we place in His hands.

Humble Generosity

When Mary broke her greatest treasure and lavished it on the Lord, she laid down her hopes and her dreams. For that perfume, valued at an entire year's wages, may have been her dowry, part of the assets she would one day take into marriage. But Mary chose to look beyond securing her future and instead lavished her best on her Lord. She chose humble generosity over selfishness, just as we must choose if we want to be free from pride.

"Do nothing out of selfish ambition or vain conceit," Paul wrote in Philippians 2:3–4, "but in humility consider others better than yourselves. Each of you should look not only to your own interests, but also to the interests of others."

These verses have been my lifelong prayer. Not only do they address my particular form of pride — the arrogant hunger for success and attention — but they also point out the kind of humility God's people need to have.

The world has had enough of the up-and-comers, the pushers and the shovers, the proud and the confident who would sooner walk over someone than help them up. What the world needs, what the world is looking for, is authentic Christianity. The heart of a Savior, willing to lay down His life to save the world . . . exemplified by a humble and generous people who are willing to lay down their own agendas in order to love the world back to God.

What does that kind of life look like? You might be surprised at how fulfilling humility can be. I like the way Andrew Murray puts it:

Humility is perfect quietness of heart. It is to expect nothing, to wonder at nothing that is done to me, to feel nothing done against me. It is to be at rest when nobody praises me, and when I am blamed or despised. It is to have a blessed home in the

Lord, where I can go in and shut the door, and kneel to my Father in secret, and am at peace as in a deep sea of calmness, when all around and above is trouble.[11]

As a result of this restful peace, our lives become a "fragrant offering" (Ephesians 5:2). Full of the "aroma of Christ" which, according to the apostle Paul, *"through us* spreads everywhere the fragrance of the knowledge of him" (2 Corinthians 2:14–15, emphasis mine).

Through us. When we willingly bend and bow, when we embrace God's breaking as our making, when we make ourselves of no reputation, something beautiful happens. The life of Christ is released in us. And the fragrance . . . well, it is intoxicatingly attractive. It turned the world upside down two thousand years ago, and God wants to use the fragrance of Christ to do so again. But it only comes through brokenness, through the genuine beauty of true humility.

SOBER JUDGMENT

Thinking too highly of ourselves. Thinking too little of ourselves. Both are dangerous pastimes for a believer in Jesus Christ. Perhaps that is why Romans 12:3 advises us to "think of yourself with sober judgment, in accordance with the measure of faith God has given you."

This sober judgment — this clear-eyed self-analysis — helps us look at ourselves honestly. It enables us to step back and make an objective evaluation of our gifts and our callings, our weaknesses as well as our strengths. And it never forgets to factor in God.

For only in faith, with sober judgment and reliance on the Holy Spirit, can we ever manage to see ourselves as we really are.

In 1717, when King Louis XIV died, his body was laid in a golden coffin. The Sun King had ruled France long and well, and his court was the most magnificent monarchy in Europe.

Surrounded by mourners, his body was carried to the great Cathedral of St. Denis. Prideful to the end, Louis had specified that the cathedral be lit very dimly so that the single candle above his coffin would shine all the brighter. The crowds who attended the king's funeral waited in hushed darkness for Bishop Massilon to begin the funeral mass.

The bishop walked over to the coffin. Then he slowly reached down to snuff out the candle.

"Only God is great!" he said.[12]

A dramatic comment on Louis' reign . . .

and an important lesson for all of us would-be sun kings.

There is only one God.

And it isn't me.

13
THE FLESH-WOMAN DIET

Train yourself to be godly. For physical training is of some value, but godliness has value for all things, holding promise for both the present life and the life to come.

1 TIMOTHY 4:7–8

I'm on a diet. Just the word makes me hungry. But the grace of God which brings salvation has appeared to me, and it is helping me say no to ungodliness — and to Sausage & Egg McMuffins with cheese. It is helping me to live an upright and holy life in this present age. Yea, even though I am surrounded by a case of Frappuccinos bought on sale at Costco and several boxes of Girl Scout cookies, I will fear no evil. For Thou art with me. Thy rod and Thy staff, they comfort me. . . .

I am so glad God doesn't leave me to myself when it comes to transformation. He really is a very present help in times of trouble, temptation, and triple-fudge brownies. But I have to cooperate with grace — adding my "try" to the "umph!" of the Spirit. For without a little discipline on my part and a whole lot of help from God, I will remain the same. Frustrated and depressed. Way behind schedule on my holy makeover.

All because I choose a life of ease rather than a life that pleases God.

CRUNCHING FOR JESUS

Discipline is such a four-letter word. Not only does it have negative connotations; it requires W-O-R-K! My idea of discipline tends to be more like that of Phyllis Diller, who once defined exercise as "a good brisk sit."[1] But as my derrière will attest, sitting only makes the problem grow. The sad truth is, if we want to be what Christ has called us to be, we will have to stop being spiritual couch potatoes and get into the gym of the Holy Spirit. For that is the only way to "work out" what God has so generously "work[ed] in" (Philippians 2:12–13).

Remember Andrea Miller's sit-up epiphany back in chapter 2? Where she expected instant transformation and instead got called to do a little work? I think most of us think that way at some time or another. I call it the "Fairy-Godmother Syndrome." We don't want to be challenged; we just want to be changed. Don't tell us to work out our salvation, God. Just wave Your wand, sprinkle pixie dust, and voilà! We'll be what we've always wanted to be — Cinderella Christians complete with a new gown, glass slippers, and a glistening coach to ride in to the ball.

Unfortunately, midnight always tolls. If we haven't experienced a true holy makeover, the heat of trials and the harsh reality of life will strip us down to our rags and leave us to find our way home barefoot and weeping. Wondering if all we experienced when we came to Christ was just a dream.

Our heavenly Father is not a fairy godmother. He is much too wise to give us the easy way. The instant fix. For He knows that we need to learn discipline if we are to grow into the beautiful women He wants us to be.

Perhaps that's why 1 Timothy 4:7 tells us to "exercise" ourselves to "godliness" (NKJV). Because something happens — both physically and spiritually — when we say no to our flesh.

I'm discovering that on my diet. Although I still crave a morning mocha from Star, my favorite barista, I've seen astonishing results after cutting out sugar for only one week. I can feel my ribs and move my wedding ring! Who knew it was possible? Imagine what could happen if I actually exercised!

All that — just from saying no to Flesh Woman in one little area of my life.

But listen to what the Bible says in the next verse of 1 Timothy 4: "For physical training is of some value, but godliness has value for all things, holding promise for both the present life and the life to come" (verse 8).

When we train our lives toward holiness, we gain greater results than what we experience physically when we get in shape. We all know that getting our body fit affects other areas of our lives — even little things, like being able to tie our shoes or scratch our backs. But pursuing godliness goes far beyond that. It has value for *all* things, the Bible says — not just for eternity and our lives with God in heaven, but for our lives here on earth. Right now.

That's a reason to exercise! And you've got your own personal trainer if you'll have Him. Just ask the Holy Spirit. He's more than willing. He can give you the want-to as well as the ability to obey all that God commands.

Are you ready? You can do this! It's time for more than a "good brisk sit."

THE PRICE OF CHANGE

Mark Twain once suggested that the way to build character is to "do something every day that you don't want to do."[2] I think he was on to something. Because sometimes we really have to push ourselves in order to pay the price of change. Yielding to God by refusing our flesh is not an easy process. But it is more important than we know.

One of the most powerful illustrations of that truth I ever witnessed came in a sermon I once heard. Or, rather, watched.

Pastor Ed Kreiner is small of stature, but a mighty man of God. One evening at our church, he spoke on the importance of yielding daily to Christ in both the big and little decisions that come our way. A powerful idea in and of itself — but it was the way he chose to illustrate the sermon that has stayed with me thirteen years after I first heard it.

How we respond to the Holy Spirit's leading determines whether we walk in freedom or bondage, Pastor Ed said. Because whenever we resist the conviction of the Holy Spirit, we are really saying no to God and yes to Satan. And each time we do that, hell clamps chains on our souls.

As Pastor Ed recited different scenarios, he acted out what our descent into bondage looks like. Standing in the middle of the stage, he began by talking about the way the Holy Spirit speaks to us:

God says, *I want you to share Christ with your co-worker.* We respond with excuses and reasons why that wouldn't be wise. And suddenly our left arm is fastened behind us. . . .

To illustrate, Pastor Ed whipped his arm back and clamped it tightly behind his back.

Give a few bucks to that man begging for change. But we resist compassion, countering that there are plenty of jobs available if he wanted to work. Unbeknownst to us, our right arm joins our left. . . .

Now off balance, with both arms clasped behind him, Pastor Ed staggered a bit.

Forgive your child for her careless remark. We refuse. Our feet are bound together. *Admit that you lied.* We say we will, but we procrastinate to save our pride. And suddenly we are on our back with our knees tied to our chest. . . .

By this time our speaker was lying on the stage like a trussed-up turkey. As he struggled to speak from his awkward position, he reminded us that just as one choice followed by another had brought us down into bondage, one choice followed by another would bring us out.

Call your mom and ask forgiveness, God instructs us. Whew. That's a tough one, but we obey. Suddenly the band around our cramped soul is loosened, and we can breathe once again.

Drop off a meal to the neighbor who's threatening to sue. We prepare lasagna, knock on the door, and find the family visited by tragedy and in need of some TLC. We stick around, they are blessed, and we find we're able to stand.

Pray for your husband instead of complaining when you pick up his dirty socks. We bend our knee and bow our hearts. Suddenly the handcuffed feeling leaves, and we're free to love him inwardly as well as outwardly.[3]

When Pastor Ed finished, he was once again standing up on the stage. And everyone in the congregation was feeling just a little more determined to say yes to the Holy Spirit. Because while change is costly, the price of not changing is even higher. It is the difference between lying helplessly hogtied to our cherished sins and walking victoriously free from hindering habits.

Once again, holiness is all about choices. One choice after another. Saying yes to God and saying no to Satan.

It really is that simple — even when we're confronted by forms of bondage we've struggled with for years.

WHEN YOU'RE TEMPTED

One of my favorite verses is 1 Corinthians 10:13 — "No temptation has seized you except what is common to man. And God is faithful; he will not let you be tempted beyond what you can bear. But when you are tempted, he will also provide a way out so that you can stand up under it."

No matter what temptation I currently face, it isn't something new. For Satan isn't very inventive. He tends to use the same things over and over, generation after generation. Doubt, discouragement, pride, prejudice, frustration, fear, lust, hatred, envy — they've all been felt before, and they will be felt by those who follow us. But what we do with these temptations is crucial if we want to become more like Jesus.

My friend Cheryl has a wonderful testimony. It's not a poof-magic-wand conversion. She didn't meet Jesus on Tuesday and become different on Wednesday. Hers was a more gradual transformation. In fact, she'll admit she spent many Sunday mornings up in our balcony nursing a hangover. She wanted a different life, but she didn't know how to get one.

Still, God kept wooing Cheryl, and she kept responding as best she could. Even when Flesh Woman seemed to have the upper hand.

"I had a problem with alcohol, and I knew it," Cheryl says. "I kept begging God to take it away. But I worked in a restaurant that had a bar, and every Friday night I'd find myself having drinks with friends. Then I would beat myself up with guilt and despair" — which, of course, didn't help.

In the midst of the battle with her flesh, Cheryl memorized 1 Corinthians 10:13 and began asking God, "Show me the way of escape. You promise You will provide a way out, Lord. Help me see it."

One Friday as Cheryl was getting ready to go pick up her paycheck at the restaurant, her middle son, Matthew, asked to go along.

"He'd been asking for weeks," Cheryl said, "and I always put him off because I knew I'd probably end up drinking. But that night when he asked, I suddenly realized — here's my way out! It had been in front of me all along."

From then on, Matthew was Cheryl's

Often, in our pursuit of holiness, we experience moments so filled with power that we are enabled to do what we could not do before. We find ourselves in holy places where "heaven touches earth and we happen to be standing there," as my friend Michael Snider puts it. If you've ever experienced an extra ability to overcome sin or a sudden lack of desire for a once cherished indulgence — that was a space of grace. To maintain it:

- ***Don't ignore it.*** This space of grace is a gift from God. Give Him praise and thanks. Then walk carefully in His provision (Romans 1:21).
- ***Don't misinterpret it.*** We often attribute God's gift of freedom to will power we worked up on our own.

Friday-night buddy. And wouldn't you know it — the cycle of that particular sin in her life began to be broken. Cheryl couldn't sit around and drink with her little boy watching, and she certainly wasn't going to drive drunk with him in the car. With that pattern of sin no longer an option, the power of al-

Pride grows, and as a result, we are often one step away from a fall (Isaiah 2:11).

- **Don't abuse it**. When we misuse grace by willfully returning to our sin after being set free, we grieve the Spirit, and the grace to overcome is often removed (Hebrews 10:26–29).
- **Don't give up.** If you've abused God's mercy or have yet to find that gracious place, repent and keep seeking God. He *wants* to set you free (Joel 2:13)!

The God of peace will soon crush Satan under your feet. The grace of our Lord Jesus be with you.

ROMANS 16:20

cohol began to lose its grip on her.[4]

What "way out" is God providing for you in your current situation? Ask the Holy Spirit for eyes to see it. God is faithful to His Word — and He will help you find it. And when you do, don't wait to act. Take full advantage of the escape route the Lord has so graciously provided.

As you do, you may find freedom waiting for you in other areas of your life as well.

ONE LINK BREAKS ANOTHER

"Jesus breaks every fetter . . . and He sets me free!"[5]

I love that old song, for it really is what Christ came to do. To a world imprisoned by its own sin and lust-filled desires, Jesus comes with a key. He unlocks the door of our bondage and invites us to step out and be free.

But I'm learning to let God choose what fetters He wants to break. Because sometimes, I've learned, we wear ourselves out fighting the wrong battle.

I first learned this principle about eight years ago. I was struggling with my weight (lifelong story) and felt absolutely helpless. Nothing I tried worked, mainly because I didn't try anything for very long. I'd start, but I just couldn't maintain the discipline to keep going.

I reached the point where all I could do was pray like the blind man did in Mark 10:47: "Jesus, Son of David, have mercy on me!" Over and over in the midst of my despair, I echoed the words of the repentant tax collector, "God, have mercy on me, a sinner" (Luke 18:13).

Jesus heard my cry. And He brought deliverance — but not in the way I expected. For instead of helping me handle my weight issue, the Lord began to convict me of my choice of reading material.

You see, at the time I was basically addicted to Christian fiction.

Now, there is nothing wrong with a wholesome story. The problem lay in the fact I couldn't read just one novel at a time — much less a few pages before bed. No, I was a binge reader. Which meant one book right after another. Forget housework, forget cooking, and "Don't bother me! I'm reading."

Basically, fiction was the way I checked out of life. It was my drug of choice, my escape valve from stress or monotony. You see, my Flesh Woman just happened to have a literary bent.

But I didn't think of it that way, of course. I thought I just loved to read — and reading is good, right? So when God asked me to embark on a yearlong fiction fast, I nearly hyperventilated.

No historical novels? No Frank Peretti? No Francine Rivers? It seemed like an awful lot for God to ask. After all, I only read Christian authors. I could feel the rationalizations lining up in my heart, eager to present their case before God.

At the same time, I could feel grace being released in my heart. Grace to obey. Grace to let go.

It wasn't easy. There were plenty of moments when I found myself longing to settle down with a good story and leave the world behind. Plenty of times when I just had to set my jaw and stride past the fiction section of the Christian bookstore on my way to pick up something for the church.

Yet strangely, at the same time, it wasn't *that* hard. I found I could do it. I didn't have that old sense of failing almost before I began.

For what God had asked, God also enabled.

And the strangest thing happened on the way back from my fiction fast. Several strange things, in fact. For one, God began awakening in me a new hunger for His Word — and I actually had time to partake! But, stranger still, with the discipline of the fiction fast came discipline in other areas of my life. Particularly in my eating.

Because I had learned to say no to Flesh Woman in the area of mental escape, I was being empowered to say no to the other cravings of my lower nature. I actually started an exercise program and stuck to it. Within eight months, I had lost thirty-five pounds and dropped three sizes. I could tie my shoes! I could scratch my back!

When I obeyed God in the specific area He pointed out, it was as though a single link in the chain that bound me snapped. But soon other links lost their power as well, and I began walking in a freedom I'd never experienced before.

All because I let God choose the battle. I obeyed what He commanded rather than assuming I knew what He wanted.

The battle really is the Lord's (1 Samuel 17:47)! And sometimes what appears to be a sideline skirmish may be the struggle that wins the war.

Which is why I'm convinced that obedience really is the key to life-transforming discipline. It's not a matter of just toughing it out, but of following the Spirit's lead.

And refusing to give up — even when we fail.

Determining to — with God's help — try, try again.

THE YO-YO PRAYER

God healed Cheryl's addiction to alcohol, but for some reason her soul-tie to smoking refused to go. She had wept and confessed.

She'd tried chewing gum and wearing nicotine patches. But this stronghold had a strong hold on her life.

"I hated that I had to sneak out of church so I could get my smoke," Cheryl says. "But I'm so glad people loved me in spite of my addiction."

At some point each year, Cheryl would ask for prayer: "I really believe God wants me to stop smoking." And each year we would pray. There were periods of victory, but something would always happen. Some new stress, some new crisis would cause Cheryl to go back to the familiar comfort of her Misty menthols.

But a Christian friend told her, "Don't quit quitting." So Cheryl persevered.

Today she has been smoke-free for nearly two years.

"I don't know exactly what happened," Cheryl says. "But I didn't quit quitting, and somewhere God met me in the middle of all that and set me free."

Cheryl's story reminds me of a transformation tool God has taught me over the years. I call it the "Yo-Yo Prayer." And, unlike yo-yo dieting, this method actually works!

Perhaps like Cheryl, like me, you've tried for years to give a certain issue over to God. A habit, an attitude, an addiction. Or an area of fear and doubt God has brought to your attention and asked you to surrender to Him.

"I'll be different, Lord," you promised. And for a while you were.

But just when you thought you'd finally gained victory over that issue, there it was again. The habit or situation you once laid down was somehow picked up again and you wonder if you were ever truly free. Which is exactly what Satan wants you to think.

"You're such a hypocrite," he hisses in your heart. "See? I told you nothing would ever change. You're playing games with God and fooling yourself. You'll never be free."

But the real lies, of course, are Satan's — and you must take them to Jesus immediately. For if you listen to such blasphemy, you will forever remain encumbered by the old "yoke of bondage" (Galatians 5:1, NKJV).

You *really* did give it to God. And He *really* is changing you. It's just that your Flesh Woman saw a chance to reclaim that territory, and she pounced on the opportunity.

So there it is. All that ugliness. All that pain. Once again in your hands. So what do you do with it?

Well, you can stick it in your pocket and pull it out once in a while to play with.

You can put it on a shelf and try to muster

up the discipline never to touch it again.

Or you can give it back to God — immediately!

I've found that the quicker I return what I've somehow stolen back from God's hands, the quicker I have peace in my heart. But in order to give it back, I have to ignore the lies of the enemy and keep agreeing with God.

"All right, Lord. I don't know how I ended up with this, but here it is. It has no place in my life. So I'm giving it back to You — now!"

As I've faithfully and diligently repented and turned issues over to God — no matter how many times I have had to repeat the "Yo-Yo Prayer" — I've found that the power these issues once held over me is diminished each time I give them away.

For when I give my problem issue to God rather than obsessing about the fact that I somehow reclaimed it, the chain around my heart is loosened.

Finally one day, when I give it to Him yet again, it doesn't return. And I realize it is truly gone. Forever over and done with.

No more yo-yo.

And no more bondage.

BROKEN CHAINS AND PERPETUAL FASTS

Once the power of a stronghold has been broken in my life, I've sometimes been able to resume the activities God asked me to previously forgo.

My fiction fast, for example, is now over, though it lasted a full four years. Not so much because God demanded it, but because I simply didn't desire it. The hunger had been filled by running to His Word rather than running away in my mind.

When I finally felt free to resume my recreational reading, it was because I felt exactly that — free! Fiction had lost its addictive power over me. I'm now able to enjoy a novel without devouring it to the exclusion of everything else. And rather than gobbling down title after title like potato chips, I can go a month or two without reading any fiction at all.

Because now novels are simply books to me. Not chains. That particular battle has been fought, won, and left behind — at least for the time being.

But that's certainly not true of all the weak areas and bad habits of my life. Some activities, I've come to realize, will always be off-limits for me. Self-pity, for instance, as well as careless eating.

But whether I'm set free from their power or have to exercise conscious restraint for the rest of my life, I've found that the Yo-Yo Prayer is an important ingredient in my per-

Though you won't find it on the magazine stand, the most effective Flesh-Woman diet I've ever tried is the regimen outlined in Isaiah 30:20. Though it limits your intake to only two kinds of food — bread and water — it is amazingly efficient in trimming lower-nature fat and building spiritual muscle. Don't worry about shopping for the ingredients. Life — and even God Himself! — tends to drop them at your door.

FIRST ON THE MENU: THE BREAD OF ADVERSITY

Adversity means "misfortune; calamity; an adverse event or circumstance." (The Hebrew word in the Old Testament for adversity denotes anything from a tight place to a pebble in the shoe.) While adversity is not a widely requested dish, God seems to use it often in the lives of His choicest people. Adversity not only reveals what we are made of but makes us more than we were. "Because," as James 1:3–4 says, "you know that the testing of your faith develops perseverance. . . . so that you may be mature and complete."

Second Menu Item:
The Water of Affliction

Affliction refers to "a distressed or painful state; misery." Hard to swallow, this is not our beverage of choice. From the Hebrew word meaning "to force or hold fast," *affliction* refers to those times when life squeezes us uncomfortably, even painfully. But when we embrace affliction as an opportunity to share in the sufferings of Christ, we will also "share in His glory" Romans 8:17 tells us. The sweetness of Christ will come out of our lives instead of bitterness. And God will be glorified.

"Although the Lord gives you the bread of adversity and the water of affliction," Isaiah 30:20 tells us, "your teachers will be hidden no more; with your own eyes you will see them." Far from punishment, adversity and affliction are designed to bring wisdom — because this food once intended for prisoners (1 Kings 22:27) can help set you free from Flesh Woman's rule.

But how you receive these two gifts makes all the difference! Adversity and affliction can either make you bitter, or they can make you better.

It's up to you.

Before I was afflicted I went astray, but now I obey your word. You are good, and what you do is good; teach me your decrees.

PSALM 119:67–68

sonal version of the Flesh-Woman Diet — because it's really an exercise in saying a repeated and persistent yes to God and no, no, no to my flesh. I've also learned that when I say yes to God in both the big and the little things of life, God says yes to me. Enabling and strengthening me, setting me free to do things I could never do on my own.

For "God is within her," the psalmist says. "She will not fall" (Psalm 46:5).

Because I'm His

When baby Joshua joined our family nearly four years ago, he brought more joy than I ever thought possible. Which is saying a lot. At forty years of age and with two nearly grown teenagers, I never expected to be shopping for cribs and colleges at the same time. (Although a friend did point out it could be worse — I could have been shopping for diapers and Depends.)

But more than joy, Joshua brought me a new understanding of God's love that I'd never considered before.

After Josh was born a month early, the doctors immediately knew something wasn't quite right. Eliminating more serious conditions, they diagnosed him with hypotonia. Low muscle tone. Rather than the tight little bundle of baby I was used to holding, Joshua felt more like a rag doll, loose and limp in my arms. He was slow to nurse, slow to roll over, slow to sit up, slow to do many things. Rather than doing movements natural for most babies, Josh's muscles had to be taught, even awakened, through physical therapy. At three-and-a-half years of age, he still has delays in motor skills as well as speech development.

But do you know what? It doesn't matter. I don't bother comparing Josh to other kids because Josh isn't like other kids. Josh is Josh. I don't keep a list of things babies should do at one or two or three years of age. It's all immaterial. Josh will do it when Josh can. And we'll do — and are doing — everything possible to help him. After being an uptight mom the first time around, constantly comparing to see how my kids measured up to others their age, I can't tell you how freeing this has been.

In some ways, these four years with Josh have been the most enjoyable years of my life. Why? Because we celebrate everything! Every little advance is met with great joy and applause. And I've recently realized that loving Josh has taught me a wonderful lesson about how God loves me.

That realization came three years ago in Gold Beach, Oregon. My sister, Linda, had come along to watch Josh while I spoke at a women's retreat. When I went back to the hotel room after the first evening session, Linda was so excited.

"You won't believe what Joshua did!" she said dragging me to where he sat playing with some toys. That in itself was a miracle, for Josh had only recently mastered the art of sitting up. But my sister had something new to show me. "Watch this!" Linda cleared the space around him, then took his favorite toy and placed it in front of him, just out of reach. Josh looked at her, then at me. Then with a little smile, he bent forward and stretched out nearly flat to grab the toy that rested beyond his toes. I was amazed. He'd never done that before. But that was only the beginning. There was more to come.

Little by little, grunting and groaning, my sweet boy slowly worked his hands back toward his body. Beads of perspiration broke out on his forehead as he, still grasping the toy, worked himself back into a sitting position. The whole process took at least thirty seconds, ten times the amount of time another child would have required. But rather than being disappointed, Linda and I whooped and hollered and cried our eyes out.

"Woohoo! That's my boy!" I said, hugging Josh. It was amazing. It was wonderful. It was a milestone, a moment of pure joy I'll never forget. And with it came a revelation from the Lord that has changed my life. As I lay in bed that night still rejoicing over Joshua's accomplishment, I felt God whisper to my spirit, *That's how I feel, you know.*

What do You mean, Lord? I asked.

The joy you feel watching Joshua do something you know is difficult — that's how I feel when I see you stretch beyond what you've tried before. When you believe Me for something that seems impossible . . . trust Me in the midst of difficulties . . . do what I ask even though you don't feel able . . . that's how I feel.

My heart swelled with the thought and

caught in my throat. That I could bring that much joy to the Lord had never occurred to me.

With the sounds of waves outside echoing the waves of gratitude in my heart, I wept quietly, mouthing words of praise to the One who knew me so intimately and yet loved me so completely.

It wasn't until I shared the thought with the women the next morning that a fuller revelation of the truth finally hit me. The women nodded and smiled through the story, and many even wept. But I suddenly realized that they could never understand the immensity of it all. Neither could Linda. Not really. No one could.

Why? Because Joshua belongs to me. He *belongs* to me.

That's why God rejoices over our every little step. That's why He tirelessly spends time exercising our faith and stretching us in order to expand our limits. That's why, when we fall, He helps us, picks us up, and encourages us to try again.

He doesn't compare us to anyone else. He doesn't have a list of what Christians should be and do at certain phases of their Christian walk. He accepts us individually and works with us where we are. Yet He constantly challenges us to go beyond what we are. And He throws a great big party whenever we reach a milestone or make a yo-yo spiritual break-through.

Why? Because we belong to Him. We *belong* to Him.

"Woohoo! That's My girl!" He says.

"Did you see that?" He asks, turning to the angels and pointing to earth. Pointing to you and to me.

"That's My girl."

14
SPEAKING LOVE

May the words of my mouth and the meditation of my heart be pleasing in your sight, O LORD, my Rock and my Redeemer.
PSALM 19:14

It had been a difficult day. Overwhelmed by responsibilities and tired from the busyness of life, I was tempted to give up. No matter how much I did, it wasn't enough. Nobody appreciated it anyway. *Maybe I'll go on strike like that mom in Minnesota,* I grumbled to myself. *Then they'll realize how much I do around here.*

As I continued my full-blown pity party, the feelings not only escalated; they multiplied. Like mice at the pet store — one moment you have two, the next, twenty-four. Home wasn't the only place I was feeling overworked and underappreciated. A church event I was in charge of was proving difficult as well. *Let's see how they do when I decide*

I'm too busy to help, I fumed. Then there were my friendships. *Why do I always have to be the one who calls?*

The day was going downhill fast. But then I checked the mail, and there it was — my message from heaven. A little note of encouragement written by a friend. Twelve lines — no more. But in those dozen lines came hope. As I read it and then reread the note, each love-laced word seemed to come from God's heart to mine.

See, Joanna? I haven't forgotten. You matter to me.

I still have that little card with the bouquet of flowers on the front. It still refreshes my heart. And it also reminds me how much power resides in a few well-chosen words.

THE MINISTRY OF ENCOURAGEMENT

"A word aptly spoken is like apples of gold in settings of silver," Proverbs 25:11 tells us. As a writer, I love that proverb because it emphasizes how giving just the right word at just the right time is not only an art — it is a ministry.

I don't know if my friend Cindy realized how deeply her note would affect me. After all, she'd written it several days before, and I wasn't going through a low time then. But God knew what I would need and when I would need it, and so, with a gentle nudge of His Spirit, He brought me to Cindy's mind. And Cindy, in response, took action — not only by praying for me, but by taking the time to write a note that spoke to the very heart of my need.

How wonderful it is to be part of the body of Christ! To know I'm not alone, that I have sisters and brothers in the Lord who want the best for me, is one of the sweetest gifts of being a Christian — as well as one of the most important responsibilities. For to give courage — to, literally, "in"-courage others through our words, our prayers, and our support — is an integral part of our calling as Christians.

Encouragement, or exhortation, is listed as one of the motivational gifts in Romans 12:6–8 — right along with prophesying, serving, leading, giving, teaching, and showing mercy. And while some people are specifically Spirit-gifted in this area, we are all called to the ministry of encouragement — to, as Hebrews 10:24 puts it, "consider how we may spur one another on toward love and good deeds."

The Greek word for encourage is *parakaleo,* which means "to call near, invite." Not coincidentally, the word is very close to the Greek name for the Holy Spirit: *paraklete,* "the one who comes alongside." When we exhort one another, when we encourage and cheer one another on, we are doing the work of the Holy Spirit. And important work it is.

For we all need someone who believes we are more than we appear to be.

A REBORN ENCOURAGER

His real name is nearly forgotten. But the legacy of Joseph, a Levite from Cyprus, lives on. We know him by a nickname — a nickname that so described who this man was that it replaced the name he was given at birth.

We call him Barnabas, which means "Son of Encouragement."

And encourage was exactly what he did. He specialized in seeing the potential in people and then doing what he could to make that potential a reality.

So, when the disciples were afraid to meet with Saul, the famous persecutor of the church, it was Barnabas who brought them all together in Acts 9:26–28. He confirmed the remarkable testimony of the man who had been Christianity's deadliest foe. And Saul (later renamed Paul), who would author much of the New Testament, was welcomed into the family of God.

When Gentiles began coming to Christ in Antioch, it was Barnabas whom the apostles in Jerusalem sent to encourage the baby church there. And "a great number of people were brought to the Lord" (Acts 11:24) — mostly because of Barnabas. Seeing the growth of the church, Barnabas tracked Paul down in Tarsus and took him to Antioch, where together they discipled and taught the people who would first wear the name "Christian."

It was this remarkable ability to recognize potential in people and encourage them to grow that caused Barnabas to part ways with Paul in Acts 15:36–39 and partner with his disgraced cousin John Mark. Paul didn't want to take a chance on the young man who had "deserted them in Pamphylia." But where Paul saw disqualification, Barnabas once again saw possibility. As a result, two missionary journeys were launched instead of one, and the work of Christ was furthered.

Barnabas's faith must have been well-placed, for even Paul changed his mind about John Mark. Near the end of his life, it was this young man whom Paul asked for, calling him "a fellow worker" and "a comfort" (Colossians 4:10–11). And later, possibly in cooperation with Peter, Mark authored the gospel that bears his name.

Because of one man's gift of encouragement, two men who might have been left behind, Paul and John Mark, were given the gift of a second chance. We are called to do the same. To believe the best about people rather than the worst. Despite their reputations, despite their questionable past performances. To look at people through the eyes of God and see what He sees.

Assets, not liabilities.

Beloved children in need of grace and mercy . . . and a big dose of truth-filled love.

Speaking the Truth in Love

Encouragement, you see, is more than cheerleading. It is more than telling people what they want to hear. It often involves what the Bible calls "speaking the truth in love" (Ephesians 4:15).

Author and speaker Jill Briscoe tells an interesting story about a friend who did just that for her. A student at Homerton College in Cambridge, England, Jill had just become a Christian and had thrown herself passionately into soul winning. After her first "grand success" in sharing the gospel, Jill rushed to tell the person who had led her to Christ. But instead of patting her on the back, her friend rebuked her. "Stop bragging about it. If God has used you, then be grateful, but remember He only uses the stupid so people will know it was His power that did it all."

When I read Jill's story, I must admit I was taken aback by her friend's response. Jill's enthusiasm seemed so natural, so commendable. But, as Jill admitted, her friend's diagnosis was right on the mark: "I had too soon ceased to be thrilled about Wendy coming to the Lord and started being proud of myself for leading her there." Pride is a rotten thing, her friend was trying to remind her. And God hates it.[1]

I don't know many people who would speak as honestly as Jill Briscoe's friend did — and I fear we are the poorer for it. While perhaps she could have worded her rebuke more gently, that woman's truthfulness still seems healthier than the "tolerance" I often see (or show!), which is often just a fear of rejection or reluctance to get involved. We don't confront because we don't want to lose relationship. Bottom line: we love ourselves more than we love others.

So I'm impressed by Jill's friend's willingness to speak an uncomfortable truth, but I'm even more impressed by Jill's willingness to hear it. She embraced her friend's rebuke and repented of her pride. Her heart was made right with God. And, more important, she didn't hold a grudge against her friend or come back with accusations of her own.

I have to ask myself — am I as willing to

accept correction as Jill Briscoe was? I want to be. I need to be. So I've been asking God to send me friends who don't always tell me what I want to hear. Who are willing to tell me the truth about myself even when the truth hurts.

There is something so important and healthy about giving other Christians whom we respect the permission to bring correction into our lives. For we all have blind spots when it comes to our true spiritual condition. We all need perspective. That's what Jill's friend gave her. That's what each of us needs — and what each of us needs to give.

EMBARRASSED TO LIFE

What would happen if we Christians loved one another enough to get involved in each others' lives? I don't mean that spiritualized voyeurism so many people call "concern" — the unhealthy desire to be in the know about other people's problems. And I don't mean the overly confident part of our woman's intuition that compels us to give everyone advice — whether or not people want it. Nor do I mean the unholy inclination to control and dominate, nitpick and demean. Instead, I'm speaking of the mature love of a godly friend who humbly asks, "Have you considered this? Have you looked at that?"

I love it when people encourage me. Even a few words can help me out of a blue mood or calm my frustrations. And I've found that speaking words of encouragement to someone else can be a surefire spirit lifter.

When people share their hopes and dreams with you, be the one to point out the wonderful possibilities. Plenty of others will point out the problems.

As busy women, we are sometimes reluctant to give encouragement because then we feel obligated to get involved and take on the other person's challenges. But encouragement doesn't mean doing other people's work or making their dreams come true. It doesn't mean becoming one person's full-time cheerleader. There are

I'm so thankful that someone took time to correct me when I was a young pastor's wife. Though this incident is embarrassing to share, I believe her loving confrontation may have saved me in more ways than one. My core need for approval was leading me down some dangerous paths, and she cared enough to take me by the shoulders and

simple ways to encourage that take very little time — pointing out a child's talent or capability, reminding a discouraged friend of the successes she has already achieved, or helping a teen articulate the next few steps needed to reach her goals. Just listening intently with words like "tell me more" can be an encouragement. So can a gentle nudge to urge someone to do what she needs to do.[2]

— Alice Gray, from *The Worn Out Woman*

Therefore encourage one another and build each other up, just as in fact you are doing.

1 THESSALONIANS 5:11

speak some sense into me.

"Joanna, I know you don't mean to," my friend said as we sat on the riverbank during a long-ago youth camp, "but you're a flirt. You like to laugh and tease with the guys. And while it may mean nothing to you, it's wrong, and you need to stop."

I was mortified. I didn't know what to say.

Though I wanted to defend myself, to plead my innocence, her words had shone a light on a giant blind spot in my heart — a great gaping hole in my soul I had truly been unaware of until that moment. Despite being married and very much loved, the awkward teenager inside of me still craved attention and admiration from the opposite sex.

I cried, and we prayed. God heard, and He forgave. I walked away from that encounter a different woman — Praise the Lord!

Oh, there are times when Flesh Woman still tries to exert her need to sparkle and shine, but there is a deep abhorrence and holy fear in my heart that I would ever again betray my husband — and my Lord! — by looking to other men for attention and approval rather than to the lovers of my soul.

Had someone not cared enough to speak the truth, though she knew it would hurt, I shudder to think what could have happened because of that vulnerable, weak place in me.

"Faithful are the wounds of a friend," says Proverbs 27:6 (NKJV). "Friendly" wounds that heal rather than scar — life-giving words that speak the truth in love.

QUALIFIED TO CONFRONT?

If we want to be the people God designed us to be, we must be willing to engage in godly confrontation — or, as my father puts it, "care-frontation." But to do that, we may need to check our attitudes at the door, admit our biases, drop our agendas, and do some serious praying.

"Brothers, if someone is caught in a sin," Galatians 6:1–2 says, "you who are spiritual should restore him gently. But watch yourself, or you also may be tempted. Carry each other's burdens, and in this way you will fulfill the law of Christ."

Note the warning in this verse. Paul states two important qualifications for truth telling. First, it must be done gently and with the right motives — to restore the other person to where she should be. The New Living Translation says that we are to "gently and humbly help that person back onto the right path" (Galatians 6:1).

The second qualification is even more important: we must be "spiritual" — or, as the New Living Translation puts it, "godly." If we confront or correct someone in the wrong spirit — out of our own envy and pride, for instance — we are likely to fall into the same snare we're trying to rescue our friend from. If we ourselves aren't in right relationship with the Lord, our best efforts will be nothing more than the blind leading the blind.

How do we know that our hearts are right enough to try to "right" someone else? I think the key is found in the last verse of the previous chapter, Galatians 5:26. It comes immediately after Paul's description of the fruit of the Spirit (also needed to make our hearts right). This verse provides a simple checklist for examining our attitude toward a person needing correction: "Let us not become conceited, provoking and envying each other."

Clearly, before we open our mouths to say something to an erring brother or sister, we'd do well to examine *why* we feel compelled to speak:

- *"Let us not become conceited . . ."* Do I feel I am better than this person and incapable of this sin?
- *"provoking . . . each other."* Is my main motivation for confrontation to prove the other person is wrong and I am right? Do I hope the person will argue so I can convince him or her of the sin?
- *"envying . . . each other."* Do I secretly want to see the other person humiliated? Is my truth telling motivated in any way by jealousy, a desire to get even, or a need to see the other person exposed?

It's the motivation, you see, that makes all the difference. Calvin Miller explains it like this: "Malicious truth gloats like a conqueror. Loving truth mourns that it must confront and show a brother his error. Malicious truth struts at its power. Loving truth weeps to find that the correction it inspires may for a while cause great pain. Malicious truth cries, 'Checkmate, you are beaten!' Loving truth whispers, 'I correct you with the same pain you feel. But when the pain is over, we shall rejoice that honesty and love have been served.' "[3]

In order to ensure that we only confront in the right kind of spirit, someone suggested that we don't do it at all unless we have spent time fasting and praying about the matter first. That's wise advice, because the disciplines of prayer and fasting help us identify our true motivation. If we're willing to give up a meal, that means we're willing to get serious with God about another person's soul rather than acting on a fleshly desire to eat someone for lunch.

It may well be, in fact, that we are being called to pray *instead* of confront. Oswald Chambers says discernment — that is, insight into a situation and wisdom to see right from wrong — is God's call to intercession, never to fault-finding.[4] Knowing something doesn't necessarily mean we are called to intervene in a situation. We may only be asked to pray — for prayer is the most powerful type of intervention in the world. It's yet another way our words can speak love and encouragement to another.

SOUND CHECK

Our words carry so much power. Power to heal. Power to destroy. And while encouragement and honest communication are vital, we need more than that. We need a pure spirit behind all our conversations. For unless the Spirit of God rules our tongues, we will almost certainly end up speaking words that bring death rather than life (Proverbs 18:21).

In my experience, nothing is a more accurate indicator of my spiritual condition than the words I speak. When I'm tired and frustrated, the fatigue and exasperation show in my speech. When I'm busy or pressed for time, my language becomes clipped or dismissive. I've found that my lack of time alone with the Lord will make itself known in my words as well. I'm less gracious. I find fault more. There is an edge to my voice rather than the softness that comes from being rightly related to God.

Evelyn Christenson noticed this too, in a

slightly different context. She writes, "My spiritual barometer for years has been 1 John 1:4: 'These things [are written] that your joy may be full' (KJV). I can always measure the amount of time I'm spending in the Scriptures by how much joy (not superficial happiness, but deep down abiding joy) I have. When I find a lack of joy in my life, the first thing I check is how much time I'm spending in God's Word!"[5]

The point is, whatever I've stored up — wherever I've set my mind and whatever I've focused my heart on — is what will come out of my life. That is what will be revealed either in the words I say or in how I say them.

How does your life sound? What if a hidden microphone were recording every exchange in your house? at your job? in your marriage? What if someone threatened to play those recordings back on the local nightly news? How much would you pay to have the tapes destroyed?

The thought of having to give account for our words is enough to make most women break out in a cold sweat! Yet that is exactly what the Bible says we will have to do one day: "But I tell you that men will have to give account on the day of judgment for every careless word they have spoken," Matthew 12:36–37 tells us. "For by your words you

Keep still! When trouble is brewing, keep still! When slander is getting on its legs, keep still! When your feelings are hurt, keep still till you recover from your excitement at any rate! Things look different through an unagitated eye.

In a commotion once I wrote a letter and sent it, and wished I had not. In my later years I had another commotion and wrote another long letter; my life had rubbed a little sense into me, and I kept that letter in my pocket until I could look it over without agitation, and without tears, and I was glad I did — less and less it seemed necessary to send it. I was not sure it would do any harm, but in my doubtfulness I learned reticence, and

will be acquitted, and by your words you will be condemned."

Wow. Does that hit you like it hits me? Although I am saved by grace and I am bound for heaven, the Bible says I will nevertheless be held accountable for the way I speak and the things I say. Not only for those words meant to hurt and cut, but also for those careless, off-the-cuff comments I blurt out

eventually it was destroyed.

Time works wonders! Wait till you can speak calmly and then perhaps you will not need to speak. Silence is the most powerful thing conceivable, sometimes. It is strength in its grandeur; it is like a regiment ordered to stand still in the mad fury of battle. To plunge in were twice as easy. *Nothing is lost by learning to keep still.* [6]

— From *Streams in the Desert* and *Springs in the Valley*

Set a watch, O LORD, before my mouth; keep the door of my lips.

PSALM 141:3 (KJV)

without thinking. My thoughtless sarcasm. Pointless babbling. Those little zingers at other people's expense. The white lies and embroidered truths. They're all on the record.

Our words are that important. They aren't just bits of fluff and stuff floating around, harmless flotsam resulting from frustration or the careless flapping of the jaw. They count. And we must take responsibility for our words if we ever hope to be changed for the better.

RESPONSIBLE TONGUE MANAGEMENT

It is amazing that something so small can be so important.

Though the tongue weighs in at just under two ounces, this little muscle holds enormous potential not only for good, but also for destruction.

No wonder the Bible refers to it so often. Over 1,000 times in Scripture, we see the influence of this verbal instrument. Both the tongue and the lips are mentioned around 100 times each in the King James version of the Bible, the mouth and lips more than 400 times, and our words more than 500. In the book of Proverbs alone, there are about 119 references to the tongue and its use.

James, the brother of Jesus, didn't mince words when he addressed the need for discipline of the mouth. "If anyone considers himself religious and yet does not keep a tight rein on his tongue," James 1:26 says, "he deceives himself and his religion is worthless."

A strong statement, perhaps — but necessary. For the devastation caused by loose-lipped Christians is incalculable. Reputations have been destroyed. Churches split. Homes broken, marriages toppled, friendships ruined — all because we've bought into the lie that if we think it, we should say it. That everyone has a right to hear our opinions. That freedom of speech means the freedom to say whatever to whomever whenever we want.

I don't suppose there is any one of us who wouldn't benefit from following James's advice on reining in our tongues, muzzling our mouths, and watching our words.

"We all stumble in many ways," James 3:2 acknowledges. "If anyone is never at fault in what he says, he is a perfect man, able to keep his whole body in check."

Purify the tongue and you purify the person, James advises. So how do we do that?

It may be as simple as keeping our mouths shut.

Note that I said simple. Not easy.

Controlling my tongue, in fact, has been one of the hardest exercises of my spiritual life. I'm rarely at a loss for words. My husband says I must be a descendant of Babylon — because I just babble on and on. A dangerous tendency, for as Proverbs 10:19 says: "When words are many, sin is not absent, but he who holds his tongue is wise."

Fortunately, the Word of God is filled with

instructions on how to manage this "restless evil, full of deadly poison" (James 3:8). Here are just a few that have helped me in my daily quest to tame my tongue:

1. *Take responsibility for your words and begin to exercise restraint* (Psalm 39:1). After a lifetime of having to eat my words, I'm slowly learning that less can be more. Silence really can be golden, and the simple fact that I have an opinion doesn't mean I have to share it. (Now that's a novel idea for the quiet-impaired.) When I let my mouth run unrestrained, I usually end up in trouble. I walk away feeling a bit empty, even embarrassed. For though I may not be aware of the specific details of the offense, I know that somewhere, somehow, I have hurt the Lord.

2. *Listen more and speak less* (James 1:19). When we focus on listening to people rather than on coming up with an appropriate response, we show that we value them and lessen the likelihood that we will misspeak. So many misunderstandings — as well as anger and broken relationships — grow out of the fact we don't really hear what the other person is saying.

3. *Get rid of iffy language and inappropriate humor* (Ephesians 5:3–4). Cursing and taking the Lord's name in vain — we know displeases God. But so does any off-color re-

mark, sexual innuendo, or dirty joke. Trying to be funny can be dangerous. Too often we resort to worldly humor, or we make other people take the brunt of our "fun." Neither glorifies the Lord. In fact, each grieves the Holy Spirit. So although laughter is a true gift from God — especially the ability to laugh at ourselves — we need to be sure our humor is clean and not demeaning.

4. *Refuse to gossip* (Leviticus 19:16, NLT). Gossip can be addictive. Knowing things that no one else knows gives us a feeling of power and leverage. How do we stop it? As someone once said, "If you don't want garbage in your garbage can, put a lid on it." In other words, don't entertain the conversation. Stop it before it begins. If we would challenge one another in this area, the destructive grapevine that too often spreads trouble in the church would be cut off at the roots.

5. *Avoid arguments* (2 Timothy 2:23). Some of us love nothing more than a good difference of opinion. Whether we're arguing about politics or theological differences, the more heated the debate, the better we like it. Unfortunately, God isn't fond of arguing, for controversy rarely benefits relationships. Instead, it polarizes our differences and causes disunity. It makes us love our opinions more

than we love one another. And that is not only dangerous to our souls; it damages the body of Christ.

BUILD UP — DON'T TEAR DOWN

Of all the many passages in the Bible concerning the tongue, perhaps Ephesians 4:29 best sums up what a Christian should sound like: "Do not let any unwholesome talk come out of your mouths, but only what is helpful for building others up according to their needs, that it may benefit those who listen."

I find this advice very helpful. For it stresses that unwholesome talk is determined not only by its content; it is also measured by its effect. Does my conversation benefit the people who listen to me or does it cause harm? Do people walk away from me feeling affirmed and built up or feeling uneasy and somehow undone?

I want my speech to edify people, especially those in my home. For that is where I most often fail to discipline my tongue. I tend to dump my frustration on the people I love best. And while I may feel better after getting everything off my chest, the person who has to dig out from under my dumping session certainly isn't relieved.

Because women tend to be more verbal

than men, I've often wondered whether Proverbs 14:1 — "The wise woman builds her house, but with her own hands the foolish one tears hers down" — was really talking about words. Because word by word, you and I either build up our families or tear them apart.

I cringe to think of some of the ways I have hurt my family by failing to discipline my tongue. Too often my words take the form of

- irritable outbursts ("Get in here right this minute!")
- subtle (or not-so-subtle) criticism ("Are you really going to wear that?")
- argument ("But you said you'd take care of the situation!")
- blame ("If you would listen, I wouldn't have to scream!")
- whining and complaining ("Nobody helps me around here! Can't you see I'm trying to write this book about having a Mary spirit?")

Until I take responsibility for this negative talk, I'll never change. My home and my whole life will continue to suffer from the destructive influence of my tongue.

So what's the best way to take responsibility for our words? The same way I take responsibility for any of my sins: through repentance.

"God is faithful to reveal junk that has come out of my mouth that I forgot about," Chip Ingram writes in *Holy Transformation*. "It's like playing a little videotape. And I deal with them and I tell Him I'm sorry. When appropriate, I go back to people whom I have offended to apologize. If I keep account of my words and take care of them, I know I won't have to give an account to my heavenly Father for an out-of-control mouth."[7]

A SPIRIT THAT REFRESHES

"Let your conversation be always full of grace," Paul writes in Colossians 4:6. In the end, that's what I want for all the words that come out of my mouth. I want my speech to be full of love even when I'm offering correction. Full of mercy and forgiveness, for God has had mercy upon me. Words fewer in number, but richer in truth and love.

That's why my daily prayer since I was a teenager has been David's prayer in Psalm 19:14 — "May the words of my mouth and the meditation of my heart be pleasing in your sight, O LORD, my Rock and my Redeemer."

I want my words to count for the Lord's purposes, not undermine them.

I want to be a Barnabas — an encourager, the kind of person who reaches out to others, who leaves people feeling refreshed and revived.

I want to be a Cindy — sensitive to the leading of the Holy Spirit. Taking time to write a note or make a phone call. Giving a word in season. Sending a golden apple to a hungry heart.

And I want to be like the friend who confronted my flirting — willing to speak truth gently, humbly, and, above all lovingly.

For I'm convinced my words make a difference. Not only to people, but also to God.

"Like the coolness of snow at harvest time is a trustworthy messenger to those who send him," says Proverbs 25:13. "He refreshes the spirit of his masters."

Do you realize that when we bless one another, we bless the Lord? Whenever we obey the Spirit's leading and speak truth and encouragement into one another's lives — or close our mouths and avoid speaking harmfully — we fulfill the law of Christ. For nothing brings the Father more joy than seeing His kids get along.

When we love one another in word and in deed, we refresh the Lord.

And "he who refreshes others will himself
be refreshed" (Proverbs 11:25).

15
WEARING JESUS

*Clothe yourselves with the Lord Jesus Christ,
and do not think about how to gratify the
desires of the sinful nature.*
ROMANS 13:14

The beggar could hardly believe his luck!

Just that morning he'd been prowling the streets looking for food, scrounging in Dumpsters, and begging at back doors of restaurants. But tonight he would be dining with a king.

"Your presence has been requested" was the only explanation the driver of the long, black limo gave when he opened the sleek door and helped him in.

When they arrived at the palace, a butler showed him to his room and brought in a set of new clothes for the man to wear. The beggar accepted the garments but carefully rolled up the rags he'd been wearing and tucked them under his arm. After all, he never knew when he might need them.

That night, clothed in a fine tuxedo, the beggar sat by the king himself. Rich paintings and expensive chandeliers hung all around him. Bowls and platters of the finest food lined the expansive table. But most beautiful of all was the kind attention the king gave the nervous man — asking him questions, drawing out details about the beggar's life he had never shared with anyone.

"I hope you will stay," the king said as the meal was about to end. "I would like you to consider this your home."

So the beggar remained. He lived for years in the king's palace and dressed in the king's finery. Every night he dined at the king's table — not as a guest, but as a friend. Yet he insisted on carrying his bundle of rags everywhere he went. For he never knew when he might need them.

Many years later, when the man died, they buried him with his bundle of rags. For the torn, tattered, rolled-up clothes had become his identity. "The ragman," they called him. And everyone mourned, including the king.

For his friend, the beggar, could have been so much more if he'd only been able to let go of what he once was.[1]

It's hard to let go of the familiar, the comfortable, and the tried. We'd rather stay the way we are than pay the price to change. Yet if we are ever to be all God intends us to be, we are going to have to let go of the old to make room for the new.

My little Joshua is having trouble with the concept, especially when it comes to his Superman pajamas. He loves those jammies so much that he wants to wear them night and day. The only problem is — it's a problem!

Even if I wanted Joshua to wear his pajamas to preschool, it wouldn't work. For he's outgrown the blue-with-red-trim shirt and pants. A large expanse of his cute little belly is exposed at all times, and the pant legs are nearly up to his knees. Not appropriate for school or for Montana's wintry weather.

But even if the pajamas fit, I wouldn't want Joshua to wear them all the time. Because nightclothes are for night, and day clothes are for day, and he needs to learn the difference.

The same is true of us as Christians. As we grow in the Lord, certain attitudes and behaviors no longer fit us as children of the King. And our dark, silly clothing of the night is no longer appropriate for children of the day. "For you were once darkness, but now you are light in the Lord," Ephesians 5:8 says. "Live as children of light."

That's why the Bible tells us over and over that it's time to change our wardrobe. It's time to put off the old and put on the new, as Paul puts it in Ephesians 4:22, 24:

> You were taught, with regard to your former way of life, to put off your old self, which is being corrupted by its deceitful desires . . . and to put on the new self, created to be like God in true righteousness and holiness.

Unfortunately, too often we try to put the new on *over* the old. Unwilling to let go of the tried and the familiar, we try to camouflage our old selves under spiffy new togs. But it just doesn't work. We end up looking rumpled and uncomfortable, struggling to move rather than able to run free.

The only way to experience the new life God offers is to discard our rags — our superhero pajamas — so we can be clothed with Christ alone.

CLEANING OUR CLOSETS

Every year or five, I get the urge to spring clean. The clutter finally overwhelms me, and I know it's time to act. And so, armed with a trash bag, I go through the house doing what FlyLady calls the "27 Fling Boogie."

Now, you might be wondering, who is she and what in the world is that?

Well, first of all, I must confess: I am a recovering slob. Though I've always dreamed of a neat and orderly home, one where you can find a Tylenol when you need one, that particular accomplishment has always remained just out of my reach. But I've made it a life goal and a daily prayer. For I've found that chaos in the home often leads to chaos in my heart. And while external clutter paralyzes me, order sets me free.

Organization still doesn't come naturally to me, but I'm getting better at it. I'm not nearly as scattered and messy as I used to be. I was very excited a few years ago when I discovered Marla Cilley's book *Sink Reflections* and her FlyLady Web site.

Home-organizational-expert Marla, a.k.a. FlyLady, actually recommends strategies the Lord had been teaching me. (That makes me an expert too, right?) I loved the practicality and humor of her approach to housekeeping, and checking in with her Web site from time to time has helped me stay motivated to keep my life in order.[2]

The 27 Fling Boogie is one of the tactics

FlyLady suggests for cleaning out the clutter that dominates so much of our lives. It's really simple: "Grab a garbage bag and boogie!"[3] The idea is to set a timer for fifteen minutes, run through your house, and pick out twenty-seven items to throw away. After you throw that bag in the trash, you get another bag, set the timer again, go back through, and pick out twenty-seven things to give away.

Easy, right? Well, it's a little harder than it sounds, because most of us get attached to our physical junk. Our attics and basements are full of stuff we don't need. Not to mention all the other nooks and crannies that make up our homes.

Unfortunately, we get accustomed to the clutter in our spiritual lives as well. Like an overstuffed closet, our hearts are often filled with piles of bad habits and unforgiven grievances and fears; our minds with a jumbled mess of impure thoughts and baggage from the past. We even have piles of un-godly attitudes and wrong reactions littering the floor of our lives like dirty clothes, easily accessible when something happens and we need to throw something on.

I've found that if I don't make a point of regularly cleaning out all the lower-nature junk from my spiritual closet, I will usually default to the easiest and most familiar responses. And those are rarely the responses of a Christlike heart.

So what items do I need to discard? Throughout this book, we've talked about a lot of possibilities — all of which are fit for our spiritual trash bags. And Scripture is full of additional suggestions.

In Ephesians 4:31, for instance, Paul suggests a great version of the 27 Fling Boogie: "Get rid of all bitterness, rage and anger, brawling and slander, along with every form of malice." Elsewhere he urges, "Let us put aside the deeds of darkness. . . . Let us behave decently, as in the daytime, not in orgies and drunkenness, not in sexual immorality and debauchery, not in dissension and jealousy" (Romans 13:12–13).

All those are fairly dramatic examples of what needs to go — though I must admit I've tried on a few of those attitudes when it was convenient. Your list may seem tamer, more mundane than Paul's. You may even struggle to come up with twenty-seven items to discard. But I can tell you from experience that even one or two pieces of junk can clutter your life, trip you up spiritually, and leave you less effective for the Lord.

But of course it isn't enough to just remove negative behaviors and patterns. We also

Here are some ideas for cleaning up your heart. Ask the Lord to help you, then start tackling one item at a time.

1. *Jealousy.* (You are all you get to be — enjoy it!)
2. *Perfectionism.* (Desire to do your best but then accept the best you can do.)
3. *Regrets.* (You can't undo mistakes, but you can learn from them.)
4. *Shame.* (If you've asked God for forgiveness, accept that you've been forgiven!)
5. *Blame.* (Stop pointing the finger at everyone else.)
6. *Coarse joking.* (Crude humor rarely uplifts; it only demeans.)
7. *Self-hatred.* (Forgive yourself and move on. God has!)
8. *Gossip.* (If it can't be said in front of the person, don't say it.)
9. *Fear.* (Stop and pray before fear takes hold.)
10. *Short temper.* (Count to ten or give yourself a time out.)

11. *Fantasies.* (Don't miss life by habitually checking out.)
12. *Envy.* (Learn to want what you have.)
13. *Lies.* (Discard the habit of half truths, exaggerations, and full-fledged deception.)
14. *Swearing.* (Eliminate even sugarcoated words like *gosh* and *heck!*)
15. *Complaining.* (Don't nurse it or rehearse it . . . disperse it.)
16. *Guilt trips.* (Don't book travel for yourself and don't send others.)
17. *Ingratitude.* (Look for things to be thankful for — tell someone about it!)
18. *Comparison.* (Accept yourself and appreciate others.)
19. *Impatience.* (Develop long-suffering without the whine.)
20. *Careless words.* (Ask, "Does this really need to be said?")
21. *Passivity.* (Tie up loose ends by taking action.)
22. *Laziness.* (Do one thing today you don't want to do.)
23. *Worry.* (Add "Dear Jesus" to your fear and turn it into prayer.)

24. **Greed.** (Give something you love away.)
25. **Negativity.** (Train yourself to look for the good in situations.)
26. **Self-Pity.** (Cry for five minutes if you must, then blow your nose and move on!)
27. **Lust.** (Eliminate the I-must-have-it-now desire for people and things.)

Let us cleanse ourselves from everything that can defile our body or spirit. And let us work toward complete purity because we fear God.

2 CORINTHIANS 7:1, NLT

need to replace the negative with the positive. For when we completely rid our closets of old behaviors, petty habits, and rotten attitudes, and fill them with Christlike patterns outlined in Scripture, we're more likely to put on the right behavior when company knocks at the door.

When the old is no longer available, it's that much easier to put on the new.

THE DESIGNER'S WARDROBE

So what are the best-dressed Christians wearing these days? In Colossians 3:12 Paul lists five basic wardrobe essentials: "Therefore, as God's chosen people, holy and dearly loved, clothe yourselves with compassion, kindness, humility, gentleness and patience." All qualities Jesus modeled for us. Qualities the Holy Spirit wants to impart into our lives.

The first quality, *compassion,* has to do with how we respond to the needs of others. It is the ability to see and feel their pain — a tenderness of heart that hurts when someone else is hurting and that is deeply compelled to relieve the suffering.

Jesus constantly wore compassion during His earthly ministry. His heart ached for the crowds He ministered to, for "they were harassed and helpless, like sheep without a shepherd" (Matthew 9:36). Because of His compassion, He multiplied the loaves and fishes and fed the hungry multitudes (Matthew 14:13–21; 15:29–39). He healed the leper and the two blind men because He felt their pain (Mark 1:40–42; Matthew 20:29–34).

And because of His compassion, Christ calls us to do the same. "Do you see their pain?" Jesus asks concerning the people around us. "What do you have to give?" And when we respond with our own compassion, doing what we can, Jesus does what He did with the little boy's lunch in John 6:9–11. No matter how small our offering, Jesus will bless and multiply it.

It's important to remember that compassion is more than a feeling. It is a feeling that produces action. For it isn't enough to say, "Be warm and be fed." Putting on Christ means we must go beyond kind words and even heartfelt concern. We must do what Jesus would do and reach out to ease the pain of those around us.

Kindness is the next item of clothing Paul recommends. Archbishop Trench once defined it as "a lovely word for a lovely quality. It was used to describe wine that has grown mellow with age and has lost its harshness."[4] More specifically, kindness is a quality of benevolence, of wishing others well and desiring to do them good. Whereas compassion is basically a reaction to others, kindness is an attitude toward them. But, like compassion, kindness requires an others-centered point of view. It considers other people's feelings and other people's needs.

The Bible tells us it is "God's kindness" that leads us to repentance (Romans 2:4) — and that's important for us to remember. It is so easy to develop a holier-than-thou attitude toward people who aren't living as they should. But true Christlike kindness does more to disarm a scoffer than all our lofty arguments ever could. For while people might be able to dispute our logic, it's more difficult to dismiss genuine loving-kindness. As someone once said, "No one cares how much you know until they know how much you care."

Humility is the third garment Paul mentions. We spent a lot of time discussing this quality in chapter 12. But the importance of humility can never be overstated, especially since it's a quality the world has never understood. Most people assume that humility means weakness, but Jesus turned that assumption on its head by showing the true power of humility. He was humble and lowly of heart (Matthew 11:29). Rather than demanding His rights, He laid down His life — and He calls His followers to do the same. For humility — a holy unawareness of self, a whole life focused on God — has always been the hallmark of a true Christian.

Gentleness has been just as misunderstood as humility. It too has been equated with weakness. People assume that the gentle and the meek are life's natural victims. But the gentleness Christ calls us to and enables us to display is just the opposite. It is strength under control, the choice not to use one's power against another. As one of the fruits of the Spirit, gentleness has to be cultivated. It doesn't just happen.

"Let your gentleness be evident to all," Philippians 4:5 says. "The Lord is near." That last phrase tells us why we can put on this kind of gentleness. For when we understand our position in Christ — that God is for us, that He is able to help and protect us — we won't need to fight or argue or jockey for position. We will be free to be gentle. For the Lord is near. He will take care of what needs to be taken care of.

The final item of clothing we Christians are called to put on is *patience.* Kent Hughes defines this quality as "long-suffering in the face of insult or injury" and states that "it means more than just enduring difficulties or passive resignation to the circumstances. It is based on a lively, outgoing faith in God and is to be exercised toward 'everyone,' as Paul instructs us in 1 Thessalonians 5:14."[5]

Patience isn't passive resignation at all, but peaceful relinquishment. It involves placing our lives and the lives of others in the Lord's hands. Trusting Him with our agendas, our timetables, and our reputations. Relying on God so we neither fear nor become uneasy over delays. Patience sets us free to wait rather than mutter; it enables us to be patient with others because God has been so patient with us.

This loving absence of complaint is a quality Christ modeled for us. We learn how to do it by watching Him. But it's not just a matter of mimicking what we see. It's something deeper and more transformative.

I like to think of it as wearing Jesus.

DRESSING UP AS CHRIST

I get a kick out of designer clothing. As I watch wispy models saunter up and down the runway in creations that seem to go out of their way to be different as well as extreme, I have to wonder who buys this stuff. And do they ever wear it?

Just the other day, *Today* featured some up-and-coming Italian designers. Some of the outfits were actually cute. But then out came a woman completely engulfed in fabric from head almost to her toes. The skirt — gathered so tightly below the knee that the poor model had to shuffle her feet like a geisha girl — resembled the bottom of a hot dog. But it was the top that really stole the show. Like a flying-nun habit gone terribly wrong, the stiff white collar of the blouse stood straight up in front of the model's face, leaving only her eyes to peek out above it.

"Pretty hard to drink coffee in that, I guess," quipped Matt Lauer. The model smiled and nodded — or at least I think she smiled. You couldn't tell.

Romans 13:14 gives us a sane and wonderful fashion alternative to either the old-and-outdated or the seriously weird: "Clothe yourselves with the Lord Jesus Christ," Paul writes, "and do not think about how to gratify the desires of the sinful nature."

Do you want to wear the latest fashion? Do you want to turn heads and set trends? Put on Christ. There is nothing more beautiful than His nature draped around ours. He always fits. Far from confining, His nature is freeing, and He never hides who we are. Instead, when we are clothed in Christ, we become everything He is. The beauty that is part of our heritage as God's creation is finally released. Revealed to the world. And it is so absolutely appealing, so beautiful, that people can't help but be attracted.

And, yes, it feels a little strange at times. It takes some getting used to.

In fact, C. S. Lewis wryly calls the whole process of "dressing up as Christ" an "outrageous piece of cheek." After all, he writes in *Mere Christianity,* "you are not a being like The Son of God, whose will and interests are at one with those of the Father: you are a bundle of self-centered fears, hopes, greeds, jealousies, and self-conceit all doomed to death. . . . But the odd thing is, that He has ordered us to do it."[6]

Lewis explains that our dressing up like Christ is a lot like children playing games — frivolous at times, but an important part of growing up. Playing with dolls helps little kids become good parents. Pretending to run a shop or teach a class prepares little people for future occupations. And choosing to act like Christ, to take on His qualities even when we may not feel like it — well, that is an important part of becoming like Him.

"Very often the only way to get a quality in reality is to start behaving as if you had it already," C. S. Lewis concludes. "When you are not feeling particularly friendly, but know you ought to be, the best thing you can do very often is to put on a friendly manner and behave as if you were a nicer person than you actually are. And in a few minutes, as we have all noted, you will be really feeling friendlier than you were."[7]

Dressing up like Christ may feel awkward at first. You may feel a bit silly and out of place — like a little girl wearing your mother's best dress and heels. You may stumble and fumble a bit. You may need to pull up the skirt so you can walk and push back the stylish hat that keeps falling over your eyes. But keep on walking. Keep on stumbling and fumbling. You'll grow into your new nature! Before long, you'll be walking with confident beauty and relaxed assurance.

It may not be your nature now, but it will be one day. Keep wearing Christ.

He really looks good on you!

CLOTHED AND READY TO GO

When we put on Christ — when we put on His heart and His attitudes — something marvelous happens! We are able to act in ways that don't come naturally. Paul implies that, when we put on the qualities of compassion, kindness, humility, gentleness, and patience he describes in Colossians 3:12, we will be able to *respond* rather than *react* to life. For one thing, we will be able to "bear with each other" (verse 13).

I don't know about you, but I could use some help with that one. For on my own, I'm more likely to *be* a bear than to bear with someone else's behavior, attitudes, and annoying statements. I'm more likely to insist that everyone put up with me than to put out any effort to put up with them. The following little paragraph made me laugh, but it also sums up the kind of self-centered existence to which I'm naturally inclined:

> If you're a bear, you get to hibernate. You do nothing but sleep for six months. I could get used to that. And another thing: before you hibernate, you're supposed to eat yourself stupid. That wouldn't bother me either. If you're a mama bear, everyone knows you mean business; you swat anyone who bothers your cubs. If your cubs get out of line, you swat them, too. Your husband expects you to growl when you wake up. He expects you to have hairy legs and excess body fat. He likes it. I wish I were a bear![8]

Wearing Christ means we don't have the luxury of such silliness. Besides, I've found that living selfishly rarely brings me happiness or satisfaction. For I wasn't created for me-centered living. Neither were you. We were created to give our lives away. To bear with one another.

When we clothe ourselves with the attitudes Paul recommends, the ones Christ practiced and modeled for us, we are able to live and love without making demands. And we are freed to serve without resenting the demands others place on us.

"Bear with each other and forgive whatever grievances you may have against one another," Colossians 3:13–14 says. "Forgive as the Lord forgave you. And over all these virtues put on love, which binds them all together in perfect unity."

Now that is an outfit I want to wear! Tender yet tough. Willing to get dirty yet Teflon coated. Quick to forgive but slow to give up. Willing to let go of offenses in order to hold on to relationships. And love makes the whole outfit work. Holding everything in place, belting it all together in heavenly perfection.

Making us look more and more like Jesus — and less and less like the world.

WHAT'S YOUR COLOR?

Remember color draping back in the eighties? Those parties where we'd gather and munch tortilla chips and seven-layer dip as we watched the experts drape one of us with various colors?

We'd ooh and aah as the lab-coated instructors told us what kind of makeup to wear, which colors to avoid — the ones that drabbed us out — and the must-have colors that would make us shine. Then we'd fork over a hefty eighty or ninety bucks and go home with a color chart the size of a small brick — which we were told to carry in our purses at all times. (After all, you never knew when you might stumble across that perfect blouse in that perfect shade — or meet a mugger on your way home from the mall. With one well-placed swing of your brick-laden purse, your color analysis would take care of them both!)

The whole point of color draping was that certain colors are suited to each individual's personal coloring. Each of us is made to wear certain hues.

Well, that may be true in the natural realm. But spiritually speaking, we were all created to wear white. In the Bible, white denotes the righteousness of Christ. It's the color of His robes, His garments. We His people — His church, His Bride — are privileged to wear His color. And, best of all, the Lord provides the clothes. He doesn't expect us to come up with them on our own. All He asks is that when He provides them, we put them on.

Jesus told a sobering story in Matthew 22:1–14. It is the story of a wedding feast given by a king for his son. Many people were invited, but verse 3 tells us "they refused to come." Oh, they had their excuses. One had business; the other had to tend to his field. Some ungrateful few actually beat up the one who brought the invitation. Finally, the king told his servants to go out to the street corner and gather as many people to come as they could.

And so they came, verse 10 tells us, "both good and bad, and the wedding hall was filled with guests." But as the king mingled with the crowd, he noticed a man not wearing wedding garments. He was clothed. But not correctly.

"Friend," the king asked, "how did you get in here without wedding clothes?" The man was speechless.

Then the king told the attendants, "Tie him hand and foot, and throw him outside, into the darkness, where there will be weeping and gnashing of teeth."

"For many are invited, but few are chosen" (Matthew 22:12–14).

That sounds harsh to our Western ears, but it is important to understand that in Bible times, wealthy hosts often provided clothing for their guests. Having brought people off the streets to attend his son's wedding feast, the host couldn't have expected that they would have the proper clothes. So the king made provision. He went out of his way to supply everything his guests needed. And yet the man, considering what he had on to be good enough, hadn't bothered to put on the gift.

How it must hurt God's heart when we refuse the garments He has laid out for us through His Son. When we look down at our righteous rags and declare them good enough. Or when, like the beggar man we met at the first of this chapter, we wear our new clothes but forever hang on to the old. All of this must cause the Lord great pain.

We may get to heaven, but we won't be new creatures. Not if we settle for the ecru and cream of our own human whiteness rather than accepting the pure white garments of righteousness that have been washed in the blood of the Lamb.

But worst of all, we'll walk through life a pale imitation of what we might have been.

CLOTHED IN WHITE

Have you ever seen an angel? I have. Oh, he probably wasn't the celestial sort, but for a brief moment in Paris's Charles de Gaulle International Airport, he certainly appeared to be.

You couldn't help but notice Jason. A medium-height, stocky young black man, he had a face that glowed with joy. I saw him from across the crowded room while 147 of us waited to see what would become of our

In his book *The Tale of the Tardy Oxcart and 1,501 Other Stories,* Chuck Swindoll gives five suggestions to overcoming habits that keep us from walking in victory. Five ways to help us put off the old person so we can put on the new.

- ***Stop rationalizing.*** Refuse to make comments like: "Oh, that's just me. I'm just like that — always have been, always will be. After all, nobody's perfect." Such excuses take the edge off disobedience and encourage you to diminish or completely ignore the Spirit's work of conviction.
- ***Apply strategy.*** Approach your target with a rifle, not a shotgun. Take on each habit one at a time, not all at once.
- ***Be realistic.*** It won't happen fast. It

flight back to the United States. He wore a white sports jersey. Maybe that's why he glowed. But I was fairly certain it was something more.

won't be easy. Nor will your resolve be permanent overnight. Periodic failures, however, are still better than habitual slavery.

- ***Be encouraged.*** Realize you're on the road to ultimate triumph . . . for the first time in years! Enthusiasm strengthens self-discipline and prompts an attitude of stick-to-itive-ness.
- ***Start today.*** This is the best moment thus far in your life. To put it off is an admission of defeat and will only intensify and prolong the self-confidence battle.[9]

Rid yourselves of all the offenses you have committed, and get a new heart and a new spirit.

EZEKIEL 18:31

In a crowd of frustrated, weary travelers — myself included — Jason exuded a peace and a joy that seemed almost inappropriate. After all, we'd just spent eight hours waiting for a flight that was finally canceled. Now we were waiting for word on what our fate would be.

I watched as the young man helped people with their carry-on luggage. He stepped aside to allow those more aggressive to get farther in line. But it wasn't until we ended up seated next to each other on the bus that would take us to a hotel for the night that I confirmed what I had suspected.

Jason was a Christian. And, not only that, he was clothed with Christ.

"I've been in Italy for six weeks studying the culture," he told me. "But not knowing the language or any of the other students, I ended up spending most of my time with the Lord. It was incredible!" He laughed. Then he told me about the sweet times he'd spent with his Master . . . the songs he'd written . . . the new passion and vision he was taking home to the ministry with youth he'd established in Mississippi.

Jason had spent six weeks with Jesus. And, oh, you could tell!

While I had been praying that the Lord would redeem my time in the airport and use me for His glory, Jason had been a living example of Jesus. While I had rushed to get my place in line, Jason had stepped back and served. While I had run over people's toes

430

with my rolling luggage, Jason had no carry-ons to wrestle with. No bundle of rags. He traveled light.

And, as a result, he *was* Light. Clothed in white. Jesus Christ Himself, loving and helping people right there in the middle of the Charles de Gaulle Airport.

Humbled, I went to my hotel room that night. I was embarrassed by how easily I forget that I have been called to be Jesus to my world. That, when I willingly take off self and put on Christ, something wonderful happens: I am transformed.

I'm a beggar girl, made a princess, still walking and living among other beggars. Free to love and accept them because I have found the love and acceptance of the King. Clothed in compassion, kindness, humility, gentleness, and patience. Able to bear with others, to forgive them as I have been forgiven, to love them with Christ's all-embracing love.

Looking just like Jesus. Wearing Him. *Becoming* Him.

All dressed up. Without the pretend.

16
STEP BY STEP

And we, who with unveiled faces all reflect the Lord's glory, are being transformed into his likeness with ever-increasing glory,which comes from the Lord, who is the Spirit.

2 CORINTHIANS 3:18

After being bound in darkness for so long, the light was nearly blinding. But as the Man pulled her to her feet, gently smoothing her wild hair, she could feel His love. The demons had not been kind. Many years of torment had left her only a shell.

The demons had taken. This Man only gave. His words, His acceptance, the smile in His eyes welcomed her back to life. For the first time in years, she felt a stirring of hope. As if the person she used to be and the person His eyes told her she could now be were about to meet.

As she stood to her feet and looked Him in the face, she realized the fear was gone. So was the seething self-hatred. Only hope remained. And, to her surprise, a small bubble of joy slipped out in breathless laughter.

He laughed as well. For they both knew something marvelous had happened.

She'd been set free.

ANOTHER MARY — A BRAND-NEW LIFE

When Mary Magdalene met Jesus, she experienced an extreme makeover. A makeover no television show, no plastic surgeon, no Hollywood dentist could ever hope to match. For this was not a makeover on the outside. This was a transformation that went to the deepest places of the heart. A healing that mended every fragmented part of her personality. A deliverance that shattered every stronghold of darkness and set her free from seven demons (Luke 8:2). A love that melted every stony wall that circled her heart.

For God is thorough. He heals to the utmost. He knows what we need and how to provide it. And God longs for us to let Him do exactly that in our lives.

While most of us have never experienced the bondage of demon possession like Mary Magdalene, many of us are just as bound. Bound by bitterness and doubt. Bound by pride and fear and unbelief. Even now, we stand with one foot in our prison cell while Jesus beckons us to walk out in freedom. Unfortunately we can't seem to figure out how to leave one life to enjoy the other.

We simply don't understand how to live free.

Sadly, it is possible for Christians to walk in and out of church Sunday after Sunday yet still live bound to the past by regret and shame. Tormented by fear and worry about the future. Shackled by frustration and discontentment with where we are and what we have now.

We go through the motions of worship, sitting when we're supposed to sit and standing when we're supposed to stand. Even singing when we're supposed to sing. But the song on our lips never quite reaches our heart. And because we secretly fear there is no other option, we settle for what we can get. Religion. Ritual. A form of godliness without any power at all. Borderland.

Trapped between the no longer and the someday. Lost in the not yet.

Never even dreaming what it would be like to live our lives in complete abandonment to God.

If nothing else, I hope this book has awakened a hunger in your heart and a realization that in Christ there is more than you've dared hope for! More freedom. More joy. Life so much richer and more abundant that your heart may laugh with the wonder of it all!

For it is that kind of life — that kind of holy makeover — that Christ wants for every one of us. The same kind of transformation that made Mary Magdalene into a whole new person and launched her on an adventure she'd never regret.

CHANGED AND REARRANGED

We really don't know much about Mary Magdalene. Religious tradition has branded her a prostitute, for she was from Magdala, a region known for that dark trade. But nothing in the Bible tells us that was the case. All the long years of demon possession had surely caused her much pain and perhaps even shame.

But once she met Jesus, none of that mattered.

And the same is true for you and me.

Our past doesn't matter. Whether it was dark and sordid or just boring and dead, we all need a Savior. We all need Jesus. Only He can set us free from captivity to ourselves and to the things that bind us.

Only He can change us from the inside out.

I'll never forget a transformation I witnessed several years ago. My friend Jane has always been pretty, but as an outdoorsy girl from Ohio, she didn't spend a lot of time on her looks. So when she was given a chance at a spa weekend, she threw caution to the wind and put herself in the capable hands of the beautician, nail tech, and makeup artist. Three hours later, she emerged like a butterfly from a cocoon.

All we could do was stare. Her brown hair, which she usually kept tied back in a knot, fell loose just above her shoulders, curling softly and framing her face. Mascara and a little eyeshadow highlighted her brown eyes. A dusting of blush and some soft pink lipstick — and my sweet Janie girl was transformed into a drop-dead-gorgeous vision of loveliness!

I can't even explain the change. It was breathtaking. All we could do was tell her over and over how beautiful she was. And all she could do was cry. "Stop it, you guys!" she said as she flapped her hands and tried to wipe her eyes. "I don't know what to do when you say that."

And with those words the truth was out. For though we all secretly dream of being beautiful, when it happens we have no idea how to handle it.

Sometimes it seems safer to stay the way we are. We'd rather only dream of lasting change than tackle the hard work and emotional adjustment true transformation requires.

LETTING GOD MESS WITH US

Once Mary Magdalene put herself in the hands of the Master, she could no longer go back to the way she used to live. She couldn't keep the same friendships. She couldn't frequent the same places. For her old life had been lived in darkness — and now she was a child of the Light.

You and I may have to make similar adjustments as we move into our own transformations. Like Mary, we must learn to walk in the light and, like little Joshua, to take off our jammies and put on some real clothes. We must learn, like my Ohio friend, how to live beautifully in the real world — so unmindful of ourselves that we transparently reflect Christ.

All of this involves stepping out of our comfort zones, allowing God to stretch and challenge us in ways we haven't been challenged before.

For Mary of Bethany, transformation meant leaving her "learner" position for the active role of servant, anointing Jesus as He

Lord, you know better than I know myself that I am growing older and will someday be old. Keep me from getting talkative, particularly from the fatal habit of thinking that I must say something on every subject and on every occasion.

Release me from craving to straighten out everybody's affairs. Make me thoughtful, but not moody; helpful, but not bossy. With my vast store of wisdom it seems a pity not to use it all, but you know, Lord, that I want a few friends at the end. Keep my mind from the recital of endless details — give me wings to come to the point.

I ask for grace enough to listen to the tales of others' pains. Seal my lips on my own aches and pains — they are increasing, and my love of rehearsing them is becoming sweeter as the years go by. Help me to endure them with patience.

I dare not ask for improved memory, but

made His way to the cross. (Her sister, Martha, of course had to put aside her "get it done" agenda and learn to sit at the Lord's feet.)

Mary, the mother of Jesus, had to lay down

for a growing humility and a lessening cocksureness when my memory seems to clash with the memories of others. Teach me the glorious lesson that occasionally it is possible that I may be mistaken.

Keep me reasonably sweet. I do not want to be a saint — some of them are so hard to live with — but a sour old woman is one of the crowning works of the devil.

Give me the ability to see good things in unexpected places, and talents in unexpected people. And give me, O Lord, the grace to tell them so.[1]

— Written by an anonymous
seventeenth-century nun

*Charm is deceptive, and beauty is
fleeting; but a woman who fears
the Lord is to be praised.*

PROVERBS 31:30

her reputation in order to carry Christ to the world.

And Mary Magdalene had to leave her familiar world of darkness and demons to follow her new Lord.

You may also be called to make some difficult adjustments. But I can promise you, the results will be worth it. You see, the Holy Spirit is in the process of doing something extraordinary in your life. C. S. Lewis describes it this way in *Mere Christianity:*

Imagine yourself as a living house. God comes in to rebuild that house. At first, perhaps, you can understand what he is doing. He is getting the drains right and stopping the leaks in the roof and so on.

You knew that those jobs needed doing and so you are not surprised. But presently he starts knocking the house about in a way that hurts abominably and does not seem to make sense. What on earth is he up to? The explanation is that he is building quite a different house from the one you thought of — throwing out a new wing here, putting on an extra floor there, running up towers, making courtyards.

You thought you were going to be made into a decent little cottage, but he is building up a palace. He intends to come and live in it himself.[2]

Imagine! You and me — dwelling places for almighty God. Impossible? Not with Christ as the cornerstone and the Holy Spirit at work in us right now, laying brick by brick, tile by tile. Putting down carpet and hanging drapes. All for one purpose — to make our lives fit for the King.

No wonder the process is frustrating at times. If you've ever experienced a remodeling project in your home, you well know how overwhelming it can be. Sometimes it seems that you'll be pushing aside tarps and breathing paint fumes forever. Sometimes you think you'd rather eat Big Macs for the rest of your life than wash another set of dishes in the bathtub. Sometimes you wonder why you wanted a change in the first place.

The truth is, it takes time to transform the ordinary into the extraordinary. It takes perseverance. And even when the Holy Spirit does the heavy lifting, transformation is often inconvenient and downright messy.

Which means that one of the biggest challenges many of us face in our own transformation is learning to be patient with the process.

STEP BY STEP

I appreciate the honesty with which so many Christian writers have shared their lives with us. From the perspective of history, though,

441

it may seem like these folks were always holy, always passionate in their pursuit of Christ. But they, like us, had days when it seemed they would never achieve the surrender they desired.

One of my heroes in the faith is Amy Carmichael, a missionary who gave her life to the children of India. Though she struggled with illness throughout most of her ministry, she saved more than a thousand children from temple prostitution. Despite being bedridden for the last twenty years of her life, Amy wrote thirty-five books, many of which still touch lives today.

The children she rescued called her Amma — "mother." Because of her passionate pursuit of Christ, Amy was a spiritual mother to many more,[3] including her biographer Elisabeth Elliot, who writes, "Amy Carmichael became for me what now some call a role model. But she was far more than that. . . . She showed me the shape of godliness."[4]

But that doesn't mean Amy Carmichael always felt totally consecrated and utterly committed to God. From a page in her journal, we get a peek into a heart that struggled just as we do:

Sometimes when we read the words of those who have been more than conquerors, we feel almost despondent. I feel that I shall never be like that. But they won through step by step.

By little bits of wills
Little denials of self
Little inward victories
By faithfulness in very little things.

They became what they are. No one sees these little hidden steps. They only see the accomplishment, but even so, those small steps were taken.

There is no sudden triumph
no [sudden] spiritual maturity.
That is the work of the moment.[5]

Are we willing to dedicate ourselves to little steps? To the hidden work God wants to do in each of us?

Realizing that God is more interested in the process than the product has transformed my walk with Christ because it allows me to concentrate on obedience, not perfection. The goal of perfection only points out how far I have to go, but obedience marks how far I have already come. Perfection frustrates and torments. Obedience releases and makes whole.

I can't become everything I ought to be overnight. But I can proceed step by step if I'm obedient to what God asks of me today.

Charlie Shedd once wrote: "Lord, help me understand what you had in mind when you made the original me."[6] That prayer speaks to my heart. For as I glimpse what God sees and respond in obedience to that understanding, God will not only show me more. He will enable me to live in the light I have.

Baby steps, perhaps. But steps all the same.

FOLLOWING CHRIST

Most of us won't experience the immediate transformation that Mary Magdalene did the day she met Jesus. For most of us, our holy makeover will be more like what Amy Carmichael described: a gradual, step-by-step process.

But that was probably true for Mary as well. Because her transformation didn't stop on the day she was delivered from demons. It unfolded as she continued to follow Jesus. Closely. Step by step.

Now there have been all kinds of speculation, much of it ridiculous, about the nature of Mary's relationship with the Lord. But what we do know from the biblical account is that once Mary met Jesus, she followed Him for the rest of His life. She appears again and again in the background — supporting Jesus's ministry just as the other women who traveled with Jesus did, "out of their own means" (Luke 8:1–3). No doubt working hard gathering food, baking bread, washing clothes. Walking countless miles in a day. Facing rejection from people who either knew about her past or scorned her present.

And yet she persevered, staying close to her Lord.

Learning from Him.

Trying to be like Him.

Step by step.

Like Amy and like Mary, I'm finding it is most often the little bits of self-denial, the faithfulness in little things that God uses in my life to change me. Rather than transporting me from where I am to where I need to be, the Holy Spirit has graciously taken my hand and led me there.

This option takes longer. And I don't always understand the path. But I'm coming to appreciate that God is up to more than just what I see. He is working "all things . . . together for good" (Romans 8:28, NKJV). And sometimes the "all" takes time. But if, like Mary Magdalene, I keep on following, I'm amazed by how well it all works out.

FLESH-DRIVEN OR SPIRIT-LED?

Remember the church building program I told you about in the first chapter of this book? Now, three years later, our new facility is almost complete. But even more exciting to me is the fact that we get to keep our existing church building for a youth and ministry outreach center. That means we will be able to fulfill the dreams and visions we had in the beginning, the very dreams and visions that had to be scaled back because of finances. In His mysterious and marvelous way, God has opened a door to more ministry opportunities for less money — and right in the middle of town rather than on our new, less accessible campus.

I had a dream, you see, but God had a better idea. Which is usually the case. So often we feel frustrated in our walk with God because of what seem like roadblocks and detours. We feel as though God has forsaken us — or, worse, that we somehow misinterpreted His will. One way or another, our joy is depleted, our passion runs dry, and we settle for motions rather than movement in our walk with God.

However, we have a choice. We always have a choice. Either we can trust the Spirit's leading, or we can insist on going our own way. But let me tell you — only one choice leads to life. The other marks a gradual descent toward spiritual death, for no one can refuse God's will and prosper.

When I finally — and grudgingly — surrendered my dreams for our church building to God, I was giving them up for good. I had no idea He would resurrect them — and in a way that would be better for everyone. God really did have a better idea, but I couldn't see it until I chose to obey and follow.

We miss so much when we insist on being flesh-driven rather than Spirit-led. When we power walk in a Martha spirit — pushing, striving, and conniving — rather than adopting a Mary spirit that says, "Wherever You lead me, Lord. I just want to be close to You," we miss out on so many of God's good ideas . . . and our chance to be a part of them.

That is why I keep on praying, "Lord, change me."

I want to have a heart that ponders rather than fears.

A heart that believes that God will do what He says He will do, though everything around me shouts to the contrary.

I want a Mary spirit. Oh, I'm glad God understands my Martha-ness and that He is not put out with me when I dream big dreams and go full tilt. But I'm also glad He doesn't allow me to continually operate in Martha overdrive.

In His mercy, God confounds me. He reins

me in and prunes me back. And He leads me on, often along paths I don't understand. For He has much more in mind for me and for His kingdom than I can see or even know.

So I'm learning not to get uptight when things don't go my way. For if I can, like the Marys we've studied, keep in step with the Spirit, He will show me which path to take. And, better yet, I'll receive what my spirit longs for.

A gentle, beautiful life, inside and out. A soul at rest and a body in motion. A life lived in the presence of my precious Lord.

And always, as I follow His footsteps, the promise of something astonishing and new.

WHERE IT ALL LEADS

On that dark Sunday morning two thousand years ago, as Mary Magdalene made her way to the tomb, she never expected to go away running, even dancing with joy. But that is exactly what happened. And that is the underlying truth that makes all our transformations possible — the glorious reality that death (especially death to ourselves!) will always be swallowed up by victory. And the sorrow which once threatened to undo us will be the very thing that makes us proclaim God's glory.

Case in point. It took my friends and me several years of prayer and pain before we began to experience healing for all we had been through. Though our friendships had been restored, much of the ministry we'd been involved in lay dormant and still.

But then Sunday happened. The crisp November day seemed so ordinary. When I walked into church that morning, I had no idea I'd witness a resurrection. Chatting before the service with two friends who'd been involved in the situation, I mentioned a new worship song we were going to sing. One line spoke of the need to dance over the graves in our lives.

"When I first heard that song," I told my friends, "I felt like we were supposed to sing that part together. I don't know about you, but in my mind I've visited the grave of what happened far too often grieving over what we lost. But I think God wants to do something this morning."

My friends agreed. We had all prayed and repented for our part in the situation, but we all sensed there was something in the spiritual realm left undone.

The music began, and when we got to that particular line, the three of us somewhat respectable women began to leap up and down and dance on the grave of our mutual pain.

We sang the song loudly and triumphantly. And somewhere in the middle of it, I felt something change in my spirit. As though there had been a divine shift in heavenly places.

"Did you feel that?" I asked my friends when the song ended. The other two nodded, wide-eyed. Tears ran down my face as I realized that God had done in a moment what I had tried to do for years. He'd long been in the process of changing me and healing our relationships. But that morning something dead was resurrected. Something lost was redeemed. Nothing would be the same.

And it hasn't been. New life is springing up all over the place.

So if I could encourage you with any one truth, it would be this: Don't miss your moment. Don't miss what God is wanting to do in your life. Right here. Right now. Right in the midst of your frustration, your pain, your everyday realities.

Follow Jesus closely, as Mary Magdalene did. Give Him your entire life, both the good and the bad — and you'll be transformed. Your tomb will be emptied, your darkness transfigured. For with Jesus, death is always swallowed up by victory (1 Corinthians 15:54).

In Everything I Do

You are a good girl trying to do good things. But you are operating in a Martha spirit, and it won't be received. It can't be received.

Those were the words the Lord whispered to me the day He convicted me of my driven Marthalike tendencies. And those are the words I check my heart with today. For as I mentioned at the beginning of this book, I don't want to wake up twenty years from now the same woman I am today. I want to wake up tomorrow — and the day after that and the day after that — a little more like Jesus and a lot less like me.

I want my offerings to the Lord to be both acceptable to Him and easily received by those around me. I want to be led by the Spirit. For when I am, it is Christ who enters the room first, and not me. Everything I do and say and am comes cloaked in His presence, His sweetness, His life. As a result, He is glorified and I am made new. I want everything I do to be Spirit inspired, Spirit driven, Spirit breathed. Even the mundane, ordinary things. Silly as it sounds, I want to walk in the power and anointing of the Holy Spirit as I do the dishes, vacuum the house, pay the bills, and scrub the toilet.

"Does God care about all of that?" you might ask. I think He does. For when I insist on living part of my life on my own, I separate my life into the secular and the sacred, and keep Jesus from being part of all I am. And when I do that, I miss out on the power of the Holy Spirit, who wants to invade and pervade every corner, every outlet of my life today — and to prepare me for my life to come.

A life where there will be no more tears. No more sorrows. No more Flesh Woman. An eternal honeymoon with our Lord.

Jude 24–25 tells us:

Now to Him who is able to keep you from
  stumbling,
And to present you faultless
Before the presence of His glory with ex-
  ceeding joy,
To God our Savior,
Who alone is wise,
Be glory and majesty,
Dominion and power,
Both now and forever.
Amen. (NKJV)

I love that passage because it reminds me of the ultimate goal of our holy makeovers. One day you and I are going to be led by our Bridegroom, Jesus Christ, to meet His Dad. But instead of feeling awkward and ugly,

Lord Jesus, I give You my life.

I invite You to have Your way in me.

Take me and break me. Shake me and make me.

Fill me and spill me. Change me and re-arrange me.

But whatever You do, Lord . . . don't leave me the same.

Spirit of wisdom and revelation, I welcome Your work.

Open my eyes so I can see . . . my ears so I can hear . . .

I choose truth over comfort, challenge over complacency.

Lord, make me forever Yours.

And most of all, make me like You.

Amen.

marred and incomplete in the presence of such perfection, we'll be able to stand clear-eyed and confident. Not only because we're dressed in gowns of absolute purity and righteous magnificence, made by Christ Himself. But also because we already *know* the Father.

The holy makeover God started so long ago will now have been made perfect. And we will finally hear those words our hearts have somehow ached to hear from the moment we were born.

"Well done, good and faithful servant! . . . Come and share your master's happiness" (Matthew 25:23).

But the transformation that will culminate in heaven must start here on earth with one simple prayer: "Lord, change me!"

And oh, dear beloved of God, if we will only ask — He will. He will!

APPENDIX A
STUDY GUIDE

There is so much life-changing power in Scripture! God promises that His Word "will accomplish what I desire and achieve the purpose for which I sent it" (Isaiah 55:11). This fourteen-week Bible study is designed to help you dig deeper into the scriptural principles undergirding each chapter of *Having a Mary Spirit*. (Group leaders, if a twelve-week format works better for you, you'll find directions at the end of this guide for adaptation.)

I recommend using a translation of the Bible that you enjoy and understand. Also have a notebook and pen for recording your answers. Before each lesson, examine God's Word and ask the Holy Spirit to increase your understanding, then apply the truths you discover.

Each lesson starts with questions for individual reflection or group discussion and then moves to a "Going Deeper" study of

Scripture. At the end of each lesson, you'll have an opportunity to write about or discuss what most impacted you in that chapter. The stories, quotes and sidebars within the chapters may provide further opportunities for discussion or reflection.

As we reprogram our hearts and our minds to operate according to God's truth, our lives are changed. This study may feel a bit personal at times, and you may find that your natural self (I call her "Flesh Woman") puts up a fight. But that is because she knows she'll lose ground as the Holy Spirit leads you into all truth. Prayerfully commit yourself to this study. Give God access to every part of your life. And prepare to be changed . . .

For God has a holy makeover waiting for you!

WEEK ONE

Read chapter 1, "A Mary Spirit," and chapter 2, "Change Me, Lord."

Questions for Discussion or Reflection

1. If you could change one thing about yourself, what would it be?

2. How do you tend to view God? As I did — up in the sky with a holy fly swatter,

waiting for me to make a mistake? As loving, but detached and distant from what's going on in your life? Or actively involved in your life, wanting to help you succeed?

Going Deeper

3. To which of the types of Pharisees listed on pages 11–12 do you most relate? Why?

4. What realities do the following scriptures say humans tend to whitewash, and what is the actual truth?
   Matthew 23:25 _____
   1 John 1:8 _____
   Revelation 3:17_____

5. What does James 2:10 say about our inability to achieve self-induced holiness?

6. Read Brother Lawrence's story on page 16. How would your life be different if, after confessing your sin to God, you gave yourself "no further uneasiness about it"?

7. Read Philippians 3:12–14. Circle key words and meditate on these verses —

457

really think about what is being said. Then memorize the passage phrase by phrase. Write it on an index card and refer to it frequently, repeating it until it becomes a part of you. (For pointers on memorizing Scripture, see Appendix E.)

8. What spoke most to you in these chapters?

WEEK TWO

Read chapter 3, "Twisted Sisters."

Questions for Discussion or Reflection

1. What does your Flesh Woman look like most often? A tattoo-and-leather biker chick? A well-dressed church lady? Or something else?

2. Read "Profiling Flesh Woman" on pages 28–29. Which of these traits does your Flesh Woman often exhibit?

Going Deeper

3. According to each of the scriptures listed below, which kingdom or throne do we need to surrender to Christ? Choose from the following list: (a) our speech, (b) our thoughts, or (c) our behavior, and write the letter in the

458

blank below:

___ Colossians 1:21

___ Romans 3:13–14

___ Luke 1:51

___ Titus 1:16

___ Mark 7:21

___ Jeremiah 9:5

4. Consider the "good dog/bad dog" story on page 35. How do you feed the good dog in your life? How can you weaken the influence of the bad dog?

5. What does each of the following verses say about handling our lower nature?
Romans 13:14 _____
Galatians 5:13 _____
Colossians 3:5 _____

6. Look at the sidebar "Conviction versus Condemnation" on page 37. How do these two things work in your life? Which side do you want to live on? Why?

7. Aren't you glad God looks at us through the blood of Christ? Write out the following passages and then meditate on the one that speaks most to you, prayerfully thanking Jesus for what He

has provided.

Romans 4:7–8 _____

Romans 8:1–3 _____

1 John 3:1–2 _____

8. What spoke most to you in this chapter?

WEEK THREE

Read chapter 4, "Spirit Check."

Questions for Discussion or Reflection

1. As you were growing up, what irritated you most about your brother and/or sister? What irritated them? (If you were an only child, perhaps you tangled with an annoying cousin or friend.)

2. What kinds of situations bring out the Twanda/Flesh Woman in you?

Going Deeper

3. Referring to the New International Version of 1 John 2:16, summarize the way this verse describes carnal, worldly living. (If you don't own an NIV, you can access it online at www.biblegateway.com.)

4. What does the Bible say about the fol-

lowing kinds of wrong spirits?
Competitive (Ecclesiastes 2:22)

_____

Controlling (1 Peter 4:15)

_____

Critical (Isaiah 58:9)

_____

Contentious (2 Timothy 2:23)

_____

Discontented (Philippians 4:12)

_____

5. Based on Philippians 2:1–4, list the characteristics Christians should have. What attitudes did Christ display (verses 5–8), and what were the results (verses 9–11)?

6. Read Psalm 139:23–24. Rewrite these verses in your own words and then pray them to the Lord.

7. Jesus said He had to go away so the Holy Spirit could come. In what ways does the Holy Spirit help us?
John 14:26 _____
Acts 1:8 _____
Romans 8:26-27 _____
1Corinthians 2:10, 12 _____
Circle the kind of help you need most

right now.

8. What spoke most to you in this chapter?

Week Four

Read chapter 5, "Fault Lines."

Questions for Discussion or Reflection

1. Looking back on your life, to what sort of things have you looked for a sense of identity and self-worth? What do you think your core issue might be?

2. Which of the "Four False Beliefs" listed on pages 62–63 tends to influence you most?

Going Deeper

3. The following verses describe some possible fault lines or core issues in our lives. Read the passages and list the core issue described and the result we might encounter if we ignore God's warning signs:

Scripture	Core Issue	Potential Result
1 Timothy 6:10	_____	_____
1 Kings 11:1–4	_____	_____
John 12:43	_____	_____

4. In order to heal our fault lines, God often has to discipline us. Read Hebrews 12:5–11. Which phrases speak most to you? Which ones, if any, make you uncomfortable? Why?

5. What did God promise in Jeremiah 24:6–7 that He will do for us? What is our part in the process (verse 7)?

6. Often the difficulties we face in life are actually preparation for a greater work God wants to do through us. Consider the following people in the Bible. Describe the method God used and the situation for which they were being prepared.

David

Method (1 Samuel 17:34–37)

_____

Situation (verses 45–50)

_____

Joseph

Method (Genesis 39:20–23)

_____

Situation (Genesis 41:37–40)

_____

Jesus

Method (Matthew 4:1–11)

_____

7. Read 2 Corinthians 12:7–10. What fault line was God addressing in Paul? How did Paul look at his difficulties and weak spots?

8. What spoke most to you in this chapter?

WEEK FIVE

Read chapter 6, "Dying to Live."

Questions for Discussion or Reflection

1. If your Flesh Woman were starring in a major motion picture, would it be a romance, an action thriller, a horror flick, or a comedy? Explain?

2. What kind of "muscle memory" behavior do you struggle with (page 80)? Where do you think it came from (e.g., was it ingrained by repetition, inherited from family patterns or genetic traits, influenced by society), etc.?

Going Deeper

3. What do the following verses have to say about sin's work *in* us?

464

Romans 6:16_____

Romans 7:17–20 _____

James 1:15 _____

4. What do the following verses have to
say concerning Christ's work *for* us?
Romans 8:1–2_____
2 Corinthians 5:21 _____
1 John 2:1 _____

5. Read Romans 6:11–13. List the five
things Paul tells us to do — and not to
do!

6. In what specific ways would your life be
different if you truly understood you
are no longer under Puppet Master's
reign but under grace (Romans 6:14)?

7. Have you ever experienced the "white
funeral" described in the sidebar on
page 91? If you feel you are ready to
take that kind of step, write out an obit-
uary using your own words and details.
It might look something like this:

*On _____ (date), _____ (your
name), died to her wants and prefer-
ences. She died to the world. She died to
others' opinions. As of this moment, she*

has determined to live only for Christ.
(signed)

---

8. What spoke most to you in this chapter?

WEEK SIX
Read chapter 7, "A Willing Spirit."

Questions for Discussion or Reflection

1. Though we want to do God's will, each of us probably has one or two things about which we've said, "God, I'll do whatever you want, but please don't ask me to . . ." Mine was "I'll go anywhere but Africa!" What's yours?

2. Try to imagine what it would have been like to be Mary — to have an angel tell you you're going to be the mother of the Son of God. How would you have felt when you heard Gabriel's announcement? What would you have said in response to the angel?

Going Deeper

3. God often asks us to do things that don't make sense to us. What were the following people asked to do, and what

was the result?
Abraham (Genesis 12:1–5; Galatians 3:6–9) _____

(Judges 7:1–22)

_____

Philip (Acts 8:26–39)

_____

4. Sometimes we don't feel qualified to be used by God. What qualifications did Paul say he had in Philippians 3:4–6? How did he view them in verses 7–8?

5. Sometimes we fear that the price of saying yes might be too high. According to 2 Corinthians 11:23–28, what difficulties did Paul face in order to follow the call of God on his life? What does 2 Timothy 4:6–8 say about Paul's response and what his reward would be?

6. Read 1 Corinthians 6:19–20. What three facts about our relationship to God does this passage list? According to the verses, what should be our response?

7. Read Isaiah 6:8. Do you sense God asking you to do something specific at

this particular moment? It may not be as grand as what is described in this scripture, but in order to say yes to this call, what would be your next step? Write out a prayer consecrating your life to God and His purposes, asking that He lead you as you obey.

8. What spoke most to you in this chapter?

WEEK SEVEN

Read chapter 8, "Mind Control."

Questions for Discussion or Reflection

1. If you could trade mental capabilities with anyone in the world, past or present, who would it be?

2. What does most of your self-talk sound like? In other words, how do you treat yourself in your mind? What kind of repetitive tapes do you tend to play? How do they affect you?

Going Deeper

3. Read Uncle Screwtape's letter to Wormwood on page 110. What does Satan usually do to distract you from hearing God's voice?

4. Read Ephesians 4:25–32. List some changes in behavior that should result from our being "made new in the attitude of [our] minds" (verse 23). Circle the changes you would like the Holy Spirit to help you with.

5. Read the Joyce Meyer quote on page 115. How would you characterize the effectiveness of your mental border patrol. Nothing slips by? Policed somewhat diligently? The guards are usually on a coffee break? Protection is nonexistent?

6. What do the following verses say about the importance of our minds and what we think about?
   Isaiah 26:3 _____
   Matthew 16:23 _____
   Romans 8:6 _____

7. Identify a negative thought that the Enemy often uses against you. Using the "Five *R*s for Managing Your Thoughts" on page 118, consider how you would take that thought captive. The next time it attacks, go through these steps. Take it to Christ and let Him deal with it. Accept His freedom

and forgiveness and don't be entangled by this particular lie anymore.

8. What spoke most to you in this chapter?

WEEK EIGHT

Read chapter 9, "Guarding the Wellspring."

Questions for Discussion or Reflection

1. What kind of boundaries or restrictions did you experience as a child growing up? How did you feel about them then, and how do you feel about them now?

2. Read the "Others May —You Cannot" sidebar on pages 130–31. Why do you think God convicts some people of certain things while He doesn't seem to convict others?

Going Deeper

3. Praise God we are no longer under the law! But the Bible is clear that we must manage our freedom correctly to avoid (a) harming ourselves, (b) harming others, or (c) hurting God. For each of the scriptures listed below, write a, b, or c to indicate who's affected by the be-

havior discussed.
___ 1 Corinthians 8:9
___ 1 Corinthians 10:23
___ Hebrews 6:6
___ 1 Peter 2:15–16
___ Romans 14:13
___ 1 Thessalonians 4:7–8

4. Paul warned in 1 Corinthians 4:4 that we can't trust our consciences completely. Still, the conscience is an important gift from God. What do the following verses say about it?
Acts 24:16 _____
Hebrews 9:14 _____
1 John 3:21–22 _____

5. Consider Lauraine's story on pages 128–29. Are you reaping the consequences of your own actions or someone else's actions? What new attitude could you "sow" today that would affect tomorrow's harvest?

6. God blesses those who keep His Word. Match the benefits below to the following scriptures: (a) Joshua 1:8; (b) 2 Peter 1:4; (c) 1 Timothy 4:16; (d) James 1:25.
___ Partake in divine nature

___ Be blessed in what one does
___ Be successful
___ Escape corruption
___ Save oneself and others
___ Prosper

7. List the temptations and experiences that tend to block or taint the living water in your life. Read 1 John 1:9. Take a moment to ask the Holy Spirit, our Keeper of the Spring, to purify your heart and to make you aware when those things try to reenter your life.

8. What spoke most to you in this chapter?

WEEK NINE

Read chapter 10, "A Fearless Beauty."

Questions for Discussion or Reflection

1. How would you rate yourself on the fear-filled worrier scale? Let 1 be "I don't worry at all" and 10 be "I worry about everything!"

2. How do you rate yourself, naturally speaking, on the scale of being quiet and gentle — with 1 being a little lamb

and 10 being a tiger? Perhaps another animal describes you best. If so, what is it?

Going Deeper

3. Read Proverbs 31:10–31. Which aspects of this woman's description fall into the "gentle beauty" categories suggested by 1 Peter 3:3–6 (listed below)? Be creative. There are no right and wrong answers!

Beauty inward not outward

_____

Gentle and quiet spirit

_____

Puts hope in God

_____

Submissive to husband

_____

Does what is right

_____

Doesn't give way to fear

_____

4. What do the following verses say about whom we are to submit to and why?
Romans 13:1 _____
1 Peter 2:18, 20 _____
Ephesians 5:21 _____
Hebrews 12:9 _____

5. How does John 15:9–10 explain the connection between loving and obeying?

6. What does 1 John 3:1 tell us about the love God has for us? Why is it hard to receive this kind of love? What would change about us if we really did?

7. If you've ever lived under the dark cloud I describe on page 142 (or know someone who has) look at how The Message paraphrases Romans 8:1–2. Underline key phrases or words. Then thank Christ for what He's done for you.

With the arrival of Jesus, the Messiah, that fateful dilemma is resolved. Those who enter into Christ's being-here-for-us no longer have to live under a continuous, low-lying black cloud. A new power is in operation. The Spirit of life in Christ, like a strong wind, has magnificently cleared the air, freeing you from a fated lifetime of brutal tyranny at the hands of sin and death.

8. What spoke most to you in this chapter?

Read chapter 11, "Rooting Out Bitterness."

Questions for Discussion or Reflection

1. Have you ever struggled to forgive someone, as R. T. Kendall did? What truth finally turned your heart around? If you're struggling with forgiveness issues right now, what part of his advice spoke to you?

2. Read "Avoiding the Shriveled Soul Syndrome" sidebar on pages 156–57. Which weed-control strategy described could you use the most right now? Why?

Going Deeper

3. What does Matthew 6:14–15 say about our need to forgive?

4. Read Kendall's "daily commitment to forgive" on page 160. Which of the following release points are the hardest for you to accept? Why?
   - "They won't get caught or found out."
   - "Nobody will ever know what they did."

475

- "They will prosper and be blessed as if they had done no wrong."

5. According to Romans 12:14–21, how are we to respond to difficult people? Make a list of responses from the passage and underline the item that comes easiest to you. Circle the one that is most difficult. Ask God to help you grow in every area.

6. Read the story about Booker T. Washington on page 167. While he had every reason to be offended, he chose not to. What Hebrews 12:14–15 steps could you take to avoid bitterness taking root the next time someone acts in an offensive manner toward you?

7. When you are faced with a hurt you can't seem to overcome, Donna Partow suggests writing the other person's side of the story. Looking at the situation from his or her perspective can bring understanding, and understanding can bring healing. Take a moment to write down the other person's perspective. Resist adding editorial comments. Doing this exercise doesn't mean the other person was justified in hurting

you, but it may help you let it go. After you finish, give both sides of the story to God — and do your best to leave them in His hands.

8. What spoke most to you in this chapter?

Week Eleven

Read chapter 12, "Broken and Blessed."

Questions for Discussion or Reflection

1. Write down or share (with discretion, of course) your most embarrassing moment or the funniest thing that ever happened to you.

2. Take the "Pride Test" on pages 170–71. In what two areas would you most like to grow?

Going Deeper

3. What was the downfall of the following people in Scripture? What happened as a result?
   Uzziah
   Downfall (2 Chronicles 26:16–18):

   _____

   Result (verses 19–21):

   _____

Haman
Downfall (Esther 3:5; 5:11–13):

_____

Result (Esther 7:9–10):

_____

Pharisees
Downfall (Mark 12:38–40):

_____

Result (verse 40):

_____

4. Read King Nebuchadnezzar's story in Daniel 4:28–37. Think about a time when God humbled you. What did you learn through the process? Write out verse 37, replacing the king's name with your own and underlining the final phrase.

5. Look up the word *humble* in a concordance. Find two verses that speak to you and write them out.

6. On page 179, Screwtape introduces the devious weapon of false humility, which is really reverse pride. Read the excerpt. Then describe (if you can) a time when Satan used this weapon against you. What other tricky ways has Screwtape found to tempt you to be proud?

7. Read Micah 6:8. Using the following prompts, write a prayer describing how you want, with the Lord's help — to display the qualities this verse recommends. (Use a dictionary to look up terms if necessary.)

Lord, I want to act justly by

_____

I want to show I love mercy by

_____

I want to walk humbly by

_____

8. What spoke most to you in this chapter?

WEEK TWELVE

Read chapter 13, "The Flesh-Woman Diet."

Questions for Discussion or Reflection

1. What's the strangest diet you've ever heard of? The most effective diet you've used? Do you tend to think of diets as short-term solutions or lifetime eating styles? Explain.

2. Tell of a time God provided a way out of temptation for you as He did for my friend Cheryl (page 188) or an instance

when the Yo-Yo Prayer I speak about on page 192 brought — or might have brought — change.

Going Deeper

3. Describe in detail the types of spiritual training the following verses promote:
Healthy diet (Hebrews 5:14)

_____

Running (1 Timothy 6:11)

_____

Weight training (2 Peter 1:5–8)

_____

4. Read Colossians 2:20–23. How should we view the world's approach to self-discipline? What warning signs does Colossians give for discerning what is good and what is harmful?

5. According to the following scriptures, why is the person we are on the inside more important than the person we are on the outside?
Matthew 15:17–20 _____
Matthew 23:27–28_____
Luke 6:45 _____

6. Remember my issue with Christian fiction? Is there a seemingly innocent area

of your life that God has been asking you to give up so He can give you more of Himself? If not, let the Lord know you are willing to do so if He asks. If there is an area, don't be afraid — He will help you. Write a prayer of consecration asking the Holy Spirit to enable you to follow through.

7. Read Hebrews 12:1. Memorize this passage phrase by phrase. Write it on an index card and refer to it frequently, repeating it until it becomes a part of you.

8. What spoke most to you in this chapter?

WEEK THIRTEEN

Read chapter 14, "Speaking Love."

Questions for Discussion or Reflection

1. Who is the most encouraging person you've ever met? What qualities make him or her that way? What does this person do that encourages you?

2. Read the "Keep Still!" sidebar on page 207. What methods do you use to keep yourself from saying things you

shouldn't? Do you ever have a problem with *not* saying things you should? What keeps you from speaking in such cases?

Going Deeper

3. Read James 3:2–12 and answer the following questions:
   - In verses 3–7, what metaphors did James use to describe the tongue?
   - How did James describe the tongue in verse 8?
   - What examples of the tongue's destructive power did he give in verses 9–12?
   - According to verse 2, what should we strive for, and what will result?

4. What instructions about speech did Paul give Timothy in the following verses of 2 Timothy 2?
   Verse 14 _____
   Verse 16 _____
   Verse 23 _____
   Verse 24 _____

5. If you had a thermometer that could measure the health of your speech, what would it register relative to the human body?

___ 98.6: healthy and life-giving
___ 86.3: cold and cutting
___ 104.6: hot and dangerous
___ Other:

6. Read Psalm 19:14 and Matthew 12:36–37. Write out a prayer of confession, asking God to forgive your careless use of words. Close with Psalm 19:14, written in your own words.

7. Do you have a friend who is going through a rough time? Take a moment to pray for her right now. Ask the Lord to give you a verse to encourage her. Then write a note expressing your love and God's love for her. Now go find a stamp and actually mail it. (I forget that part sometimes!)

8. What spoke most to you in this chapter?

Week Fourteen

Read chapter 15, "Wearing Jesus," and chapter 16, "Step by Step."

Questions for Discussion or Reflection

1. C. S. Lewis suggests we dress up as Christ (page 221). Read his quote

about putting on "a friendly manner." Have you ever taken this kind of "fake it till you make it" approach to change? Why does this approach help? Can you see some potential pitfalls?

2. Read "Doing the 27 Fling (Spiritual) Boogie" on pages 216–17. Select three items from this list that you could discard today. What additions could you make to the list?

Going Deeper

3. Read the description of the demon-possessed man in Mark 5:1–5. It's hard to imagine the transformation Mary Magdalene experienced when she met Christ. While your encounter was probably not that dramatic, can you remember a time when the description in Mark 5:15 of being finally dressed and in your right mind applied to you? Describe it. In what ways has knowing Christ changed you up to this point?

4. In Matthew 9:20–22, an unnamed woman with "an issue of blood" (KJV) touched the hem of Jesus's robe and was healed. We all have issues. What kind of transformations did the follow-

ing people experience when they met
Jesus?
Zacchaeus (Luke 19:1–9)

_____

Young man (Luke 7:11–15)

_____

Woman (John 8:3–11)

_____

5. While Jesus has purchased our salva-
tion, we must learn to live in the new
life He gives. What do the following
verses say we should put off and put
on?
Put Off
Ephesians 4:22 _____
Ephesians 4:25 _____
Romans 13:12_____
Put On
Ephesians 4:24 _____
Ephesians 6:14 _____
Ephesians 6:11 _____

6. Read the C. S. Lewis quote on page
232. After going through this study,
what kind of renovation do you sense
God doing in your life? What elements of change are making you uncomfortable? What signs of progress
do you see?

7. Often we Christians feel like we're playing dress-up, but the Bible is clear: "Therefore, if anyone is in Christ, [she] is a new creation; the old has gone, the new has come!" (2 Corinthians 5:17). In faith, write a description of who you are in Christ and what you want to be — the attitudes you desire to wear, the kind of faith you want to display, and so on. Now, thank God for the person He is making you!

8. What spoke most to you in these chapters?

Using This Study
in a Twelve-Week Format

Due to the number of chapters and amount of material covered, I would highly encourage group studies to use the fourteen-week format. But I realize that many groups follow a quarterly calendar and would prefer a twelve-week study. Unfortunately that requires reducing four weeks of study down to two.

While you are free to combine chapters as you wish, I suggest covering chapters 6 and 7 ("Dying to Live" and "A Willing Spirit") in week five and chapters 8 and 9 ("Mind Control" and "Guarding the Wellspring") on week six. When you do combine weeks, choose one "Discussion and Reflection" question from each chapter and three from each "Going Deeper" section. Be sure to assign the questions the week before the chapters are to be discussed so the homework doesn't feel quite so daunting.

OTHER RESOURCES

Check out www.havingamaryspirit.com for a reproducible study guide in a workbook format as well as a leader's guide. Please visit again after you've finished the book to share creative ideas and what worked well for you in your study. That way other churches and small groups can glean from your experience as well.

I love being part of the Body of Christ!

APPENDIX B
RESOURCES FOR A HOLY MAKEOVER

Below are some of the books and studies that have changed my life. This isn't an exhaustive list by any means, but it may be a starting place for your own transformation.

DEVOTIONALS

The following books and authors have become my spiritual mentors; they have opened biblical truth and principles to me on a daily basis. I highly recommend them to you. Because many are available in multiple editions, I have provided only the current publishers. A few titles are out of print but should be available at a library, used bookstore, or online.

Growing Strong in the Seasons of Life by Charles R. Swindoll. Grand Rapids: Zondervan, 1994.

Morning and Evening by Charles Haddon Spurgeon. Nashville: Thomas Nelson,

1994. (This perennial classic is available from a number of publishers. You can also find the daily readings on the Web at a number of sites, including www.ccel.org /ccel/spurgeon/morneve.d0614am.html and www.spurgeon.org/daily.htm.)

My Utmost for His Highest by Oswald Chambers. Uhrichsville, OH: Barbour Publishing. (This Christian classic, originally published in 1935, remains fresh and challenging. An updated-language version, edited by James Reimann, is available from Discovery House, 1992. You can also access daily readings of this classic work on the Internet at www.myutmost.org.)

Silent Strength: God's Wisdom for Daily Living by Lloyd J. Ogilvie. Eugene, OR: Harvest House, 1990.

Streams in the Desert and *Springs in the Valley* by L. B. (Mrs. Charles) E. Cowman. Grand Rapids: Zondervan, 1996 and 1997. (These inspirational compilations first appeared in 1925 and 1939 and are still popular today. I own them in a combined edition. James Reimann edited the updated-language versions, available from Zondervan.)

BIBLE STUDIES

Meeting weekly with other women to study

the following materials has been invaluable in strengthening my walk with Christ.

Believing God video series and workbook by Beth Moore. Nashville: LifeWay Christian Resources, 2002.

Breaking Free video series and workbook by Beth Moore. Nashville: LifeWay Christian Resources, 1999.

Experiencing God: How to Live the Full Adventure of Knowing and Doing the Will of God by Henry Blackaby. Nashville: Broadman & Holman, 1994.

Growing Strong in God's Family: A Course in Personal Discipleship to Strengthen Your Walk with God. (The New 2:7 Series, 1) from the Navigators. Colorado Springs: NavPress, 1999.

The Search for Significance: Seeing Your True Worth Through God's Eyes by Robert S. McGee. Nashville: W Publishing Group, 2003.

A Step in the Right Direction: Your Guide to Inner Happiness by Stormie Omartian. Nashville: Thomas Nelson, 1991.

BOOKS

The following books have affected my life at different times in deep ways. Again, they have been mentors to my faith and stepping-stones toward transformation.

The Applause of Heaven by Max Lucado.
Dallas: W Publishing Group, 1996.
*The Bait of Satan: Living Free from the Deadly
Trap of Offense* by John Bevere. Lake Mary,
FL: Charisma House, 2004.
Beyond Our Selves by Catherine Marshall.
Grand Rapids: Chosen Books, 2002.
The Christian's Secret of a Happy Life by
Hannah Whitall Smith. Nashville: Thomas
Nelson, 1999. (This inspirational treasure
is widely available from several publishers
and online at http://library.timelesstruths
.org/texts/The_Christians_Secret_of_a
_Happy_Life.)
*Holy Sweat: The Process of Personal Peak
Performance* by Tim Hansel. Waco, TX: W
Publishing Group, 1987.
*The Holy Wild: Trusting in the Character of
God* by Mark Buchanan. Sisters, OR:
Multnomah, 2003.
*Liberating Ministry from the Success Syn-
drome* by Kent and Barbara Hughes.
Wheaton, IL: Tyndale House, 1988.
(Don't be fooled by the word *ministry* in
the title on this one. This book is full of
wonderful ideas for the layperson too.)
Lord, Change Me! by Evelyn Christenson.
Colorado Springs: Chariot Victor, 1993.

Love Beyond Reason: Moving God's Love from Your Head to Your Heart by John Ortberg. Grand Rapids: Zondervan, 1998.

The Power of a Praying Wife by Stormie Omartian. Eugene, OR: Harvest House, 1997.

The Practice of the Presence of God by Brother Lawrence. (This little gem from a seventeenth-century monk is available from a number of publishers and online at www.ccel.org/ccel/lawrence/practice.html.)

The Pursuit of God by A. W. Tozer. Camp Hill, PA: Christian Publications or Wingspread Publishers, 1993.

Secrets of the Vine: Breaking Through to Abundance by Bruce Wilkinson. Sisters, OR: Multnomah, 2001.

Stepping Heavenward: One Woman's Journey to Godliness by Elizabeth Prentiss. Uhrichsville, OH: Barbour Publishing, 1998. (This remarkable public-domain book can also be found at www.guten berg.org/etext/2515.)

Total Forgiveness: True Inner Peace Awaits You! by R. T. Kendall. Lake Mary, FL: Charisma House, 2002.

What's So Amazing About Grace? by Philip Yancey. Grand Rapids: Zondervan, 2003.

APPENDIX C
DEVELOPING A QUIET TIME

If we want God's blessing and His fresh touch on our lives, we need to spend time with Him on a regular basis, praying and devoting time to the Word. But some people find the whole idea a bit of a challenge. Here are some things that have helped me get the most out of my special time alone with God each day.

- *Find a consistent place and time when you can be relatively undisturbed.* This may be difficult, but with a little creativity you can come up with something. Try getting up half an hour earlier or finding a quiet chair after everyone's in bed. Some people find they concentrate well in a busy but impersonal place like a park or a coffee shop. One woman I heard of used to find a quiet corner in the lobby of a large hotel! Consider your quiet time an appointment with God.

- ***Get a translation of the Bible you enjoy and understand.*** I personally like the New International Version. But you might prefer one with more traditional language (like the King James or New King James translation). For variety try one with updated language (like the New Living Translation or The Message).

- ***Begin with a simple plan.*** Reading smaller portions and going back and forth between the Old and New Testaments (Genesis, Matthew, Exodus, Mark, etc.) has helped keep me on track. You may want to start with the gospel of John or one of Paul's letters. Or read a psalm or a chapter of Proverbs each day. Some people like to use a daily reading schedule or a "passage a day" Bible.

- ***Ask the Holy Spirit to increase your understanding.*** Begin your time in the Word by first asking the Spirit to remove preconceived ideas and to teach and lead you into all truth (John 16:7, 13). He longs to give you fresh manna — a personal blessing from His Word to you. Spend a little time in silence, just waiting on the Lord and trying to tune in to His presence before you do anything else.

- **_Meditate on Scripture._** Read until God speaks to you but no more than a chapter to begin with. When you find a passage that seems to stand out, ask yourself, "what does it mean" and "how does it apply to me?" Also ask the Lord questions. Use the study notes in your Bible (if you have them) or other helps to learn more about what this scripture is saying.

- **_Make use of devotionals and other aids._** God has used books like _My Utmost for His Highest_ and others to shape my understanding of how He wants to work in my life. Bible studies and commentaries can also throw light on what you read — although your daily quiet time is best kept separate from in-depth study. The main purpose of a daily quiet time is to listen to the Word and spend time with the Lord.

- **_Keep a journal._** Writing down either the key passages you read or the scripture you meditate on can help plant the Word in your heart. Copy the passage down or paraphrase it in your own words. Then respond to God prayerfully. Write down how you plan to apply the truth you've discovered.

- **_Pray._** Respond to what the Lord has said to you in Scripture. Take time to confess your sins as the Holy Spirit brings them to mind. Present your requests and claim God's promises. Responding to what God is saying to your heart fosters the living relationship you need.

APPENDIX D
JOURNALING YOUR TRANS-
FORMATION

I have found that journaling my spiritual walk is crucial to lasting change in my life. For if I don't capture the truth as the Holy Spirit speaks it to me, I am like "a man who looks at his face in a mirror" and walks away forgetting what he's seen (James 1:23).

While I use my journal primarily to keep a record of my Bible study and prayer time, I have found it comes in handy for other purposes as well. Here are several other ideas you might want to incorporate as you journal your journey.

- As God reveals them in the Word or other sources, record special insights and areas in your life that need to change.
- Write down quotations or illustrations that speak to your heart from favorite speakers or books.
- Pour out your heart to the Lord. Then

prayerfully listen for a response. Write down what you sense God is saying.

- Detail how you see yourself changing and growing — and share your frustration as well!
- Starting on the back page of your journal, write down prayer requests. Write down the date God answers each of them.

The most important element of journaling is to be honest with the Lord. Don't let the fear of someone reading your journal keep you from being real in your details. Lock your journal up if you must, but let it be a tool of true dialogue with the Lord. For more information on using your journal and other Bible study helps, see my book *Having a Mary Heart in a Martha World: Finding Intimacy with God in the Busyness of Life.*[1]

APPENDIX E
MEMORIZING SCRIPTURE

"I have hidden your word in my heart," says Psalm 119:11, "that I might not sin against you." Memorizing Scripture is a very basic and important way to grow in our spiritual walk. I used to believe I couldn't do it. But the following steps, adapted from the Navigators' *2:7 Discipleship Course,* have helped me overcome that roadblock and begin to make God's Word my own.

- Choose a verse (or verses) you want to memorize. Write it on an index card so you can carry it around with you.
- Read the verse out loud several times. Think about what it means; focus on the message.
- Learn the reference and first phrase of the verse together as a unit.
- After you've reviewed the reference and first phrase a few times, add the next phrase. Repeat the two phrases several

times until you can say them smoothly. Gradually add phrases and repeat the reference once again at the end.

- Always review the verse using the following pattern: reference, then verse, then reference again (for instance: "John 11:35, 'Jesus wept,' John 11:35"). Don't leave out the reference. If you don't know the location of the verse, what you say will have less authority.

- Say the verse out loud whenever possible. This reinforces the passage in your mind.

- Each time you repeat the verse to yourself, ponder its application to your life. Ask the Holy Spirit to bring revelation.

- If possible, have a friend or family member help you review. Ask that person to signal mistakes but to only prompt you when you ask for it. Focus on saying the verse perfectly, word for word. It is easier to retain a verse that you have learned perfectly.

The Navigators stress that the key to memorizing Scripture is review, review, review. Even after you can quote the whole verse without making a mistake, keep on reviewing it — a minimum of once daily, but preferably several times a day:

> The more you review, the greater your retention. The most important concept is the principle of overlearning. A verse should not be considered memorized simply at the point when we can quote it accurately. Only when we have reviewed it frequently enough for it to become ingrained in our memory should we consider a verse memorized.[1]

NOTES

Chapter One: A Mary Spirit

1. Seen on a birthday card years ago.
2. Thanks to my friend Donna Partow who coined this phrase.
3. Donna Partow, "Strengthening Your Mind, Will & Emotions: He Restores My Soul," www.donnapartow.com/Renewal _soul_herestoresmysoul.html.

Chapter Two: Change Me, Lord

1. W. E. Vine, *Vine's Expository Dictionary of Old and New Testament Words* (Nashville: Nelson, 1997), 845–46.
2. Adapted from William Barclay, *The Gospel of Matthew,* rev. ed., vol. 2 (Louisville, KY: Westminster/John Knox, 2001), 283–84.
3. Oswald Chambers, *The Golden Book of Oswald Chambers: My Utmost for His Highest,* Christian Library Edition (Westwood, NJ: Barbour, 1963), January

31, June 21.

4. Donald Miller, *Blue Like Jazz: Nonreligious Thoughts on Christian Spirituality* (Nashville: Nelson, 2003), 79.

5. Miller, *Blue Like Jazz,* 79.

6. Andrew Murray and Brother Lawrence, *The Christian Classics: A 700 Club Edition with Christ in the School of Prayer and The Practice of the Presence of God* (Virginia Beach, VA: CBN University, 1978), 16–17.

7. Andrea Wells Miller, *Body Care: A Proven Program for Successful Diet, Fitness and Health, Featuring Ten Weeks of Devotions to Help You Achieve God's Plan for Your Body, Mind and Spirit* (Waco, TX: Word, 1984), 86.

8. George H. Gallup Jr., phone interview, July 21, 2006.

9. George Barna, "State of the Church 2005," www.barna.org, 37. Used by permission.

10. George Barna, "Barna by Topic: Born Again," 2005, www.barna.org/FlexPage .aspx?Page=Topic&TopicID=8. Used by permission.

11. Evelyn Christenson, *Lord, Change Me!* in *Changing Your Life Through the Power of Prayer: Three Bestselling Works Complete in One Volume* (New York: Inspira-

tional, 1993), 144.

Chapter Three: Twisted Sisters

1. Adapted from E. E. Shelhamer, "Traits of the Carnal Mind," first published by Shelhamer as a tract in the early 1900s, adapted by Christian Light Publications as "Traits of the Self-Life," www.anabaptists.org/tracts/traits.html. This version has been further adapted from the Christian Light version.

2. *Fried Green Tomatoes,* directed by Jon Avnet (City, ST: Universal Studios, 1991), quoted in "Memorable Quotes from Fried Green Tomatoes," IMDB: Earth's Biggest Movie Database, www.imdb.com/title/tt0101921/quotes.

3. *The KJV New Testament Lexicon* (based on *Thayer's Greek-English Lexicon* and *Smith's Bible Dictionary*), on Cross walk.com.http://bible.crosswalk.com /Lexicons/Greek/grk.cgi?number=4561 &version=kjv.

4. W. E. Vine, *Vine's Expository Dictionary of Old and New Testament Words* (Nashville: Thomas Nelson, 1997), 437–38.

5. Ray C. Stedman, *Authentic Christianity* (Waco, TX: Word, 1975).

6. Theologians hold differing views on

whether we are three-part persons or only two — body, soul, and spirit or body and soul/spirit. What's described here is the view that has been most helpful to me.

7. Stedman, *Authentic Christianity,* 92.

8. A. W. Tozer, *The Pursuit of God* (Camp Hill, PA: Christian Publications, 1993), 22, 29.

9. C. S. Lewis, *The Voyage of the Dawn Treader* (New York: HarperTrophy, 1994), 115–16.

10. Lewis, *Voyage,* 119–20.

Chapter Four: Spirit Check

1. Because some early manuscripts don't include these words of Jesus, recorded in verses 55–56 of the NKJV, the NIV puts them in a text note to the main passage.

2. Plato, *Dialogues: Apology,* www .quotationspage.com.

3. James Strong, *The New Strong's Exhaustive Concordance of the Bible* (Nashville: Nelson, 1995), 72, 130.

4. Mark Buchanan, *The Holy Wild: Trusting in the Character of God* (Sisters, OR: Multnomah, 2003), 22–23.

5. Beth Moore, "Goals for Breaking Free," introductory session of *Breaking Free: Making Liberty in Christ a Reality in*

Life, video series leader kit (Nashville: LifeWay Christian Resources, 1999).

6. Adapted from Catherine Marshall, *Beyond Our Selves* (Grand Rapids: Chosen Books, 1961), 143.

7. Marshall, *Beyond Our Selves,* 141.

8. Marshall, *Beyond Our Selves,* 143.

9. Oswald Chambers, *The Golden Book of Oswald Chambers: My Utmost for His Highest,* Christian Library Edition (Westwood, NJ: Barbour, 1963), October 10.

10. Marshall, *Beyond Our Selves,* 143.

11. A. R. Fausset, *Fausset's Bible Dictionary,* PC Study Bible, New Reference Library (Seattle: BibleSoft, 1998-2005).

Chapter Five: Fault Lines

1. William Barclay, *The Revelation of John,* rev. ed., vol. 1 (Louisville, KY: Westminster/John Knox, 1976), 113–14.

2. Robert McGee, *The Search for Significance: Seeing Your True Worth Through God's Eyes* (Nashville: W Publishing, 2003), 40–41.

3. Martha Tennison, sermon delivered 24 September 1999, Billings, Montana.

4. Adapted from McGee, *Search for Significance,* 27.

5. Formula adapted from McGee, *Search for Significance,* 27.

6. McGee, *The Search for Significance,* 27.

7. Adapted from McGee, *Search for Significance,* 40–41. The actual wording in the chart is McGee's, but I have changed the format and some of the headings.

8. Publisher's comments on Simon Winchester, *A Crack in the Edge of the World: America and the Great California Earthquake of 1906,* www.amazon.com/gp /product/product-description /0060571993/103-9620929-7191809.

9. Interview with Tricia Goyer, February 2006. Used by permission. Story also told in Goyer's book, *Generation NeXt Parenting* (Sisters, OR: Multnomah, 2006).

10. Barclay, *Revelation of John,* 115.

11. Brennan Manning, *The Ragamuffin Gospel: Good News for the Bedraggled, Beat-Up, and Burnt Out,* (Sisters, OR: Multnomah, 1990), 154.

Chapter Six: Dying to Live

1. Adelaide A. Pollard, "Have Thine Own Way, Lord," in *Hymns of Glorious Praise* (Springfield, MS: Gospel Publishing, 1969), 347. First published in Northfield Hymnal with Alexander's Supplement, 1907.

2. Mark Rutland, *Holiness: The Perfect Word to Imperfect People* (Lake Mary, FL: Creation House, 2005), 72.

3. Sermon delivered by Anabel Gillham, Glacier Bible Camp, Hungry Horse, Montana, April 27, 1996.

4. W. E. Vine, *Vine's Expository Dictionary of Old and New Testament Words* (Nashville: Nelson, 1997), 930.

5. Martin Luther, "Autobiographical fragment," from E. G. Rupp and Benjamin Drewery, "Luther's Theological Breakthrough," *Martin Luther,* Documents of Modern History (London: Edward Arnold, 1970), 5–7, www st-andrews.ac.uk/jfec/cal/reformat/the ologo/rupp6218.htm.

6. *Luther,* directed by Eric Till (MGM, 2004, film released 2003).

7. Hannah Whitall Smith, quoted in Bruce Wilkinson, *30 Days to Experiencing Spiritual Breakthroughs* (Sisters, OR: Multnomah, 1999), 62, 64-65.

8. Adapted from Hannah Whitall Smith, *The Christian's Secret of a Happy Life* (Nashville: Thomas Nelson, 1999), 21–22.

9. Smith, *Christian's Secret,* 22.

10. Smith, *Christian's Secret,* 35.

11. Beth Moore, "Week One Viewer

Guide," from *Believing God* video series, week one viewer guide (Nashville: Life-Way Christian Resources, 2002), 9.

12. Martin Luther, "Comments on Romans 6," *Preface to Romans,* PC Study Bible, electronic database (Seattle, WA: 2003).

13. Catherine Marshall, *Beyond Our Selves* (Grand Rapids: Chosen, 1961), 182.

14. Marshall, *Beyond Our Selves,* 182.

15. C. S. Lewis, *Beyond Personality: The Christian Idea of God* (New York: Macmillan, 1947), 40.

16. Oswald Chambers, *The Golden Book of Oswald Chambers: My Utmost for His Highest,* Christian Library edition (Westwood, NJ: Barbour, 1963), January 15.

Chapter Seven: A Willing Spirit

1. Frederick Buechner, *Peculiar Treasures: A Biblical Who's Who* (San Francisco: HarperSanFrancisco, 1993), 44.

2. Donna Otto with Anne Christian Buchanan, *Finding Your Purpose As a Mom: How to Build Your Home on Holy Ground* (Eugene, OR: Harvest House, 2004), 28–29.

3. Richard Foster, *Prayer: Finding the*

Heart's True Home (San Francisco: HarperSanFrancisco, 1992), 50.

4. Ben Patterson, "A Faith Like Mary's," *Preaching Today* Tape #87, transcript downloaded from PreachingToday Sermons.com, 4.

5. Arthur Christopher Bacon, quoted in Mrs. Charles E. Cowman, *Streams in the Desert* in *Zondervan Treasures: Streams in the Desert and Springs in the Valley* (Grand Rapids: Zondervan, 1996), 48–49.

6. *The Passion of the Christ,* directed by Mel Gibson, (20th Century Fox, 2004. Film released by Newmarket Films, 2004).

7. *Inn of Sixth Happiness,* directed by Mark Robson, (20th Century Fox, 2003, film released 1958).

8. Quoted on The Bible Channel Web site, "Missions Quotes," http://the biblechannel.org/Missions_Quotes/ missions_quotes.html.

Chapter Eight: Mind Control

1. Daniel G. Amen, M.D., *Making a Good Brain Great: The Amen Clinic Program for Achieving and Sustaining Optimal Mental Performance* (New York: Harmony Books, 2005), 20.

2. Michael Tipper, "Comparisons with the Brain," *Michael Tipper's Pages on Accelerated Learning,*www.happychild.org .uk/acc/tpr/amz/0999comp.htm.

3. Arthur S. Bard and Mitchell G. Bard, *The Complete Idiot's Guide to Understanding the Brain* (Indianapolis: Alpha Books, 2002), 77, 80.

4. Amen, *Making a Good Brain Great,* 20.

5. C. S. Lewis, *The Screwtape Letters* (Old Tappan, NJ: Revell, 1976), 22–23.

6. Oswald Chambers, *My Utmost for His Highest,* Christian Library Edition (Westwood, NJ: Barbour, 1963), December 1.

7. Joyce Meyer, *Battlefield of the Mind: Winning the Battle in Your Mind* (New York: Warner Faith, 2002), 65.

8. Tim Hansel, *Holy Sweat* (Waco, TX: Word, 1987), 102–3.

9. Hansel, *Holy Sweat,* 103.

10. Sermon delivered by Anabel Gillham, Glacier Bible Camp, Hungry Horse, Montana, April 27, 1996.

11. Anabel Gillham, *The Confident Woman: Knowing Who You Are in Christ* (Eugene, OR: Harvest House, 1993), 85.

12. Gillham, *Confident Woman,* 100. Note that her original list included four points. I have made it into five by divid-

ing point four.

13. Neil Anderson, Mike Quarles, and Julia Quarles, *One Day at a Time: The Devotional for Overcomers* (Ventura, CA: Regal Books, 2000), 361.

14. Hansel, *Holy Sweat,* 50.

Chapter Nine: Guarding the Wellspring

1. Adapted from Peter Marshall's story told in Charles Swindoll, *Improving Your Serve: The Art of Unselfish Living,* rev. ed. (Dallas: Word, 1981), 127–28.

2. Catherine Marshall, *Beyond Our Selves* (Grand Rapids: Chosen Books, 1961), 102.

3. William Barclay, *The Letters of James and Peter,* rev. ed. (Louisville, KY: Westminster John Knox Press, 1976), 57.

4. Chip Ingram, *Holy Transformation: What It Takes for God to Make a Difference in You* (Chicago: Moody, 2003), 183.

5. Not her real name.

6. John Ortberg, *Love Beyond Reason: Moving God's Love from Your Head to Your Heart* (Grand Rapids: Zondervan, 1998), 79.

7. G. D. Watson, "Others May, You Cannot," www.bullentininserts.org, accessed June 19, 2006.

8. Herbert Lockyer Sr., ed., *Illustrated*

Dictionary of the Bible (Nashville: Thomas Nelson, 1986), 648.

9. I am grateful to Charles Crabtree for introducing me to the pendulum concept. Though it was used in a different context than what I present here, the principle has been very helpful in understanding the extremes we should avoid.

10. William Cowper, "There Is a Fountain Filled with Blood" in *Hymns of Glorious Praise* (Springfield, MO: Gospel Publishing, 1969), 95.

11. William Barclay, *The Gospel of John,* vol. 1, rev. ed. (Philadelphia: Westminster, 1975), 249–50.

12. Yes, I realize this constant desire could be a sign of a physical problem, and we've had Joshua checked. He simply loves wa-wa!

13. United Nations Children's Fund (UNICEF), "World Water Day 2005: 4000 children die each day from a lack of safe water," Newsline article on UNICEF Web site, 20 March 2005. www.unicef.org/wes/index_25637.html.

Chapter Ten: A Fearless Beauty

1. I highly recommend attending a Basic Life Principles Seminar yourself. Check out locations and dates at Bill Gothard's

Web site: www.iblp.org/iblp.

2. John Newton, "Amazing Grace," *Hymns of Glorious Praise* (Springfield, MO: Gospel Publishing, 1969), 206.

3. Joy Dawson, *Intimate Friendship with God: Through Understanding the Fear of the Lord* (Old Tappan, NJ: Chosen Books, 1986), 20.

4. H. B. Macartney, quoted in V. Raymond Edman, *They Found the Secret: Twenty Transformed Lives That Reveal a Touch of Eternity* (Grand Rapids: Zondervan, 1960), 20.

Chapter Eleven: Rooting Out Bitterness

1. R. T. Kendall, *Total Forgiveness: True Inner Peace Awaits You!* (Lake Mary, FL: Charisma House, 2002), xxiv–xxv.

2. Jordana Lewis and Jerry Adler, "Forgive and Let Live," *Newsweek,* 27 September 2004.

3. Paul Borthwick, "The Shriveled Soul Syndrome: How to Live Large for a Lifetime," *Discipleship Journal,* no. 118 (July/August 2000), www.navpress.com /EPubs/DisplayArticle/1/1.118.3.1.html.

4. Bill Gothard, *Research in Principles of Life: Basic Seminar Textbook* (Oak Brook, IL: Institute in Basic Life Principles, 1981), 90–91.

5. Max Lucado, *The Applause of Heaven* (Dallas: Word, 1996), 100.

6. Description based on information from "Deep Jungle: Monsters of the Forest," episode in the Public Broadcasting System *Nature* series (New York: Thirteen/WNET, 2005), www.pbs.org/wnet /nature/deepjungle/episode2_index.html. Additional information from "Tropical Forest," Brittanica.com Web site, www.britannica.com/eb/article-70772.

7. Kendall, *Total Forgiveness,* xxix.

8. Andy Andrews, *The Traveler's Gift: Seven Decisions That Determine Personal Success* (Nashville: Nelson, 2002), 138–40.

9. Quoted on Putting Forgiveness First Web site, www.forgivenessfirst.com/ ffidefiningforgiveness.htm.

10. Kendall, *Total Forgiveness,* 32.

11. From *Our Daily Bread,* quoted on the Bible.org Web site, www.bible.org/ illus.asp?topic_id=756.

Chapter Twelve: Broken and Blessed

1. Joanna Weaver, "The Agony of Defeat," first appeared in *HomeLife* magazine, January 2000, 58–60.

2. The general format for this test and some of the basic ideas came from

Catherine Marshall, *Beyond Our Selves* (Grand Rapids: Chosen, 1961), 184–85. However, I have rewritten the items to reflect my own understanding.

3. Rick Steves, Steve Smith, and Gene Openshaw, *Rick Steves' Paris 2006* (Emeryville, CA: Avalon Travel, 2006), 433.

4. Steves, Smith, and Openshaw, *Rick Steves' Paris,* 431.

5. Herbert Lockyer Sr., ed., *Illustrated Dictionary of the Bible* (Nashville: Nelson, 1986), 1011–12.

6. Charles Stanley, *The Blessing of Brokenness: Why God Allows Us to Go Through Hard Times* (Grand Rapids: Zondervan, 1997), 229.

7. For more on Martha's holy makeover, see *Having a Mary Heart in a Martha World* by Joanna Weaver (Colorado Springs: WaterBrook, 2000).

8. Beth Moore, *Praying God's Word: Breaking Free From Spiritual Strongholds* (Nashville: Broadman & Holman, 2000), 59–60.

9. C. S. Lewis, *The Screwtape Letters* (Old Tappan, NJ: Revell, 1976), 73.

10. Lewis, *The Screwtape Letters,* 74.

11. Andrew Murray, quoted in Paul Lee Tan, *Encyclopedia of 7,700 Illustrations:*

Signs of the Times (Garland, TX: Bible Communications, 1996), 2304.

12. Adapted from Robert J. Morgan, *Nelson's Complete Book of Stories, Illustrations & Quotes: The Ultimate Contemporary Resource for Speakers* (Nashville: Nelson, 2000), 635.

Chapter Thirteen: The Flesh-Woman Diet

1. Phyllis Diller, in "Exercise Quotes" on *All the Best Quotes,* http://chatna .com/theme/exercise.htm.

2. Quoted on *The Quotations Page,* www.quotationspage.com/quote/2164 .html.

3. Adapted from sermon by Ed Kreiner in Whitefish, Montana, date unknown.

4. Cheryl's stories in this chapter are used with her permission.

5. Janie West Metzgar, "Jesus Breaks Every Fetter," 1927.

Chapter Fourteen: Speaking Love

1. Jill Briscoe, *Thank You for Being a Friend: My Personal Journey* (Chicago: Moody Press, 1999), 68.

2. Alice Gray, in Steve Stephens and Alice Gray, *The Worn Out Woman: When Your Life Is Full and Your Spirit Is Empty* (Sisters, OR: Multnomah, 2004), 103–4.

3. Calvin Miller, "To Be Perfectly Honest," *Moody Monthly,* quoted on Bible.org, www.bible.org/illus.asp?topic_id=965.

4. Oswald Chambers, *My Utmost for His Highest,* Christian Library edition (Westwood, NJ: Barbour, 1963), May 3rd.

5. Evelyn Christenson, *Lord, Change Me!* in *Changing Your Life through the Power of Prayer: Three Bestselling Works Complete in One Volume* (New York: Inspirational Press, 1993), 164.

6. Attributed to "H. W. S." in Mrs. Charles E. Cowman, *Streams in the Desert & Springs in the Valley* (Grand Rapids: Zondervan, 1996), 18.

7. Chip Ingram, *Holy Transformation: What It Takes for God to Make a Difference in You* (Chicago: Moody, 2003), 250.

Chapter Fifteen: Wearing Jesus

1. I heard this story years ago in a sermon. Source is unknown.

2. Check out FlyLady's Web site at www.flylady.net. You'll find an online support network and hundreds of practical tips for digging out from under life.

3. Marla Cilley, *Sink Reflections* (New York: Bantam Books, 2002), 35.

4. Quoted in R. Kent Hughes, *Colossians*

and Philemon: The Supremacy of Christ,
Preaching the Word series (Westchester,
IL: Crossway, 1989), 102.

5. Hughes, *Colossians and Philemon,*
104.

6. C. S. Lewis, *Mere Christianity* (New
York: HarperCollins, 1980), 188.

7. Lewis, *Mere Christianity,* 188. Note
that actual wording is flipped. Opening
phrase in my paragraph is actually the
last phrase of Lewis's original.

8. Author unknown, on Bible.org: Trustworthy Bible Study Resources, www
.bible.org/illus.asp?topic_id=1695.

9. Charles R. Swindoll, *The Tale of the
Tardy Oxcart and 1,501 Other Stories*
(Nashville: Word, 1998), 257–8.

Chapter Sixteen: Step by Step

1. Robert J. Morgan, *Nelson's Complete
Book of Stories, Illustrations & Quotes: The
Ultimate Contemporary Resource for
Speakers* (Nashville: Nelson, 2000),
16–17.

2. C. S. Lewis, *Mere Christianity* (New
York: HarperCollins, 1980), 205.

3. "Amy Carmichael," *Wikipedia: The
Free Encyclopedia,* http://en.wikipedia
.org/wiki/Amy_Carmichael.

4. Elisabeth Elliot, *A Chance to Die: The*

Life and Legacy of Amy Carmichael (Grand Rapids: Revell Books, 1987), front cover copy.

5. Quoted in Tim Hansel, *Holy Sweat: The Process of Personal Peak Performance* (Waco, TX: Word, 1987), 130.

6. Hansel, *Holy Sweat,* 79.

Appendix D:
Journaling Your Transformation

1. Joanna Weaver, *Having a Mary Heart in a Martha World: Finding Intimacy with God in the Busyness of Life* (Colorado Springs: WaterBrook, 2000).

Appendix E: Memorizing Scripture

1. Adapted from Growing Strong in God's Family: A Course in Personal Discipleship to Introduce New Life to Your Church, the 2:7 Series (Colorado Springs: NavPress, 1987), 13, 19–20.

Dear Reader,

Once again I walk away from writing with the sense that there is so much more to say. Hard to believe, considering how long this book turned out to be! But that is the majesty and the marvelous mystery of God's amazing truth. It is so multifaceted and relevant to our lives that every day there is something new to learn and apply.

That is why I am so grateful for the sweet work of the Holy Spirit. For He goes far beyond any book, taking what belongs to the Father and making it known to us — working within us to "will and to act according to [God's] good purpose" (Philippians 2:13). Creating within us the sweet spirit of Jesus, that winsomeness we so need to win our world. A holy makeover that makes us less like us and more like Him.

Oh, how I wish I could be there to watch the beauty unfold in you!

If you have time, I'd love to hear about it. While I may not be able to answer every letter, I would be honored to pray for you. You can contact me through www.havinga maryspirit.com or reach me at:

Joanna Weaver
P.O. Box 755
Whitefish, Montana 59937
joannaweaver@hotmail.com

God is up to something marvelous in you, my friend! Whatever you do, don't miss it. Give Christ access to your deepest heart, and He will bring His light and His life to your darkest places. Changing you forever into the person you were always meant to be.

And isn't that the whole point after all?

Becoming His,
Joanna

May God himself, the God of peace, sanctify you through and through. . . . The one who calls you is faithful and he will do it.

1 Thessalonians 5:23–24

ABOUT THE AUTHOR

Joanna Weaver is a pastor's wife, a Bible study leader, and an author whose works include the best-selling *Having a Mary Heart in a Martha World* and the award-winning gift book *With This Ring.* Her articles have appeared in such publications as *Focus on the Family, Guideposts,* and *HomeLife.* She and her husband, John, have been in full-time ministry for twenty-four years. They live with their three children in Whitefish, Montana.

The employees of Thorndike Press hope you have enjoyed this Large Print book. All our Thorndike and Wheeler Large Print titles are designed for easy reading, and all our books are made to last. Other Thorndike Press Large Print books are available at your library, through selected bookstores, or directly from us.

For information about titles, please call:

(800) 223-1244

or visit our Web site at:

www.gale.com/thorndike
www.gale.com/wheeler

To share your comments, please write:

Publisher
Thorndike Press
295 Kennedy Memorial Drive
Waterville, ME 04901